BERTRAND RUSSELL

ON ETHICS, SEX, AND MARRIAGE

We have, in fact, two kinds of morality side by side: one which we preach but do not practice, and another which we practice but seldom preach.

From "Chinese Morals"

The morality which I should advocate does not consist simply of saying to grown-up people or to adolescents: "Follow your impulses and do as you like." There has to be consistency in life; there has to be continuous effort directed to ends that are not immediately beneficial and not at every moment attractive; there has to be consideration for others, and there should be certain standards of rectitude. . . . But this does not mean that we should be dominated by fears which modern discoveries have made irrational.

From "Morality and Instinct"

BERTRAND
RUSSELL

ON ETHICS, SEX, AND MARRIAGE

edited by
Al Seckel

PROMETHEUS BOOKS
59 John Glenn Drive • Amherst, New York 14228-2197

Dedicated to my friends
Ron and Marilyn

Published 1987 by Prometheus Books
59 John Glenn Drive, Buffalo, New York 14228-2197
716-691-0133. FAX: 716-691-0137.

Library of Congress Catalog Card Number: 87-60825
ISBN 0-87975-400-1

Printed in the United States of America on acid-free paper.

Cover illustration by Paul Seckel

Bertrand Russell
(1872–1970)

Bertrand Russell's parents, Viscount John Amberley and Viscountess Kate Amberley, were married in 1864 and less than one year later they celebrated the birth of their first born, named Frank. Russell's father was a gentle and austere freethinker who stood for Parliament in 1868 but was defeated, the apparent result of his unpopular support of birth control and a pending bill in Parliament that would have legalized the holding of debates on Sundays.

Six years after the viscount had his political ambitions dashed, the Amberleys rejoiced at the arrival of their second son Bertrand on May 18, 1872. His birth was the apparent result of a failure in that unmentionable practice of birth control, the advocacy of which had led his father into political isolation. Russell's life was to begin with tragedy, for at the tender age of two he lost his mother to diptheria and then at the age of three he was orphaned by his father, who succumbed to a weakened condition. Though Russell's father had made provision for the upbringing of his sons, their grandparents, Lord John and Lady Frances Russell, successfully contested their son's will thereby winning custody of the boys. Lord Russell died in 1878 leaving Bertrand's care and education to Lady Frances who, although of Scottish Presbyterian background, had Unitarian leanings and raised the young man in that spiritual environment.

Young Bertrand's childhood at Pembroke Lodge was a regimented existence of puritan piety, austerity, and loneliness; hardly an atmosphere conducive to free thought. He found the loneliness unbearable. "There were family prayers at eight o'clock every morning. Although there were eight servants, food was always of Spartan simplicity, and

i

even what there was, if it was at all nice, was considered too good for children. Cold baths all the year round were insisted upon. ... My grandmother never allowed herself to sit in an armchair until the evening. Alcohol and tobacco were viewed with disfavor although stern convention compelled them to serve a little wine to guests. Only virtue was prized, virtue at the expense of intellect, health, happiness, and every mundane good."[1]

Dreading the influence of public schools, Lady Frances saw that Bertrand was tutored at home. This was to be the beginning of the intense philosophical reflection that was so crucial to Russell's later career. At the age of eighteen he left the confines of Pembroke Lodge and entered Cambridge University to pursue mathematics. There he found the intellectual freedom and liberal scholarly environment that would allow him to flourish.

Though a shy and somewhat awkward young man, in 1892 Russell's emotions were aroused by Alys Pearsall Smith, daughter of an American Quaker family. Over the arguably justifiable objections of his family, the two were married in 1894. Having become the beneficiary of a large legacy from his father, Russell was able to pursue whatever life course he desired. While his new wife engaged herself in social issues and the special causes of a woman of leisure, Bertrand sought satisfying intellectual work—more specifically the area of economics. Between 1895 and the turn of the century Russell investigated the German Social Democratic Party, about which he devoted a book on the future of German politics (*German Social Democracy*). He also wrote works on the foundations of geometry, the philosophy of Leibniz, and the philosophy of mathematics. The latter work was eventually to lead Russell to his magnum opus, *Principia Mathematica,* a three volume work co-authored with Alfred North Whitehead and published between 1910 and 1913.

Russell's political awakening came in 1901 during the Boer War in South Africa. Initially an imperialist, upon reflection he rejected what he considered an unjust war in *A Free Man's Worship*. His concern for political and social questions prodded Russell to stand for Parliament in 1907 on a platform that advocated women's suffrage. Unfortunately, and like his father before him, Russell's political aspirations were dashed when he was defeated nearly three to one in the polls. With the First World War looming overhead Russell's dedication to social issues grew more intense. An interest in mass psychology led him to advocate pacifism in the face of rampant nationalistic war-mongering. The majority of human beings in Western culture were filled with destructive and perverse impulses, and no scheme for reform would achieve a beneficial improvement in human affairs until the psychological structure of the average person was suitably transformed through an education that stressed rational thought, a skeptical attitude, cooperation rather than competition, and kind feelings instead of strife and prejudice.

This dedication to the cause of peace was not espoused without considerable risk: Russell was derided by friends and foes alike; dismissed from Cambridge University, where former teachers turned their backs on him; prevented from lecturing at Harvard University by a British government that revoked his passport; and generally held in low esteem by those in power. He was widely known not only for the support he gave to the women's movement and the No-Conscription movement, but also for his public writing in support of conscientious objectors. In 1918 he was sentenced to six months imprisonment for pacifist articles that were thought to be subversive. Undaunted, and with the help of influential friends, Russell endured his confinement in prison, where he used his time wisely in the completion of two books, *An Introduction to Mathematical Philosophy* and *An Analysis of Mind,* published in 1919 and 1921 respectively.

The Great War profoundly changed Russell's outlook on both his own life and the direction in which his work should proceed. He ceased to be academic and took to writing a new kind of book. He changed his whole conception of human nature, and became for the first time deeply convinced that puritanism does not make for human happiness. Through the spectacle of death, Russell acquired a new love for what was living. During this period of redirection, he grew increasingly discontented with his wife Alys, and drifted in and out of a series of affairs. Russell remarked to one of his female companions, "Chastity, I gave it a good try once, but never again." In 1919 he met Dora Black, who was to become his second wife.

Upon being invited to join a Labor delegation to the Soviet Union in 1920, Russell eagerly accepted in the hope of seeing the fruits of a revolution that he had ardently welcomed. While there he was gravely disappointed in the new regime. Upon his return to England, Russell was to swim once more against the tide of prevailing opinion by publishing his critical assessment of Bolshevik failures to meet expectations, from which his prophetic work *The Practice and Theory of Bolshevism* (1920) was the published result. Finding himself isolated by conservatives on the Right and Bolshevik sympathizers on the Left, Russell retreated from public view, accepting a one-year teaching position at the University of Peking in 1921.

In 1927, Russell, now the proud father of two, became increasingly interested in education and sexual morality. His controversial views were closely linked with his observation of the joy people took in fighting and killing during the war. He believed that these characteristics were largely the outcome of experiences and teachings people were exposed to at an early age. A peaceful and happy world could not be achieved without drastic changes in education. In sexual matters, although not only these, irrational prohibitions and dishonesty were exceedingly harmful. Conventional education was judged to be at fault, through its general tendency to cramp creative impulses and to discourage a spirit of free inquiry.

Although puritanical moralists professed to be violently shocked by Russell's views on sex and education, it is worth emphasizing that his recommendations are not extreme and his writings on sex form only a small segment of his published works. As Russell later stated in an interview, "I should deal with sexual morality exactly as I would with everything else. I should say that if what you are doing does no harm to anybody there's no reason to condemn it. And you shouldn't condemn it merely because some ancient taboo has said that this is wrong. You should look into whether it does harm or not, and that's the basis of sexual morality as of all others."[2] It would be overly simplistic to regard Russell as an "advocate of wild living." On the contrary, he had no such intentions. In *Marriage and Morals* he wrote: "There has to be consistency in life; there has to be continuous effort directed to ends that are not immediately beneficial and not at every moment attractive; there has to be consideration for others; and there should be certain standards of rectitude. But this does not mean that we should be dominated by fears which modern discoveries have made irrational."[3] Russell could see nothing wrong in sexual relations before marriage, and he advocated temporary childless marriages for most university students. It is wrong to regard Russell as an enemy of the institution of marriage, though he did object to continuing a marital relationship when no love was left. What shocked people a great deal was his remark that a permanent marriage need not exclude a few temporary extramarital affairs.

Russell's views on education were so revolutionary in the twenties that he and wife Dora decided to open their own private school. Alas, it was not a success. In fact, it claimed a large amount of time and financial resources. In addition, the school attracted a fair number of problem children, and Russell had great difficulty in effecting his idea of the right balance between freedom and discipline. Though Russell left the school in 1932, it continued in Dora's hands into the 1940s, even after their marriage had ended. In 1938, Russell married his third wife, Patricia Spence, who had been a teacher at the school.

Russell's views on sexual morality and religion featured prominently in the 1940 case involving the City College of New York. When Russell was teaching at the University of California in Los Angeles, he was unanimously invited by the board of higher education in New York to join the staff of the City College to teach a graduate course in logic and mathematics. This appointment was intended to give the school great prestige, for by this time, Russell had achieved an outstanding international reputation as a brilliant scholar and lecturer in these esoteric fields. A protest against his appointment was soon started in the New York papers by Bishop Manning of the Anglican Church who declared that "Russell was a recognized propagandist against both religion and morality and who specifically defends adultery."[4] A taxpayer's suit to annul the appointment was filed in the New York Supreme Court by Miss Jane Kaye, whose daughter was about to attend City College.

At trial Russell's books were described as "Lecherous, salacious, libidinous, lustful, venerous, erotomanic, aphrodisiac, atheistic, irreverent, narrow-minded, bigoted, untruthful . . . and bereft of moral fiber."[5] It was further alleged that Russell had written salacious poetry, conducted a nudist colony in England, and condoned homosexuality. The judge, a Roman Catholic, delivered the historic verdict: Russell's appointment was to be annulled on three grounds: (1) Russell was not an American; (2) he had not been given a competitive examination on logic and mathematics, and (3) his books were immoral and full of filth.[6]

The bombing of Hiroshima and Nagasaki in 1945 forced Russell to speak out on the dangers of nuclear war, and by 1949 he had become so respectable in the eyes of the English Establishment that members of Parliament felt that he should be given the Order of Merit, England's highest honor to a civilian. The very next year, he was to receive the Nobel Prize for Literature in recognition of his "Philosophical works . . . of service to moral civilization."[7]

Russell continued to dedicate himself to the inherent dangers of nuclear weapons well into the 1950s. His enormously successful broadcast on December 23, 1954, entitled "Man's Peril," paved the way for a collaboration with noted physicist Albert Einstein on the famous Einstein-Russell Declaration, a document signed by many renowned scientists and presented to world leaders in the hope of curbing nuclear proliferation.

Russell was active in the nuclear arms debate for the remaining years of his life. He launched the Pugwash Movement to gather the world's leading scientists together to bring to their respective governments the disinterested ways and means to avert a nuclear disaster. He was elected president of the Campaign for Nuclear Disarmament in 1958, and in October of 1962 Russell played an instrumental role in the peaceful resolution of the Cuban Missile Crisis. During this time, Russell's efforts and influence had considerable impact on Soviet Premier Khrushchev's willingness to compromise.

During the middle and late 1960s Russell was one of the first to raise public doubts about international involvement in Viet Nam, doubts that culminated in his work *War Crimes in Viet Nam* (1968). His public spiritedness remained undaunted even as he aged well into his nineties. It was an alert Russell who on the afternoon of January 31, 1970, dictated a message to be read to the International Conference of Parliamentarians in Cairo, a statement that in vintage Russell form condemned Israel for its bombing of Egypt.

Two days later, on February 2, 1970, Russell fell ill in the morning and retired to his bed. He was dead within an hour. In accordance with his wishes, he was buried without a religious ceremony.

NOTES

1. Bertrand Russell, *Portraits From Memory* (London: George Allen and Unwin, 1956), p. 9.

2. Bertrand Russell, "Taboo Morality," this volume p. 184.

3. Bertrand Russell, "Marriage and Morals," this volume p. 265.

4. John Dewey, *The Bertrand Russell Case* (New York: Viking Press, 1941), p. 19.

5. Barry Feinberg and Ronald Kasrils (eds.), *Bertrand Russell's America: 1896-1945* (London: George Allen and Unwin, 1973), p. 153.

6. Dewey, pp. 213-225.

7. Ronald Clark, *The Life of Bertrand Russell* (New York: Alfred Knopf, Press, 1976), pp. 512-513.

Acknowledgments

No one person could bring together such a collection of essays without assistance. First and foremost, I owe a debt of gratitude to my wife Laura and to Steven L. Mitchell, college division director of Prometheus Books, for their advice and opinions. Both spent many hours reading through pages of proofs, correcting numerous errors, and making helpful suggestions. My appreciation extends as well to Dr. Paul Kurtz, president of Prometheus Books, for the encouragement he gave and for his willingness to undertake this project. I also want to thank my close friends, John Edwards, Robert Finn, Eric and Shelley Mjolsness, Ron and Marilyn Crowley, and Robert Davis (former president of the Bertrand Russell Society) for all of their valuable insights and comments throughout the preparation of this volume. In addition, my appreciation extends to Dr. Harry Ruja who has provided me with helpful advice and important bibliographic information.

I would like to express appreciation to the Bertrand Russell Archives at McMaster University in Hamilton, Ontario, Canada, and in particular to Archivist Dr. Kenneth Blackwell, for providing copies of several of Russell's more obscure essays and for suggesting that Russell's unpublished essay "Morality and Instinct" be included in this volume.

Contents

Acknowledgments   *vii*

Preface   11

PART ONE: ETHICS

Introduction   15

  1. The Elements of Ethics   17
  2. Science and Ethics   57
  3. Power and Ethical Rules   69
  4. Sources of Ethical Beliefs and Feelings   87
  5. Is There Ethical Knowledge?   99

PART TWO: MORAL RULES

Introduction   109

  6. What Makes a Social System Good or Bad?   115
  7. Moral Standards and Social Well-being   129
  8. New Morals for Old   149
  9. How Will Science Change Morals?   155
 10. Morality and Instinct   167
 11. Moral Codes   173
 12. Taboo Morality   179
 13. Chinese Morals   189

PART THREE: SEXUAL MORALITY

Introduction   199

14. Education Without Sex Taboos   201
15. Why a Sexual Ethic Is Necessary   207
16. The Place of Sex Among Human Values   213
17. Our Sexual Ethics   221

PART FOUR: MARRIAGE AND DIVORCE

Introduction   231

18. Marriage and the Population Question   233
19. The Ostrich Code of Morals   249
20. My Own View of Marriage   255
21. Marriage and Morals   261
22. Is Modern Marriage a Failure?   271
23. Do I Preach Adultery?   301
24. A Liberal View of Divorce   307

PART FIVE: HAPPINESS

Introduction   313

25. What Makes People Unhappy?   315
26. How to Be Free and Happy   323

Bibliography of Russell's Published Books   335

Selected Reading on Russell's Life and Views   338

Index of Names   341

Subject Index   345

Preface

During the first two-thirds of the twentieth century Bertrand Russell, through numerous publications as well as public lectures and debates across the United States and Britain, consistently advocated ideals and expressed beliefs that made him one of the most formative influences on the modern mind and society. Perhaps more than any other person of his time Russell influenced future generations to adopt a saner and more tolerant attitude toward marriage, divorce, and sexual morality.

Although numerous Russell anthologies and collections have appeared over the decades, it is curious that, so far, his writings on ethical theory, practical morality, marriage, divorce, and sexual ethics have not been collected into one handy reference volume. Indeed, most of the essays selected for this volume have hitherto been practically inaccessible, published, as they were, many years ago in widely dispersed and now almost unobtainable journals. The present volume also includes a recently discovered unpublished manuscript by Russell entitled "Morality and Instinct."

Russell, a philosopher with numerous honors and achievements to his credit, including the Nobel Prize for Literature, was an important social influence. The essays presented here were chosen for their contribution to social thought *at the time they were written,* and should be considered in this context.

During the first two-thirds of the twentieth century, especially in the United States, Bertrand Russell's outspoken views on marriage, morality, and sex were the subject of bitter controversy. Puritanical moralists, who believed that morality was a subject that ought not to be questioned, derived no pleasure from reading Russell's terse criticisms of traditional mores.

It is not surprising that Russell encountered his most vitriolic opposition when the topic of sexual morality arose. But sex is just one moral concern among many. As the selections that follow amply demonstrate, Russell had a deep concern for moral problems encountered during the course of human conduct and an acute interest in the ethical principles offered by theorists in an attempt to forge solutions to pressing dilemmas.

Russell had one constant preoccupation in his philosophical outlook: he struggled to determine how much can be said to be known and with what degree of certainty or doubt. He once wrote: "I wish to propose for the reader's favorable consideration a doctrine which may, I fear, appear wildly paradoxical and subversive. The doctrine in question is this: that it is undesirable to believe a proposition when there is no ground whatever for supposing it true."* Russell was quite right in saying that if this doctrine were to become generally accepted, it would absolutely revolutionize human life.

The essays included in this volume illustrate another side to Russell's skeptical outlook; they chronicle the efforts of one of the clearest philosophers of our time to struggle with one of the central problems of our time: how to justify passionately-held moral convictions when all the evidence seems to lead to moral skepticism.

---

*Bertrand Russell. *Skeptical Essays* (London: George Allen and Unwin, Ltd., 1928), p. 11.

Part One

Ethics

Introduction

Parts 1 and 2 of this volume concern Russell's views on ethics and morality. One might begin by asking: What is the difference between the two subjects?

As a provisional definition, ethics consists of general principles that help to determine rules of conduct. The task of philosophers who address the subject of ethics is to analyze moral rules and to attempt to discover general principles that determine or underlie specific rules of conduct—in other words, to provide a basis from which such rules can be deduced. It is not the business of ethics to arrive at actual rules of conduct that suggest how a person should behave in specific situations: "Thou shalt not steal" or "One should keep one's promises." The development of mores is the province of morality. Finally, as Russell pointed out, it is not the business of ethics to justify the moral rules of those in power.

Although ethics has traditionally been a department of philosophy, Russell had mixed feelings about its proper status throughout his career. In his earliest writings on ethics, which were heavily influenced by his colleague George Edward Moore, Russell viewed ethics as an exact science: ethical theory contained value propositions that could be demonstrated as true *a priori*. Russell fully elaborates this theme in "The Elements of Ethics," his first important work on the subject matter, originally published in 1908 and 1910.

In 1912 the philosopher George Santayana published a book entitled *The Winds of Doctrine*. One of the essays in this book, "Hypostatic Ethics," was a brilliant attack on Russell's Mooreian analysis of the ethical concept of "Good." Santayana denied that we have any objective premises on which an ethical theory can be built. He declared that "good" and "bad" were like "right" and "left"—dependent upon an individual's point of view. Santayana's criticisms were so cogent that Russell very quickly became disillusioned with the objectivistic ethical theory he shared with Moore. In contrast, Moore, who was also aware of Santayana's criticisms, not to mention the objections that others had raised against the views he had set forth in *Principia Ethica,* continued to defend it nearly forty years after its first publication.

Throughout most of Russell's later philosophical writings he largely ignored the problems of ethics because he became convinced that this was not a legitimate part of philosophy. This was no doubt due to his dissatisfaction with his own attempts to find a rational basis for ethical principles. In 1943 he wrote that "while my own conclusions as to ethics do not satisfy me, other people's satisfy me even less."[1] And in 1948 Russell decided to leave out any discussion of ethics in his last major philosophical book, *Human Knowledge: Its Scopes and Limits.* Then, in 1954, with the publication of *Human Society in Ethics and Politics,* his last and most important book on ethics, he reaffirmed his earlier opinion that ethics does indeed belong within the domain of philosophy. Russell stated in its preface: "I had originally intended to include the discussion of ethics in my book on 'Human Knowledge' but I decided not to do so because I was uncertain as to the sense in which ethics can be regarded as 'Knowledge.'"[2]

Russell's views on ethics were constantly evolving: at one time or another he has espoused nearly all of the main theoretical positions. Thus, a survey of his thought constitutes an excellent overview of ethics.

NOTES

1. Paul Schilpp (ed.). *The Philosophy of Bertrand Russell* (Illinois: Open Court, 1971) fourth edition, p. 724.
2. Bertrand Russell. *Human Society in Ethics and Politics* (London: George Allen & Unwin, Ltd., 1954), p. v.

1

The Elements of Ethics

The separate essays that compose "The Elements of Ethics" form Russell's
first important published work on the subject of ethics and collectively
they contain his most complete and systematic early attempts to explore
the theoretical problems of ethics. Except for sections 5 and 6 below, "The
Elements of Ethics" appeared in two issues of the journal The New Quarterly *and in an issue of the* Hibbert Journal *between 1908 and 1910, under*
titles listed in the separate credit lines for each. Sections 5 and 6 had been
scheduled for publication in the New Quarterly *for September 1910 but*
that journal suspended publication in the previous May. They were made
public by Longman's Green and Company when that house published the
essays under their now famous title as the first chapter of their volume
Philosophical Essays. *Russell made various minor textual corrections and*
emendations to sections 1 through 4 in the 1910 published version. These
additions have been placed within brackets. Here for the first time the
reader is presented with the essays in their most complete form with ac-
companying footnotes that were not in the 1910 published version.

Russell begins by asking two fundamental questions: (1) What is the
nature of ethical inquiry? and (2) On what topics are there legitimate and
important questions for the theoretical ethicist to answer?

In this work, Russell defends a position closely akin to that elaborated
by his friend and colleague George Edward Moore in Principia Ethica
(1903). Although the substance of Russell's work owes a lot to Moore,
Russell's method of presentation and his arguments differ somewhat from
Moore's. (I refer the reader to Lillian Aiken's Bertrand Russell's Philosophy
of Morals *for a full discussion of the difference between Moore's* Principia
Ethica *and Russell's "The Elements of Ethics.")*

Russell writes that the substance of ethics is as independent of human
judgment as is the substance of mathematics. Right and wrong, good and
evil, are entities as unalterable as the redness of fire or the softness of
wool, and a statement involving them can be as true or false as a state-

ment involving any other fact in the universe. "Good" itself is an indefinable non-natural quality. "Thus good and bad are qualities which belong to objects independently of our opinions, just as much as round and square do; and when two people differ as to whether a thing is good only one of them can be right, though it may be very hard to know which is right."

Russell elaborates on these propositions and enters into a discussion chiefly concerned with the question of right conduct. He maintains that right action is that which produces the most good. In the case where no favorable balance of good is attainable, the right action is that which produces the smallest preponderance of evil. The degree to which some state of affairs is intrinsically good (good in and for itself), according to Russell, has an objectively true answer that is discoverable only by intuition. He is disinclined to discuss or outline actions that can be considered good. Russell justifies this omission by stating that if the reader agrees with the analysis, he can make such a list himself, and if he disagrees "without falling into any of the possible confusions, there is no way of altering his opinion."

Although Russell eventually disassociated himself from the theory that he advocates here, these early views still represent an important and complex analysis of some of the basic problems in contemporary ethical theory. They also raise genuine challenges to those ethical theories that maintain the existence of a logical connection between moral judgments and factual premises, where the latter are not necessarily confined to empirical statements, but may also include metaphysical doctrines.

It is perhaps significant that "The Elements of Ethics" was written before the First World War; for Russell often said that it was just such a global tragedy that first awakened his interest in social and political reforms. Accordingly, most of his later writings were concerned more with practice than with theory.

I. THE SUBJECT—MATTER OF ETHICS*

The study of Ethics is perhaps most commonly conceived as being concerned with the questions "What sort of actions ought men to perform?" and "What sort of actions ought men to avoid?"[1] It is conceived, that is to say, as dealing with human conduct, and as deciding what is virtuous and what vicious among the kinds of conduct between which, in practice, people are called upon to choose. Owing to this view of the province of ethics, it is sometimes regarded as *the* practical study, to which all others may be opposed as theoretical; the good and the true are sometimes spoken of as independent kingdoms, the former belonging to ethics, while the latter belongs to the sciences.

---

*Originally published as "Ethics (I)"in *The New Quarterly* 3 (February 1910): 21-34.

This view, however, is doubly defective. In the first place, it overlooks the fact that the object of ethics, by its own account, is to discover true propositions about virtuous and vicious conduct, and that these are just as much a part of truth as true propositions about oxygen or the multiplication table. The aim is, not practice, but propositions about practice; and propositions about practice are not themselves practical, any more than propositions about gases are gaseous. One might as well maintain that botany is vegetable or zoology animal. Thus the study of ethics is not something outside science and co-ordinate with it: it is merely one among sciences.

In the second place, the view in question unduly limits the province of ethics. When we are told that actions of certain kinds ought to be performed or avoided, as, for example, that we ought to speak the truth, or that we ought not to steal, we may always legitimately ask for a reason, and this reason will always be concerned, not only with the actions themselves, but also with the goodness or badness of the consequences likely to follow from such actions. We shall be told that truth-speaking generates mutual confidence, cements friendships, facilitates the dispatch of business, and hence increases the wealth of the society which practices it, and so on. If we ask why we should aim at increasing mutual confidence, or cementing friendships, we may be told that obviously these things are good, or that they lead to happiness, and happiness is good. If we still ask why, the plain man will probably feel irritation, and will reply that he does not know. His irritation is due to the conflict of two feelings—the one, that whatever is true must have a reason; the other, that the reason he has already given is so obvious that it is merely contentious to demand a reason for the reason. In the second of these feelings he may be right; in the first, he is certainly wrong. In ordinary life, people only ask why, when they are unconvinced. If a reason is given which they do not doubt, they are satisfied. Hence, when they do ask why, they usually have a logical right to expect an answer, and they come to think that a belief for which no reason can be given is an unreasonable belief. But in this they are mistaken, as they would soon discover if their habit of asking *why* were more persistent. It is the business of the philosopher to ask for reasons as long as reasons can legitimately be demanded, and to register the propositions which give the most ultimate reasons that are attainable.

Since a proposition can only be proved by means of other propositions, it is obvious that not all propositions can be proved, for proofs can only begin by assuming something. And since the consequences have no more certainty than their premises, the things that are proved are no more certain than the things that are accepted merely because they are obvious, and are then made the basis of our proofs. Thus in the case of ethics, in particular, we must ask why such and such actions ought to be performed, and continue our backward inquiry for reasons until we reach the kind of proposition of which proof is impossible, because it is so simple or so obvious that nothing more fundamental can be found from which to deduce it.

Now when we ask for the reasons in favor of the actions which moralists recommend, these reasons are, usually, that the consequences of the actions are likely to be *good,* or if not wholly good, at least the best possible under the circumstances. Hence all questions of conduct presuppose the decision as to what things other than conduct are *good* and what *bad.* What is called good conduct is conduct which is a means to other things which are good on their own account; and hence the study of what is good on its own account is necessary before we can decide upon rules of conduct. And the study of what is good or bad on its own account must be included in ethics, which thus ceases to be concerned only with human conduct.

The first step in ethics, therefore, is to be quite clear as to what we mean by good and bad. Only then can we return to conduct, and ask how right conduct is related to the production of goods and the avoidance of evils. In this, as in all philosophical inquiries, after a preliminary analysis of complex data we proceed again to build up complex things from their simpler constituents, starting from ideas which we understand though we cannot define them, and from premises which we know though we cannot prove them. The appearance of dogmatism in this procedure is deceptive, for the premises are such as ordinary reasoning unconsciously assumes, and there is less real dogmatism in believing them after a critical scrutiny than in employing them implicitly without examination.

II. THE MEANING OF GOOD AND BAD

Good and Bad, in the sense in which the words are here intended (which is, I believe, their usual sense), are the objects of ideas which everybody, or almost everybody, possesses. These ideas are apparently among those which form the simplest constituents of our more complex ideas, and are therefore incapable of being analyzed or built up out of other simpler ideas. When people ask "What do you mean by

Good?" the answer must consist, not in a verbal definition such as could be given if one were asked "What do you mean by *Pentagon?*" but in such a characterization as shall call up the appropriate idea to the mind of the questioner.

This characterization may, and probably will, itself contain the idea of *good,* which would be a fault in a definition, but is harmless when our purpose is merely to stimulate the imagination to the production of the idea which is intended. It is in this way that children are taught the names of colors: they are shown (say) a red book, and told that that is red; and for fear they should think *red* means *book,* they are shown also a red flower, a red ball, and so on, and told that these are all red. Thus the idea of redness is conveyed to their minds, although it is quite impossible to analyze redness or to find constituents which compose it.

In the case of *good,* the process is more difficult, both because goodness is not perceived by the senses, like redness, and because there is less agreement as to the things that are good than as to the things that are red. This is perhaps one reason that has led people to think that the notion of *good* could be analyzed into some other notion, such as *pleasure* or *object of desire.* A second reason, probably more potent, is the common confusion that makes people think they cannot understand an idea unless they can define it— forgetting that ideas as defined by other ideas, which must be already understood if the definition is to convey any meaning. When people begin to philosophize, they seem to make a point of forgetting everything familiar and ordinary; otherwise their acquaintance with redness or any other color might show them how an idea can be intelligible where definition, in the sense of analysis, is impossible.

To explain what we mean by Good and Bad, we may say that a thing is good when on its own account it ought to exist, [and bad when on its own account it ought not to exist]. If it seems to be in our power to cause a thing to exist or not to exist, we ought to try to make it exist if it is good, and not exist if it is bad. When a thing is good, it is fitting that we should feel pleasure in its existence; when it is bad, it is fitting that we should feel pain in its existence. But all such characterizations really presuppose the notions of good and bad, and are therefore useful only as means of calling up the right ideas, not as logical definitions.

It might be thought that *good* could be defined as the quality of whatever we ought to try to produce. This would merely put *ought* in the place of *good* as our ultimate undefined notion; but as a

the good is much wider than what we ought to try to
is no reason to doubt that some of the lost tragedies
ere good, but we ought not to try to re-write them,
uld certainly fail. What we ought to do, in fact, is
owers and opportunities, whereas the good is subject
to no such limitation. And our knowledge of goods is confined to the
things we have experienced or can imagine; but presumably there
are many goods of which we human beings have absolutely no
knowledge, because they do not come within the very restricted
range of our thoughts and feelings. Such goods are still goods, although human conduct can have no reference to them. Thus the
notion of good is wider and more fundamental than any notion
concerned with conduct; we use the notion of good in explaining
what right conduct is, but we do not use the notion of right conduct
in explaining what good is.

A fairly plausible view is that *good* means the same as *desired,* so that when we say a thing is good we mean that it is
desired. Thus anything is good which we either hope to acquire or
fear to lose. Yet it is commonly admitted that there are bad desires;
and when people speak of bad desires, they seem to mean desires for
what is bad. For example, when one man desires another man's
pain, it is obvious that what is desired is not good but bad. But the
supporter of the view that *good* means *desired* will say that nothing
is good or bad in itself, but is good for one person and perhaps bad
for another. This must happen, he will say, in every case of a conflict of desires; if I desire your suffering, then your suffering is good
for me, though it is bad for you. But the sense of *good* and *bad*
which is needed in ethics is not in this way personal; and it is quite
essential, in the study of ethics, to realize that there is an impersonal
sense. In this sense, when a thing is good, it ought to exist on its
own account, not on account of its consequences, nor yet of who is
going to enjoy it. We cannot maintain that for me a thing ought to
exist on its own account, while for you it ought not; that would
merely mean that one of us is mistaken, since in fact everything
either ought to exist or ought not. Thus the fact that one man's
desire may be another man's aversion proves that *good,* in the sense
relevant to ethics, does not mean the same as *desired,* since everything is in itself either good or not good, and cannot be at once good
for me and bad for you. This could only mean that its effects on me
were good, and on you bad; but here good and bad are again impersonal.

There is another line of argument, more subtle but more instructive, by which we can refute those who say that *good* means *desired,* or who propose any other idea, such as pleasure, as the actual *meaning* of good. This line of argument will not prove that the things that are good are not the same as the things that are desired; but it will prove that, if this were the case, it could not be proved by appealing to the *meaning* of the word "good." So far, it might be thought that such an argument could only have a purely logical importance. But in fact this is not so. Many ethical theories have been based upon the contention that "good" means so-and-so, and people have accepted consequences of this contention which, if they had relied upon inspection untrammelled by false theory, they would almost certainly have rejected. Whoever believes that "good" means "desired" will try to explain away the cases where it seems as if what is desired is bad; but if he no longer holds this theory, he will be able to allow free play to his unbiased ethical feelings [perceptions] and will thus escape errors into which he would otherwise have fallen.

The argument in question is this: If any one affirms that the good is the desired, we consider what he says, and either assent or dissent; but in any case our assent or dissent is decided by considering what the good and the desired really are. When, on the contrary, some one gives a definition of the meaning of a word, our state of mind is quite different. If we are told "a pentagon is a figure which has five sides," we do not consider what we know about pentagons, and then agree or disagree; we accept this as the meaning of the word, and we know that we are getting information, not about pentagons, but merely about the *word* "pentagon." What we are told is the sort of thing that we expect dictionaries to tell us. But when we are told that the good is the desired, we feel at once that we are being told something of philosophical importance, something which has ethical consequences, something which it is quite beyond the scope of a dictionary to tell us. The reason of this is, that we already know what we mean by the good, and what we mean by the desired; and if these two meanings always applied to the same objects, that would not be a verbal definition, but an important truth. The analogue of such a proposition is not the above definition of a pentagon but rather: "A pentagon (defined as above) is a figure which has five angles." Whenever a proposed definition sets us thinking whether it is true in fact, and not whether that is how the word is used, there is reason to suspect that we are not dealing with a definition, but with a significant proposition, in which the word professedly defined has a meaning already known to us, either as simple or as defined in some other way. By applying this test, we shall easily convince ourselves that all hitherto suggested definitions of the good are significant, not merely verbal, propositions; and that therefore, though they *may* be true in fact, they do not give the meaning of the word "good."

The importance of this result is that so many ethical theories depend upon the denial of it. Some have contended that "good" means "desired," others that "good" means "pleasure," others again that it means "conformity to Nature" or "obedience to the will of God." The mere fact that so many different and incompatible definitions have been proposed is evidence against any of them being really definitions; there have never been two incompatible definitions of the word "pentagon." None of the above are really definitions; they are all to be understood as substantial affirmations concerning the things that are good. All of them are, in my opinion, mistaken in fact as well as in form, but I shall not here undertake to refute them severally.

It is important to realize that when we say a thing is good in itself, and not merely as a means, we attribute to the thing a property which it either has or does not have, quite independently of our opinion on the subject, or of our wishes or other people's. Most men are inclined to agree with Hamlet: "There is nothing good or bad but thinking makes it so." It is supposed that ethical preferences are a mere matter of taste, and that if X thinks A is a good thing, and Y thinks it is a bad thing, all we can say is that A is good for X and bad for Y. This view is rendered plausible by the divergence of opinion as to what is good and bad, and by the difficulty of finding arguments to persuade people who differ from us in such a question. But difficulty in discovering the truth does not prove that there is no truth to be discovered. If X says A is good, and Y says A is bad, one of them must be mistaken, though it may be impossible to discover which. If this were not the case, there would be no difference of opinion between them. If, in asserting that A is good, X meant merely to assert that A had a certain relation to himself, say of pleasing his taste in some way; and if Y, is saying that A is not good, meant merely to deny that A had a like relation to himself: then there would be no subject of debate between them. It would be absurd if X said "I am eating a pigeon-pie," for Y to answer "that is false: I am eating nothing." But this is no more absurd than a dispute as to what is good, if, when we say A is good, we mean merely to affirm a relation of A to ourselves. When Christians assert that God is good, they do not mean merely that the contemplation of God rouses certain emotions in them: they may admit that this contemplation rouses no such emotion in the devils who believe and tremble, but the absence of such emotions is one of the things that make devils bad.

As a matter of fact, we consider some tastes better than others: we do not hold merely that some tastes are ours and other tastes are other people's. We may prefer bridge to poetry, but think it better to prefer poetry to bridge. And when Christians affirm that a world created by a good God must be a good world, they do not mean that it must be to their taste, for often it is by no means to their taste, but they use its goodness to argue that it *ought* to be their taste. And they do not mean merely that it is to God's taste: for that would have been equally the case if God had not been good. Thus *good* and *bad* are qualities which belong to objects independently of our opinions, just as much as *round* and *square* do; and when two people differ as to whether a thing is good, only one of them can be right, though it may be very hard to know which is right.

One very important consequence of the indefinability of *good* must be emphasized, namely, the fact that knowledge as to what things exist, have existed, or will exist, can throw absolutely no light upon the question as to what things are good. There might, as far as mere logic goes, be some general proposition to the effect "whatever exists, is good," or "whatever exists, is bad," or "what will exist is better (or worse) than what does exist." But no such general proposition can be proved by considering the *meaning* of "good," and no such general proposition can be arrived at empirically from experience, since we do not know the whole of what does exist, nor yet of what has existed or will exist. We cannot therefore arrive at such a general proposition, unless it is itself self-evident, or follows from some self-evident proposition, which must (to warrant the consequence) be of the same general kind. But, as a matter of fact, there is, so far as I can discover, no self-evident proposition as to the goodness or badness of all that exists or has existed or will exist. It follows that, from the fact that the existent world is of such and such a nature, nothing can be inferred as to what things are good or bad.

The belief that the world is wholly good has, nevertheless, been widely held. It has been held either because, as a part of revealed religion, the world has been supposed created by a good and omnipotent God, or because, on metaphysical grounds, it was thought possible to *prove* that the sum-total of existent things must be good. With the former line of argument we are not here concerned; the latter must be briefly dealt with. The belief that, without assuming any ethical premise, we can prove that the world is good, or indeed any other result containing the notion of good, logically involves the belief that the notion of good is complex and capable of definition. If when we say that a thing is good we mean (for example) that it has three other simpler properties, then, by proving that a thing has those three properties we prove that it is good, and thus we get a conclusion involving the notion of *good* although our premises did not involve it. But if *good* is a simple notion, no such inference will be possible; unless our premises contain the notion of good, our conclusion cannot contain it. The case is analogous to the case of elements and compounds in chemistry. By combining elements or compounds, we can get a new compound, but no chemical operation will give an element which was not present in the beginning. So, if good is simple, no propositions not containing this notion can have consequences which do contain it.

As a matter of fact, those who have endeavored to prove that the world as a whole is good have usually adopted the view that all evil consists wholly in the absence of something, and that nothing positive is evil. This they have usually supported by defining *good* as meaning the same as *real*. Spinoza says[2]: "By reality and perfection I mean the same thing"; and hence it follows, with much less trouble than metaphysicians have usually taken in the proof, that the real is perfect. This is the view in "Abt Vogler":

"The evil is null, is nought, is silence implying sound."

Whenever it is said that all evil is limitation, the same doctrine is involved; what is meant is that evil never consists in the existence of something which can be called bad, but only in the non-existence of something. Hence everything that does exist must be good, and the sum-total of existence, since it exists most, must be the best of all. And this view is set forth as resulting from the *meaning* of evil.

The notion that non-existence is what is *meant* by evil is refuted exactly as the previous definitions of good were refuted. And the belief that, as a matter of fact, nothing that exists is evil, is one which no one would advocate except a metaphysician defending a theory. Pain and hatred and envy and cruelty are surely things that exist, and are not merely the absence of their opposites; but the theory should hold that they are indistinguishable from the blank unconsciousness of an oyster. Indeed, it would seem that this whole theory has been advanced solely because of the unconscious bias in favor of optimism, and that its opposite is logically just as tenable. We might urge that evil consists in existence, and good in non-existence; that therefore the sum-total of existence is the worst thing there is, and that only non-existence is good. Indeed, Buddhism does seem to maintain some such view. It is plain that this view is false; but logically it is no more absurd than its opposite.

We cannot, then, infer any results as to what is good or bad from a study of the things that exist. This conclusion needs chiefly, at the present time, to be applied against evolutionary ethics. The phrase "survival of the fittest" seems to have given rise to the belief that those who survive are the fittest in some ethical sense, and that the course of evolution gives evidence that the later type is better than the earlier. On this basis, a worship of force is easily set up, and the mitigation of struggle by civilization comes to be deprecated. It is thought that what fights most successfully is most admirable, and that what does not help in fighting is worthless. Such a view is wholly destitute of logical foundation. The course of nature, as we have seen, is irrelevant in deciding as to what is good or bad. *A priori*, it would be as probable that evolution should go from bad to worse, as that it should go from good to better. What makes the view plausible is the fact that the lower animals existed earlier than the higher, and that among men the civilized races are able to defeat and [often] exterminate the uncivilized. But here the ethical preference of the higher to the lower animals, and of the exterminators to the exterminated, is not based upon evolution, but exists independently, and unconsciously intrudes into our judgment of the evolutionary process. If evolutionary ethics were sound, we ought to be entirely indifferent as to what the course of evolution may be, since whatever it is is thereby proved to be the best. Yet if it should turn out that the negro or the Chinaman was able to oust the European, we should cease to have any admiration for evolution; for as a matter of fact our preference of the European to the negro is wholly independent of the European's greater prowess with the Maxim gun.

Broadly, the fact that a thing is unavoidable affords no evidence that it is not an evil; and the fact that a thing is impossible affords no evidence that it is not a good. It is doubtless foolish, in practice, to fret over the inevitable; but it is false, in theory, to let the actual world dictate our standard of good and evil. It is evident that among

the things that exist some are good, some bad, and that we know too
little of the universe to have any right to an opinion as to whether
the good or the bad preponderates, or as to whether either is likely in
the future to gain on the other. Optimism and pessimism alike are
general theories as to the universe which there is no reason whatever for accepting; what we know of the world tends to suggest that
the good and the evil are fairly balanced, but it is of course possible
that what we do not know is very much better or very much worse
than what we do know. Complete suspense of judgment in this
matter is, therefore, the only rational attitude.

III. RIGHT AND WRONG*

The ideas of right and wrong conduct are, as we have seen, those
with which ethics is generally supposed to be most concerned. This
view, which is unduly narrow, is fostered by the use of the one word
good, both for the sort of conduct which is *right,* and for the sort of
things which ought to exist on account of their intrinsic value. This
double use of the word *good* is very confusing, and tends greatly to
obscure the distinction of ends and means. I shall therefore speak of
right actions, not of *good* actions, confining the word *good* to the
sense explained in Section II.

The word "right" is very ambiguous, and it is by no means easy
to distinguish the various meanings which it has in common par-
lance. Owing to the variety of these meanings, adherence to any one
necessarily involves us in apparent paradoxes when we use it in a
context which suggests one of the other meanings. This is the usual
result of precision of language; but so long as the paradoxes are
merely verbal, they do not give rise to more than verbal objections.

In judging of conduct we find at the outset two widely divergent
methods, of which one is advocated by some moralists, the other by
others, while both are practiced by those who have no ethical theory.
One of these methods, which is that advocated by Utilitarians,
judges the rightness of an act by relation to the goodness or badness
of its consequences. The other method, advocated by intuitionists,
judges by the approval or disapproval of the moral sense or conscience. I believe that it is necessary to combine both theories in

---

*Originally published as "Ethics (II)" in *The New Quarterly* 3 (May 1910): 131–143 order to get a complete account of right and wrong. There is, I think, one sense in which a man does right when he does what will probably have the best consequences, and another in which he does right when he follows the dictates of his conscience, whatever the probable consequences may be. (There are many other senses which we may give to the word *right*, but these two seem to be the most important.) Let us begin by considering the second of these senses.

The question we have to ask ourselves is: What do we mean by the dictates of the moral sense? If these are to afford a definition of right conduct, we cannot say that they consist in judging that such and such acts are *right*, for that would make our definition circular.

We shall have to say that the moral sense consists in a certain specific emotion of *approval* towards an act, and that an act is to be called right when the agent, at the moment of action, feels this emotion of approval towards the action which he decides to perform. There is certainly a sense in which a man ought to perform any act which he approves, and to abstain from any act which he disapproves; and it seems also undeniable that there are emotions which may be called approval and disapproval. Thus this theory, whether adequate or not, must be allowed to contain a part of the truth.

It is, however, fairly evident that there are other meanings of right conduct, and that, though there is an emotion of approval, there is also a judgment of approval, which may or may not be true. For we certainly hold that a man who has done an action which his conscience approved may have been mistaken, and that in some sense his conscience ought not to have approved his action. But this would be impossible if nothing were involved except an emotion. To be mistaken implies a judgment; and thus we must admit that there is such a thing as a *judgment* of approval. If this were not the case we could not reason with a man as to what is right; what he approves would be necessarily right for him to do, and there could be no argument against his approval. We do in fact hold that when one man approves of a certain act, while another disapproves, one of them is mistaken, which would not be the case with a mere emotion. If one man likes oysters and another dislikes them, we do not say that either of them is mistaken.

Thus there is a judgment of approval,[3] and this must consist of a judgment that an act is, in a new sense, right. The judgment of approval is not merely the judgment that we feel the emotion of approval, for then another who disapproved would not necessarily hold our judgment of approval to be mistaken. Thus in order to give a meaning to the judgment of approval, it is necessary to admit a sense of *right* other than *approved*. In this sense, when we approve an act we judge that it is right, and we may be mistaken in so judging. This new sense is *objective,* in the sense that it does not depend upon the opinions and feelings of the agent. Thus a man who obeys the dictates of his conscience is not always acting rightly in the objective sense. When a man does what his conscience approves, he does what he *believes* to be objectively right, but not necessarily what *is* objectively right. We need, therefore, some other criterion than the moral sense for judging what is objectively right.

It is in defining objective rightness that the consequences of an action become relevant. Some moralists, it is true, deny the dependence upon consequences; but that is to be attributed, I think, to confusion with the subjective sense. When people argue as to whether such and such an action is right, they always adduce the consequences which it has or may be expected to have. A statesman who has to decide what is the right policy, or a teacher who has to decide what is the right education, will be expected to consider what policy or what education is likely to have the best results. Whenever a question is at all complicated, and cannot be settled by following some simple rule, such as "thou shalt not steal," or "thou shalt not bear false witness," it is at once evident that the decision cannot be made except by consideration of consequences.

But even when the decision can be made by a simple precept, such as not to lie or not to steal, the justification of the precept is found only by consideration of consequences. A code such as the Decalogue, it must be admitted, can hardly be true *without exception* if the goodness or badness of consequences is what determines the rightness or wrongness of actions; for in so complex a world it is unlikely that obedience to the Decalogue will always produce better consequences than disobedience. Yet it is a suspicious circumstance that breaches of those of the Ten Commandments which people still hold it a duty to obey do, as a matter of fact, have bad consequences in the vast majority of instances, and would not be considered wrong in a case in which it was fairly certain that their consequences would be good. This latter fact is concealed by a question-begging addition of moral overtones to words. Thus, e.g., "thou shalt do no murder," would be an important precept if it were interpreted, as Tolstoy interprets it, to mean "thou shalt not take human life." But it is not so interpreted; on the contrary, some taking of human life is called "justifiable homicide." Thus murder comes to mean "unjustifiable homicide"; and it is a mere tautology to say, "Thou shalt do no unjustifiable homicide." That this should be announced from Sinai would be as fruitless as Hamlet's report of the ghost's message: "There's not a villain, in all Denmark, but he's an arrant knave." As a matter of fact, people do make a certain classification of homicides, and decide that certain kinds are justifiable and certain others unjustifiable. But there are many doubtful cases: tyrannicide, capital punishment, killing in war, killing in self-defense, killing in defense of others, are some of these. And if a decision is sought, it is sought usually by considering whether the consequences of actions belonging to these classes are on the whole good or bad. Thus the importance of precepts such as the Ten Commandments lies in the fact that they give simple rules, obedience to which will in almost all cases have better consequences than disobedience; and the justification of the rules is not wholly independent of consequences.

In common language the received code of moral rules is usually presupposed, and an action is only called *immoral* when it infringes one of these rules. Whatever does not infringe them is regarded as permissible, so that on most of the occasions of life no one course of action is marked out as alone *right*. If a man adopts a course of action which, though not contrary to the received code, will probably have bad consequences, he is called unwise rather than immoral. Now, according to the distinction we have made between objective and subjective rightness, a man may well act in a way which is objectively wrong without doing what is subjectively wrong, i.e. what his conscience disapproves. An act (roughly speaking, I shall return to this point presently) is *immoral* when a man's conscience disapproves it, but is judged only unwise or injudicious when his conscience approves it, although we judge that it will probably have bad consequences. Now the usual moral code is supposed, in common language, to be admitted by every man's conscience, so that when he infringes it, his action is not merely injudicious, but immoral; on the other hand, where the code is silent, we regard an unfortunate action as objectively but not subjectively wrong, i.e. as injudicious, but not immoral.

The acceptance of a moral code has the great advantage that, in so far as its rules are objectively right, it tends to harmonize objective and subjective rightness. Thus it tends to cover all frequent cases, leaving only the rarer ones to the individual judgment of the agent. Hence when new sorts of cases become common, the moral code soon comes to deal with them; thus each profession has its own code concerning cases common in the profession, though not outside it. But the moral code is never itself ultimate; it is based upon an estimate of probable consequences, and is essentially a method of leading men's judgment to approve what is objectively right and disapprove what is objectively wrong. And when once a fairly correct code is accepted, the exceptions to it become very much fewer than they would otherwise be, because one of the consequences of admitting exceptions is to weaken the code, and this consequence is usually bad enough to outweigh the good resulting from admitting such and such an exception. This argument, however, works in the opposite direction with a grossly incorrect code; and it is to be observed that most conventional codes embody some degree of unwarrantable selfishness, individual, professional, or national, and are thus in certain respects worthy of detestation.

What is objectively right, then, is in some way dependent on consequences. The most natural supposition to start from would be that the objectively right act, under any circumstances, is the one which will have the best consequences. We will define this as the *most fortunate* act. The most fortunate act, then, is the one which will produce the greatest excess of good over evil, or the least excess of evil over good (for there may be situations in which every possible act will have consequences that are on the whole bad). But we cannot maintain that the most fortunate act is always the one which is objectively right, in the sense that it is what a wise man will hold that he ought to do. For it may happen that the act which will in fact prove the most fortunate is likely, according to all the evidence at our disposal, to be less fortunate than some other. In such a case, it will be, at least in one sense, objectively wrong to go against the evidence, in spite of the actual good result of our doing so. There have certainly been some men who have done so much harm that it would have been fortunate for the world if their nurses had killed them in infancy. But if their nurses had done so the action would not have been objectively right, because the probability was that it would not have the best effects. Hence it would seem we must take account of probability in judging of objective rightness; let us then consider whether we can say that the objectively right act is the one which will *probably* be most fortunate. I shall define this as the *wisest* act. The *wisest* act, then, is that one which, when account is taken of all available data, gives us the greatest expectation of good on the balance, [or the least expectation of evil on the balance]. There is, of course, a difficulty as to what are to be considered available data; but broadly we can distinguish, in any given state of knowledge, things capable of being foreseen from things which are unpredictable. I suppose account to be taken of the general body of current knowledge, in fact the sort of consideration which people expect when they ask legal or medical advice. There is no doubt this brings us nearer to what is objectively right than we were when we were considering the actually most fortunate act. For one thing, it justifies the unavoidable limitation to not very distant consequences, which is almost always necessary if a practical decision is to be reached. For the likelihood of error in calculating distant consequences is so great, that their contribution to the *probable* good or evil is very small, though their contribution to the *actual* good or evil is likely to be much greater than that of the nearer consequences. And it seems evident that what it is quite impossible to know cannot be relevant in judging as to what conduct is right. If, as is possible, a cataclysm is going to destroy life on this planet this day week, many acts otherwise useful will prove to have been wasted labor; but since we have no reason to expect such a cataclysm, the rightness or wrongness of acts is plainly to be estimated without regard to it.

One apparent objection at once suggests itself to the definition. Very few acts are of sufficient importance to justify such elaborate and careful consideration as is required for forming an opinion as to whether they are the wisest. Indeed, the least important decisions are often those which it would be hardest to make on purely reasonable grounds. A man who debates on each day which of two ways of taking exercise is likely to prove most beneficial is considered absurd; the question is at once difficult and unimportant, and is therefore not worth spending time over. But although it is true that unimportant decisions ought not to be made with excessive care, there is danger of confusion if this is regarded as an objection to our definition of objective rightness. For the act which, in the case supposed, is objectively wrong, is the act of deliberation, not the act decided upon as the result of deliberation. And the deliberation is condemned by our definition, for it is very unlikely that there is no more beneficial way of spending time than in debating trivial points of conduct. Thus, although the wisest act is the one which, after complete investigation, appears likely to give the most fortunate results, yet the complete investigation required to show that it is the wisest act is only itself wise in the case of very important decisions. This is only an elaborate way of saying that a wise man will not waste time on unimportant details. Hence this apparent objection can be answered.

One further addition is required for the definition of the objectively right act, namely, that it must be *possible*. Among the acts whose consequences are to be considered we must not include such as are either physically impossible to perform, or impossible for the agent to think of. This last condition introduces difficulties connected with Determinism, which I have discussed elsewhere.* Ignoring these difficulties, we may say that the objectively right act is that one which, of all that are possible, will probably have the best consequences.

We must now return to the consideration of subjective rightness, with a view to distinguishing conduct which is merely mistaken from conduct which is immoral or blameworthy. We here require a new sense of *ought,* which it is by no means easy to define. In the objective sense, a man ought to do what is objectively right. But in the subjective sense, which we have now to examine, he sometimes ought to do what is objectively wrong. For example, we saw that it is often objectively right to give less consideration to an unimportant question of conduct than would be required for forming a trustworthy judgment as to what is objectively right. Now it seems plain that if we have given to such a question the amount and kind of consideration which is objectively right, and we then do what *appears* to us objectively right, our action is, in some sense, subjectively right, although it may be objectively wrong. Our action could certainly not be called a sin, and might even be highly virtuous, in spite of its objective wrongness. It is these notions of what is sinful and what is virtuous that we have now to consider.

The first suggestion that naturally occurs is that an act is subjectively right when it is judged by the agent to be objectively right, and subjectively wrong when it is judged to be objectively wrong. I do not mean that it is subjectively right when the agent judges that it is the act which, of all that are possible, will probably have the best results; for the agent may not accept the above account of objective rightness. I mean merely that it is the one towards which he has the judgment of approval. A man may judge an act to be right without judging that its consequences will be probably the best possible; I only contend that, when he *truly* judges it to be right, then

---

*"Determinism and Morals," *Hibbert Journal* 7 (October 1908): 113-121. [See section IV below.]

its consequences will probably be the best possible. But his judgment as to what is objectively right may err, not only by a wrong estimate of probable consequences, or by failing to think of an act which he might have thought of, but also by a wrong theory as to what constitutes objective rightness. In other words, the definition I gave of objective rightness is not meant as an analysis of the meaning of the word, but as a mark which in fact attaches to all objectively right actions and to no others.

We are to consider then the suggestion that an act is moral when the agent approves it, and immoral when he disapproves it; using *moral* to mean *subjectively right* and *immoral* to mean *subjectively wrong*. This suggestion, it is plain, will not stand without much modification. In the first place, we often hold it immoral to approve some things and disapprove others, unless there are special circumstances to excuse such approval or disapproval. In the second place, unreflecting acts, in which there is no judgment either of approval or disapproval, are often moral or immoral. For both these reasons the suggested definition must be regarded as inadequate.

The doctrine that an act is never immoral when the agent thinks it right has the drawback (or the advantage) that it excuses almost all the acts which would be commonly condemned. Very few people deliberately do what, at the moment, they believe to be wrong; usually they first argue themselves into a belief that what they wish to do is right. They decide that it is their duty to teach so-and-so a lesson, that their rights have been so grossly infringed that if they take no revenge there will be an encouragement to injustice, that without a moderate indulgence in pleasure a character cannot develop in the best way, and so on and so on. Yet we do not cease to blame them on that account.

Of course it may be said that a belief produced by a course of self-deception is not a genuine belief, and that the people who invent such excuses for themselves know all the while that the truth is the other way. Up to a point this is no doubt true, though I doubt if it is always true. There are, however, other cases of mistaken judgment as to what is right, where the judgment is certainly genuine, and yet we blame the agent. These are cases of thoughtlessness, where a man remembers consequences to himself, but forgets consequences to others. In such a case he may judge correctly and honestly on all the data that he remembers, yet if he were a better man he would remember more data. Most of the actions commonly condemned as selfish probably come under this head. Hence we must admit that an act may be immoral, even if the agent quite genuinely judges that it is right. Unreflecting acts, again, in which there is no judgment as to right or wrong, are often praised or blamed. Acts of generosity, for example, are more admired when they are impulsive than when they result from reflection. I cannot think of any act which is more blamed when it is impulsive than when it is deliberate; but certainly many impulsive acts are blamed—for example, such as spring from an impulse of malice or cruelty.

In all these cases where reflection is absent, and also in the case of inadequate reflection, it may be said that blame does not belong properly to the act, but rather to the character revealed by the act, or, if to some acts, then to those previous deliberate acts by which the character has been produced which has resulted in the present act. The cases of self-deception would then be dismissed on the ground that the self-deceiver never really believes what he wishes to believe. We could then retain our original definition, that a moral act is one which the agent judges to be right, while an immoral one is one which he judges to be wrong. But I do not think this would accord with what most people really mean. I rather think that a moral act should be defined as one which the agent would have judged to be right if he had considered the question candidly and with due care; if, that is to say, he had examined the data before him with a view to discovering what was right, and not with a view to proving such-and-such a course to be right.

If an act is unimportant, and at the same time not obviously less right than some obvious alternative, we shall consider it neither moral nor immoral; for in such a case the act does not deserve careful consideration. The amount of care which a decision deserves depends upon its importance and difficulty; in the case of a statesman advocating a new policy, for example, years of deliberation may sometimes be necessary to excuse him from the charge of levity. But with less important acts, it is usually right to decide even when further reflection might show the present decision to be erroneous. Thus there is a certain amount of reflection appropriate to various acts, while some right acts are best when they spring from impulse (though these are such as reflection would approve).

We may therefore say that an act is moral when it is one which the agent would judge to be right after an appropriate amount of candid thought, or, in the case of acts which are best when they are unreflecting, after the amount and kind of thought requisite to form a first opinion. An act is immoral when the agent would judge it to

be wrong after an appropriate amount of reflect
moral nor immoral when it is unimportant and a
reflection would not suffice to show whether it was

We may now sum up our discussion of right a
man asks himself: "What ought I to do?" he is as
is *right* in an objective sense. He cannot mean: "What ⌣⌣
person to do who holds my views as to what a person ought to do?"
for his views as to what a person ought to do are what will constitute his answer to the question: "What ought I to do?" But the
onlooker, who thinks that the man has answered this question
wrongly, may nevertheless hold that, in acting upon his answer, the
man was acting rightly in a second, subjective, sense. This second
sort of right action we call *moral* action. We hold that an action is
moral when the agent would judge it to be *right* after an appropriate
amount of candid thought, or after a small amount in the case of
acts which are best when they are unreflecting; the appropriate
amount of thought being dependent upon the difficulty and the
importance of the decision. And we hold that an action is *right*
when, of all that are possible, it is the one which will probably have
the best results. There are many other meanings of *right,* but these
seem to be the meanings required for answering the questions:
"What ought I to do?" and "What acts are immoral?"

IV. DETERMINISM AND MORALS*

The importance to ethics of the free-will question is a subject upon
which there has existed almost as much diversity of opinion as on
the free-will question itself. It has been urged by advocates of free-
will that its denial involves the denial of merit and demerit, and
that, with the denial of these, ethics collapses. It has been urged on
the other side that, unless we can foresee, at least partially, the
consequences of our actions, it is impossible to know what course we
ought to take under any given circumstances; and that if other
people's actions cannot be in any degree predicted, the foresight
required for rational action becomes impossible. I do not propose, in
the following discussion, to go into the free-will controversy itself.
The grounds in favor of determinism appear to me overwhelming,
and I shall content myself with a brief indication of these grounds.

---

*Originally published under this title in *Hibbert Journal* 7 (October 1908): 113-121.

The question I am concerned with is not the free-will question itself, but the question how, if at all, morals are affected by assuming determinism.

In considering this question, as in most of the other problems of ethics, the moralist who has not had a philosophical training appears to me to go astray, and become involved in needless complications, through supposing that right and wrong in conduct are the ultimate conceptions of ethics, rather than good and bad, in the *effects* of conduct and in other things. The words *good* and *bad* are used both for the sort of conduct which is *right* or *wrong,* and for the sort of effects to be expected from right and wrong conduct, respectively. We speak of a *good* picture, a *good* dinner, and so on, as well as of a *good* action. But there is a great difference between these two meanings of *good.* Roughly speaking, a *good* action is one of which the probable effects are *good* in the other sense. It is confusing to have two meanings for one word, and I shall therefore speak of a *right* action rather than a *good* action. In order to decide whether an action is *right,* it is necessary to consider its probable effects. If the probable effects are, on the whole, better than those of any other action which is possible under the circumstances, then the action is *right.* The things that are good are things which, on their own account, and apart from any consideration of their effects, we ought to wish to see in existence: they are such things as, we may suppose, might make the world appear to the Creator worth creating. I do not wish to deny that right conduct is among the things that are good on their own account; but if it is so, it depends for its intrinsic goodness upon the goodness of those other things which it aims at producing, such as love or happiness. Thus the rightness of conduct is not the fundamental conception upon which ethics is built up. This fundamental conception is intrinsic goodness or badness.

In order to be able to pass quickly to the consideration of our main theme, I shall assume the following definitions. The *objectively right* action, in any circumstances, is that action which, of all that are possible, gives us, when account is taken of all available data, the greatest expectation of probable good effects, or the least expectation of probable bad effects. The *subjectively right* or *moral* action is that one which will be judged by the agent to be objectively right if he devotes to the question an appropriate amount of candid thought, or, in the case of actions that ought to be impulsive, a small amount. The appropriate amount of thought depends upon the importance of the action and the difficulty of the decision. An act is neither moral nor immoral when it is unimportant, and a small amount of reflection would not suffice to show whether it was right or wrong. After these preliminaries, we can pass to the consideration of our main topic.

The principle of causality—that every event is determined by previous events, and can (theoretically) be predicted when enough previous events are known—appears to apply just as much to human actions as to other events. It cannot be said that its application to human actions, or to any other phenomena, is wholly beyond doubt; but a doubt extending to the principle of causality must be so fundamental as to involve all science, all everyday knowledge, and everything, or almost everything, that we believe about the actual world. If causality is doubted, morals collapse, since a right action, is one of which the probable effects are the best possible, so that estimates of right and wrong necessarily presuppose that our actions can have effects, and therefore that the law of causality holds. For the view that human actions alone are not the effects of causes, there appears to be no ground whatever except the sense of spontaneity. But the sense of spontaneity only affirms that we can do as we choose, and choose as we please, which no determinist denies; it cannot affirm that our choice is independent of all motives,[4] and indeed introspection tends rather to show the opposite. It is said by the advocates of free-will[5] that determinism destroys morals, since it shows that all our actions are inevitable, and that therefore they deserve neither praise nor blame. Let us consider how far, if at all, this is the case.

The part of ethics which is concerned, not with conduct, but with the meaning of good and bad, and the things that are intrinsically good and bad, is plainly quite independent of free-will. Causality belongs to the description of the existing world, and no inference can be drawn from what exists to what is good. Whether, then, causality holds always, sometimes, or never is a question wholly irrelevant in the consideration of intrinsic goods and evils. But when we come to conduct and the notion of *ought,* we cannot be sure that determinism makes no difference. For the materially [objectively] right action may be defined as that one which, of all that are *possible* under the circumstances, will probably on the whole have the best consequences. The action which is materially [objectively] right must therefore be in some sense *possible.* But if determinism is true, there is a sense in which no action is possible except the one actually performed. Hence, if the two senses of possibility are the same, the action actually performed is always Materially [objectively] right; for it is the only possible action, and therefore there is no other possible action which would have had better results. There is here, I think, a real difficulty. But let us consider the various kinds of possibility which may be meant.

In order that an act may be a *possible* act, it must be physically possible to perform, it must be possible to think of, and it must be possible to choose if we think of it. Physical possibility, to begin with, is obviously necessary. There are circumstances under which I might do a great deal of good by running from Oxford to London in five minutes. But I should not be called unwise, or guilty of an objectively wrong act, for omitting to do so. We may define an act as physically possible when it will occur if I will it. Acts for which this condition fails are not to be taken account of in estimating rightness or wrongness.

To judge whether an act is possible to think of is more difficult, but we certainly take account of it in judging what a man ought to do. There is no *physical* impossibility about employing one's spare moments in writing lyric poems better than any yet written, and this would certainly be a more useful employment than most people find for their spare moments. But we do not blame people for not writing lyric poems unless, like Fitzgerald, they are people that we feel could have written them. And not only we do not blame them, but we feel that their action may be objectively as well as subjectively right if it is the wisest that *they* could have thought of. But what they *could* have thought of is not the same as what they *did* think of. Suppose a man in a fire or a shipwreck becomes so panic-stricken that he never for a moment thinks of the help that is due to other people, we do not on that account hold that he does right in only thinking of himself. Hence in some sense (though it is not quite clear what this sense is), some of the courses of action which a man does not think of are regarded as possible for him to think of, though others are admittedly impossible.

There is thus a sense in which it must be possible to think of an action, if we are to hold that it is objectively wrong not to perform the action. There is also, if determinism is true, a sense in which it is not possible to think of any action except those which we do think of. But it is questionable whether these two senses of possibility are the same. A man who finds that his house is on fire may run out of it in a panic without thinking of warning the other inmates; but we *feel*, rightly or wrongly, that it was possible for him to think of warning them in a sense in which it is not possible for a prosaic person to think of a lyric poem. It may be that we are wrong in feeling this difference, and that what really distinguishes the two cases is dependence upon past decisions. That is to say, we may recognize that no different choice among alternatives thought of at any time would have turned an ordinary man into a good lyric poet; but that most men, by suitably choosing among alternatives actually thought of, can acquire the sort of character which will lead them to remember their neighbors in a fire. And if a man engages in some useful occupation of which a natural effect is to destroy his nerve, we may conceivably hold that this excuses his panic in an emergency. In such a point, it would seem that our judgment may really be dependent on the view we take as to the existence of free-will; for the believer in free-will cannot allow any such excuse.

If we try to state the difference we feel between the case of the lyric poems and the case of the fire, it seems to come to this: that we do not hold an act materially [objectively] wrong when it would have required what we recognize as a special aptitude in order to think of a better act, and when we believe that the agent did not possess this aptitude. But this distinction seems to imply that there is not such a thing as a special aptitude for this or that virtue; a view which cannot, I think, be maintained. An aptitude for generosity or for kindness may be as much a natural gift as an aptitude for poetry; and an aptitude for poetry may be as much improved by practice as an aptitude for kindness or generosity. Thus it would seem that there is no sense in which it is possible to think of some actions which in fact we do not think of, but impossible to think of others, except the sense that the ones we regard as possible would have been thought of if a different choice among alternatives actually thought of had been made on some previous occasion.

We shall then modify our previous definition of the objectively right action by saying that it is the probably most beneficial among those that occur to the agent at the moment of choice. But we shall hold that, in certain cases, the fact that a more beneficial alternative does not occur to him is evidence of a wrong choice on some previous occasion. But since occasions of choice do often arise, and since there certainly is a sense in which it is possible to choose any one of a number of different actions which we think of, we can still distinguish some actions as right and some as wrong.

Our previous definitions of objectively right actions and of moral actions still hold, with the modification that, among physically possible actions, only those *which we actually think of* are to be regarded as possible. When several alternative actions present themselves, it is certain that we can both do which we choose, and choose which we will. In this sense all the alternatives are possible. What determinism maintains is, that our will to choose this or that alternative is the effect of antecedents; but this does not prevent our will from being itself a cause of other effects. And the sense in which other [different] decisions are possible seems sufficient to distinguish some actions as right and some as wrong, some as moral and some as immoral.

Connected with this is another sense in which, when we deliberate, either decision is possible. The fact that we judge one course objectively right may be the cause of our choosing this course: thus, before we have decided as to which course we think right, either is possible in the sense that either will result from our decision as to which we think right. This sense of possibility is important to the moralist, and illustrates the fact that determinism does not make moral deliberation futile.

Determinism does not, therefore, destroy the distinction of right and wrong; and we saw before that it does not destroy the distinction of good and bad: we shall still be able to regard some people as better than others, and some actions as more right than others. But it is said that praise, and blame, and responsibility are destroyed by determinism. When a madman commits what in a sane man we should call a crime, we do not blame him, partly because he probably cannot judge rightly as to consequences, but partly also because we feel that he could not have done otherwise: if all men are really in the position of the madman, it would seem that all ought to escape blame. But I think the question of choice really decides as to praise and blame. The madman, we believe (excluding the case of wrong judgment as to consequences), did not choose between different courses, but was impelled by a blind impulse. The sane man who (say) commits a murder has, on the contrary, either at the time of the murder or at some earlier time, chosen the worst of two or more alternatives that occurred to him; and it is for this we blame him. It is true that the two cases merge into each other, and the madman may be blamed if he has become mad in consequence of vicious self-indulgence. But it is right that the two cases should not be too sharply distinguished, for we know how hard it often is in practice to decide whether people are what is called "responsible for their actions." It is sufficient that there is a distinction, and that it can be applied easily in most cases, though there are marginal cases which present difficulties. We apply praise or blame, then, and we attribute responsibility, where a man, having to exercise choice, has chosen wrongly; and this sense of praise or blame is not destroyed by determinism.

Determinism, then, does not in any way interfere with morals. It is worth noticing that free-will, on the contrary, would interfere most seriously, if anybody really believed in it. People never do, as a matter of fact, believe that any one else's actions are not determined by motives, however much they may think *themselves* free. Bradshaw consists entirely of predictions as to the actions of engine-drivers; but no one doubts Bradshaw on the ground that the volitions of engine-drivers are not governed by motives. If we really believed that other people's actions did not have causes, we could never try to influence other people's actions; for such influence can only result if we know, more or less, what causes will produce the actions we desire. If we could never try to influence other people's actions, no man could try to get elected to Parliament, or ask a woman to marry him: argument, exhortation, and command would become mere idle breath. Thus almost all the actions with which morality is concerned would become irrational, rational action would be wholly precluded from trying to influence people's volitions, and right and wrong would be interfered with in a way in which determinism certainly does not interfere with them. Most morality absolutely depends upon the assumption that volitions have causes, and nothing in morals is destroyed by this assumption.

Most people, it is true, do not hold the free-will doctrine in so extreme a form as that against which we have been arguing. They would hold that most of a man's actions have causes, but that some few, say one percent, are uncaused spontaneous assertions of will. If this view is taken, unless we can mark off the one percent of volitions which are uncaused, every inference as to human actions is infected with what we may call one percent of doubt. This, it must be admitted, would not matter much in practice, because, on other grounds, there will usually be at least one percent of doubt in predictions as to human actions. But from the standpoint of theory there is a wide difference: the sort of doubt that must be admitted in any case is a sort which is capable of indefinite diminution, while the sort derived from the possible intervention of free-will is absolute and ultimate. In so far, therefore, as the possibility of uncaused volitions comes in, all the consequences above pointed out follow;

and in so far as it does not come in, determinism holds. Thus one percent of free-will has one percent of the objectionableness of absolute free-will, and has also only one percent of the ethical consequences.

In fact, however, no one really holds that right acts are uncaused. It would be a monstrous paradox to say that a man's decision ought not to be influenced by his belief as to what is his duty; yet, if he allows himself to decide on an act because he believes it to be his duty, his decision has a motive, i.e. a cause, and is not free in the only sense in which the determinist must deny freedom. It would seem, therefore, that the objections to determinism are mainly attributable to misunderstanding of its purport. Hence, finally, it is not determinism but free-will that has subversive consequences. There is therefore no reason to regret that the grounds in favor of determinism are overwhelmingly strong.

V. EGOISM*

We have next to consider an objection to the view that objective rightness consists in probably having the best consequences on the whole. The objection I mean is that of egoism: that a man's first duty is to himself, and that to secure his own good is more imperative than to secure other people's. Extensions of this view are, that a man should prefer the interest of his family to that of strangers, of his countrymen to that of foreigners, or of his friends to that of his enemies. All these views have in common the belief that, quite apart from practicability, the ends which one man ought to pursue are different from those which another man ought to pursue.

Egoism has several different meanings. It may mean that every man is psychologically bound to pursue his own good exclusively; it may mean that every man will achieve the best result on the whole by pursuing his own good; it may mean that his own good is the only thing a man ought to think good; and it may mean, lastly, that there is no such thing as the general good at all, but only individual goods, and that each man is only concerned with what is good for himself. These meanings all presuppose that we know what is meant by "*my* good"; but this is not an easy conception to define clearly. I

---

*First published in *Philosophical Essays* by Bertrand Russell (London: Longmans, Green, and Company, 1910), pp. 40-49.

shall therefore begin by considering what it is capable of meaning.

"My good" is a phrase capable of many different meanings. It may mean any good that I desire, whether this has any further special relation to me or not. Or, again, it may mean my pleasure, or any state of mind in me which is good. Or it may include honor and respect from others, or anything which is a good and has some relation to me in virtue of which it can be considered *mine*. The two meanings with which we shall be concerned are: (1) any good I desire, (2) any good having to me some relation other than that I desire it, which it does not have to others, of the kind which makes it *mine*, as my pleasure, my reputation, my learning, my virtue, etc.

The theory that every man is psychologically bound to pursue his own good exclusively is, I think, inconsistent with known facts of human nature, unless "my good" is taken in the sense of "something which I desire," and even then I do not necessarily pursue what I desire most strongly. The important point is, that what I desire has not necessarily any such other relation to me as would make it my good in the second of the above senses. This is the point which must now occupy us.

If "my good" means a good which is mine in some other sense than that I desire it, then I think it can be shown that my good is by no means the only object of my actions. There is a common confusion in people's thoughts on this subject, namely the following: If I desire anything, its attainment will give me more or less pleasure, and its non-attainment will give me more or less pain. Hence it is inferred that I desire it on account of the pleasure it would give me, and not on its own account. But this is to put the cart before the horse. The pleasure we get from things usually depends upon our having had a desire which they satisfy; the pleasures of eating and drinking, for example, depend upon hunger and thirst. Or take, again, the pleasure people get from the victory of their own party in a contest. Other people would derive just the same pleasure from the victory of the opposite party; in each case the pleasure depends for its existence upon the desire, and would not exist if the desire had not existed. Thus we cannot say that people only desire pleasure. They desire all kinds of things, and pleasures come from desires much oftener than desires from imagined pleasures. Thus the mere fact that a man will derive some pleasure from achieving his object is no reason for saying that his desire is self-centered.

Such arguments are necessary for the refutation of those who hold it to be obvious *a priori* that every man must always pursue his own good exclusively. But, as is often the case with refutations of *a priori* theories, there is an air of logic-chopping about a discussion as to whether desire or the pleasure expected from its satisfaction ought to have priority. Let us leave these questions, and consider whether, as a matter of fact, people's actions can be explained on the egoistic hypothesis. The most obvious instances to the contrary are, of course, cases of self-sacrifice—of men to their country, for example, or of parents to children. But these instances are so obvious that the egoistic theory is ready with an answer. It will maintain that, in such cases, the people who make the sacrifice would not be happy if they did not make it, that they desire the applause of men or of their own consciences, that they find in the moment of sacrifice an exaltation which realizes their highest self, etc. etc. etc. Let us examine these arguments. It is said that the people in question would not be happy if they did not make the sacrifice. This is often false in fact, but we may let that pass. Why would they not be happy? Either because others would think less well of them, or because they themselves would feel pangs of conscience, or because they genuinely desired the object to be attained by their sacrifice and could not be happy without it. In the last case they have admittedly a desire not centered in self; the supposed effect upon their happiness is due to the desire, and would not otherwise exist, so that the effect upon happiness cannot be brought into account for the desire. But if people may have desires for things that lie outside their ego, then such desires, like others, may determine action, and it is possible to pursue an object which is not "my" good in any sense except that I desire and pursue it. Thus, in all cases of self-sacrifice, those who hold the egoistic theory will have to maintain that the outside end secured by the self-sacrifice is not desired. When a soldier sacrifices his life he does not desire the victory of his country, and so on. This is already sufficiently preposterous, and sufficiently contrary to plain fact. But it is not enough. Assuming that this is the case, let us suppose that self-sacrifice is dictated, not by desire for any outside end, but by fear of the disapproval of others. If this were so there would be no self-sacrifice if no one would know of its non-performance. A man who saw another drowning would not try to save him if he was sure that no one would see him not jumping into the water. This also is plainly contrary to fact. It may be said that the desire for approval, as well as the fear of disapproval, ought to be taken into account; and a man can always make sure of approval by judicious boasting. But men have made sacrifices universally disapproved, for example, in maintaining unpopular opinions; and very many have made sacrifices of which an essential part was that they should not be mentioned. Hence the defender of psychological egoism is driven back on the approval of conscience as the motive to an act of self-sacrifice. But it is really impossible to believe that all who deny themselves are so destitute of rational foresight as this theory implies. The pangs of conscience are to most people a very endurable pain, and practice in wrong-doing rapidly diminishes them. And if the act of self-denial involves the loss of life, the rapture of self-approbation, which the virtuous man is supposed to be seeking, must in any case be very brief. I conclude that the psychology of egoism is only produced by the exigencies of a wrong theory, and is not in accordance with the facts of observable human nature.

Thus when we consider human actions and desires apart from preconceived theories, it is obvious that most of them are objective and have no direct reference to self. If "my good" means an object belonging to me in the sense of being a state of my mind, or a whole of which a state of my mind is a part, or what others think about me, then it is false that I can only desire or pursue my good. The only sense in which it is true is when "my good" is taken to mean "what I desire"; but what I desire need not have any other connection with myself, except that I desire it. Thus there is no truth in the doctrine that men do, as a matter of fact, only desire or pursue objects specially related to themselves in any way except as objects desired or pursued.

The next form of egoism to be considered is the doctrine that every man will best serve the general good by pursuing his own. There is a comfortable eighteenth-century flavor about this doctrine —it suggests a good income, a good digestion, and an enviable limitation of sympathy. We may admit at once that in a well-ordered world it would be true, and even that, as society becomes better organized, it becomes progressively truer, since rewards will more and more be attached to useful actions. And in so far as a man's own good is more in his control than other people's, his actions will rightly concern themselves more with it than with other people's. For the same reason he will be more concerned with the good of his family than with that of people with whom he has less to do, and more with the good of his own country than with that of foreign countries. But the scope of such considerations is strictly limited, and every one can easily find in his own experience cases where the general good has been served by what at any rate appears to be a self-sacrifice. If such cases are to be explained away, it is necessary to alter the conception of "my own good" in a way which destroys the significance of the doctrine we are considering. It may be said, for example, that the greatest of goods is a virtuous life. It will then follow that whoever lives a virtuous life secures for himself the greatest of goods. But if the doctrine means to assert, as it usually does, that self-centered desires, if they are prudent and enlightened, will suffice to produce the most useful conduct, then a refutation may be obtained either from common experience or from any shining example of public merit. The reformer is almost always a man who has strong desires for objects quite unconnected with himself; and indeed this is a characteristic of all who are not petty-minded. I think the doctrine depends for its plausibility, like psychological egoism, upon regarding every object which I desire as *my* good, and supposing that it must be mine in some other sense than that I desire it.

The doctrine that my good is the only thing that I ought to think good can only be logically maintained by those who hold that I ought to believe what is false. For if I am right in thinking that my good is the only good, then every one else is mistaken unless he admits that my good, not his, is the only good. But this is an admission which I can scarcely hope that others will be willing to make.

But what is really intended is, as a rule, to deny that there is any such thing as the general good at all. This doctrine cannot be logically refuted, unless by discovering in those who maintain it some opinion which implies the opposite. If a man were to maintain that there is no such thing as color, for example, we should be unable to disprove his position, provided he was careful to think out its implications. As a matter of fact, however, everybody does hold opinions which imply a general good. Everybody judges that some sorts of communities are better than others; and most people who affirm that when they say a thing is good they mean merely that they desire it, would admit that it is better two people's desires should be satisfied than only one person's. In some such way people fail to carry out the doctrine that there is no such concept as *good;* and if there is such a concept, then what is good is not good *for me* or *for you,* but is simply good. The denial that there is such a thing as good in an impersonal sense is only possible, therefore, to those who are content to have no ethics at all.

It is possible to hold that, although there is such a thing as the general good, and although this is not always best served by pursuing my own good, yet it is always right to pursue my own good exclusively. This doctrine is not now often held as regards individuals; but in international politics it is commonly held as regards nations. Many Englishmen and many Germans would admit that it is right for an English statesman to pursue exclusively the good of England, and a German the good of Germany, even if that good is to be attained by greater injury to the other. It is difficult to see what grounds there can be for such a view. If good is to be pursued at all, it can hardly be relevant who is going to enjoy the good. It would be as reasonable for a man on Sundays to think only of his welfare on future Sundays, and on Mondays to think only of Mondays. The doctrine, in fact, seems to have no merit except that it justifies acts otherwise unjustifiable. It is, indeed, so evident that it is better to secure a greater good for A than a lesser good for B, that it is hard to find any still more evident principle by which to prove this. And if A happens to be some one else, and B to be myself, that cannot affect the question, since it is irrelevant to the general maxim who A and B may be.

If no form of egoism is valid, it follows that an act which ought to be performed may involve a self-sacrifice not compensated by any personal good acquired by means of such an act. So unwilling, however, are people to admit self-sacrifice as an ultimate duty that they will often defend theological dogmas on the ground that such dogmas reconcile self-interest with duty. Such reconciliations, it should be observed, are in any case merely external; they do not show that duty *means* the pursuit of one's own interest, but only that the acts which it dictates are those that further one's own interest. Thus when it is pretended that there are *logical* grounds making such reconciliations imperative, we must reply that the *logical* purpose aimed at could only be secured by showing that duty *means* the same as self-interest. It is sometimes said that the two maxims, "You ought to aim at producing the greatest possible good" and "You ought to pursue your own interest," are equally evident; and each is supposed to be true in all possible circumstances and in all possible worlds. But if that were the case, a world where self-interest and the general good might conflict ought not only to be nonexistent, but inconceivable; yet so far is it from being inconceivable that many people conceive it to be exemplified in the actual world. Hence the view that honesty is the best policy may be a comfort to the reluctant saint, but cannot be a solution to the perplexed logician.

The notion, therefore, that a good God or a future life can be *logically* inferred to remove the apparent conflict of self-interest and the general good is quite unwarrantable. If there were a logical puzzle, it could only be removed by showing that self-interest and the general good *mean* the same thing, not by showing that they coincide in fact. But if the above discussion has been sound, there is no logical puzzle: we ought to pursue the general good, and when this conflicts with self-interest, self-interest ought to give way.

VI. METHODS OF ESTIMATING GOODS AND EVILS*

In order to complete our account of ethics, it would be natural to give a list of the principal goods and evils of which we have experience. I shall, however, not attempt to give such a list, since I hold that the reader is probably quite as capable as I am of judging what things are good and what bad. All that I propose to do in this section is to examine the view that we can never know what is good and what bad, and to suggest methods to be employed and fallacies to be avoided in considering intrinsic goodness or badness.

There is a widespread ethical skepticism, which is based upon observation of men's differences in regard to ethical questions. It is said that A thinks one thing good, and B thinks another, and there is no possible way in which either can persuade the other that he is wrong. Hence, it is concluded, the whole thing is really only a matter of taste, and it is a waste of time to ask which is right when two people differ in a judgment of value.

It would be absurd to deny that, as compared with physical science, ethics does suffer from a measure of the defect which such skeptics allege. It must be admitted that ultimately the judgment "this thing is good" or "that thing is bad" must be an immediate judgment, which results merely from considering the thing appraised, and cannot be proved by any argument that would appeal to a man who had passed an opposite immediate judgment. I think it must also be admitted that, even after every possible precaution against error has been taken, people's immediate judgments of value do still differ more or less. But such immediate differences seem to me to be the exception: most of the actual differences are of a kind which

---

*First published in *Philosophical Essays* by Bertrand Russell (London: Longmans, Green, and Company, 1910), pp. 49-58.

argument might lessen, since usually the opinion held is either one of which the opposite is demonstrable or one which is falsely believed to be itself demonstrable. This second alternative embraces all false beliefs held because they flow from a false theory; and such beliefs, though often the direct contraries of what immediate inspection would lead to, are apt to be a complete bar to inspection. This is a very familiar phenomenon. Sydney Smith, believed to be always witty, says "pass the mustard," and the whole table is convulsed with laughter. Much wrong judgment in ethics is of this nature.

In regard to the things that are good or bad, in themselves, and not merely on account of their effects, there are two opposite errors of this sort to be avoided—the one the error of the philosopher, the other that of the moralist. The philosopher, bent on the construction of a system, is inclined to simplify the facts unduly, to give them a symmetry which is fictitious, and to twist them into a form in which they can all be deduced from one or two general principles. The moralist, on the other hand, being primarily concerned with conduct, tends to become absorbed in means, to value the actions men ought to perform more than the ends which such actions serve. This latter error—for in theorizing it is an error—is so forced upon us by the exigencies of practice that we may easily come to feel the ultimate ends of life far less important than the proximate and intermediate purposes which we consciously endeavor to realize. And hence most of what they value in this world would have to be omitted by many moralists from any imagined heaven, because there such things as self-denial and effort and courage and pity could find no place. The philosopher's error is less common than the moralist's, because the love of system and of the intellectual satisfaction of a deductive edifice is rarer than the love of virtue. But among writers on ethics the philosopher's error occurs oftener than the other, because such writers are almost always among the few men who have the love of system. Kant has the bad eminence of combining both errors in the highest possible degree, since he holds that there is nothing good except the virtuous will—a view which simplifies the good as much as any philosopher could wish, and mistakes means for ends as completely as any moralist could enjoin.

The moralist's fallacy illustrates another important point. The immediate judgments which are required in ethics concern intrinsic goods and evils, not right and wrong conduct. I do not wish to deny that people have immediate judgments of right and wrong, nor yet that in action it is usually moral to follow such judgments. What I mean is that such judgments are not among those which ethics must accept without proof, provided that (whether by the suggestions of such judgments or otherwise) we have accepted some such general connection of right action with good consequences. [See section III above]. For then, if we know what is good and bad, we can discover what is right or wrong; hence in regard to right and wrong it is unnecessary to rely upon immediate inspection—a method which must be allowed some scope, but should be allowed as little as possible.

I think when attention is clearly confined to good and bad, as opposed to right and wrong, the amount of disagreement between different people is seen to be much less than might at first be thought. Right and wrong, since they depend upon consequences, will vary as men's circumstances vary, and will be largely affected, in particular, by men's beliefs about right and wrong, since many acts will in all likelihood have a worse effect if they are generally believed to be wrong than if they are generally believed to be right, while with some acts the opposite is the case. (For example, a man who, in exceptional circumstances, acts contrary to a received and generally true moral rule, is more likely to be right if he will be thought to be wrong, for then his action will have less tendency to weaken the authority of the rule.) Thus differences as regards rules of right action are not a ground for skepticism, provided the different rules are held in different societies. Yet such differences are in practice a very powerful solvent of ethical beliefs.

Some differences as to what is good in itself must, however, be acknowledged even when all possible care has been taken to consider the question by itself. For example, retributive punishment, as opposed to deterrent or reformative punishment, was almost universally considered good until a recent time; yet in our own day it is very generally condemned. Hell can only be justified if retributive punishment is good; and the decay of a belief in hell appears to be mainly due to a change of feeling on this point.

But even where there seems to be a difference as to ends, this difference is often due to some theory on one side or on both, and not to immediate inspection. Thus in the case of hell, people may reason, consciously or unconsciously, that revelation shows that God created hell, and that therefore retributive punishment must be good; and this argument doubtless influences many who would otherwise hold retributive punishment to be bad. Where there is such an influence we do not have a genuine difference in an immediate judgment as to intrinsic good or bad; and in fact such differences are, I believe, very rare indeed.

A source of apparent differences is that some things which in isolation are bad or indifferent are essential ingredients in what is good as a whole, and some things which are good or indifferent are essential ingredients in what is bad as a whole. In such cases we judge differently according as we are considering a thing in isolation or as an ingredient in some larger whole. To judge whether a thing is in itself good, we have to ask ourselves whether we should value it if it existed otherwise than as an ingredient in some whole which we value. But to judge whether a thing ought to exist, we have to consider whether it is a part of some whole which we value so much that we prefer the existence of the whole with its possibly bad part to the existence of neither. Thus compassion is a good of which some one's misfortune is an essential part; envy is an evil of which some one's good is an essential part. Hence the position of some optimists, that all the evil in the world is necessary to constitute the best possible whole, is not logically absurd, though there is, so far as I know, no evidence in its favor. Similarly the view that all the good is an unavoidable ingredient in the worst possible whole is not logically absurd; but this view, not being agreeable, has found no advocates.

Even where none of the parts of a good whole are bad, or of a bad whole good, it often happens that the value of a complex whole cannot be measured by adding together the values of its parts; the whole is often better or worse than the sum of the values of its parts. In all aesthetic pleasures, for example, it is important that the object admired should really be beautiful: in the admiration of what is ugly there is something ridiculous, or even sometimes repulsive, although, apart from the object, there may be no difference in the value of the emotion *per se*. And yet, apart from the admiration it may produce, a beautiful object, if it is inanimate, appears to be neither good nor bad. Thus in themselves an ugly object and the emotion it excites in a person of bad taste may be respectively just as good as a beautiful object and the emotion it excites in a person of good taste; yet we consider the enjoyment of what is beautiful to be better, as a whole, than an exactly similar enjoyment of what is ugly. If we did not we should be foolish not to encourage bad taste, since ugly objects are much easier to produce than beautiful ones. In like manner, we consider it better to love a good person than a bad one. Titania's love for Bottom may be as lyric as Juliet's for Romeo;

yet Titania is laughed at. Thus many goods must be estimated as wholes, not piecemeal; and exactly the same applies to evils. In such cases the wholes may be called *organic unities*.

Many theorists who have some simple account of the sole good have also, probably without having recognized them as such, immediate judgments of value inconsistent with their theory, from which it appears that their theory is not really derived from immediate judgments of value. Thus those who have held that virtue is the sole good have generally also held that in heaven it will be *rewarded* by happiness. Yet a reward must be a good; thus they plainly *feel* that happiness also is a good. If virtue were the sole good it would be logically compelled to be its own reward.

A similar argument can be brought against those who hold that the sole good is pleasure (or happiness, as some prefer to call it). This doctrine is regarded as self-evident by many, both philosophers and plain men. But although the general principle may at first sight seem obvious, many of its applications are highly paradoxical. To live in a fool's paradise is commonly considered a misfortune; yet in a world which allows no paradise of any other kind a fool's paradise is surely the happiest habitation. All hedonists are at great pains to prove that what are called the higher pleasures are really the more pleasurable. But plainly their anxiety to prove this arises from an uneasy instinct that such pleasures are higher, even if they are not more pleasurable. The bias which appears in hedonist arguments on this point is otherwise quite inexplicable. Although they hold that, "quantity of pleasure being equal, pushpin is as good as poetry," they are careful to argue that quantity of pleasure is *not* equal, but is greater in the case of poetry—a proposition which seems highly disputable, and chiefly commended by its edifying nature. Any one would admit that the pleasure of poetry is a greater good than the pleasure of bathing on a hot day; but few people could say honestly that it is as intense. And even states of mind which, as a whole, are painful, may be highly good. Love of the dead may easily be the best thing in a life; yet it cannot but be full of pain. And conversely, we condemn pleasure derived from the love of what is bad; even if we admit that pleasure in itself is a good, we consider the whole state of mind bad. If two bitter enemies lived in different countries, and each falsely believed that the other was undergoing tortures, each might feel pleasure; yet we should not consider such a state of things good. We should even think it much worse than a state in which each derived pain from the belief that the other was in torture. It may, of course, be said that this is due to the fact that hatred in general causes more pain than pleasure, and hence is condemned broadly on hedonistic grounds, without sufficient regard to possible exceptions. But the possibility of exceptions to the principle that hatred is bad can hardly be seriously maintained, except by a theorist in difficulties.

Thus while we may admit that all pleasure, in itself, is probably more or less good, we must hold that pleasures are not good in proportion to their intensity, and that many states of mind, although pleasure is an element in them, are bad as a whole, and may even be worse than they would be if the pleasure were absent. And this result has been reached by appealing to ethical judgments with which almost every one would agree. I conclude, therefore, from all that has been adduced in this section, that although some ultimate ethical differences must be admitted between different people, by far the greater part of the commonly observed differences are due either to asking the wrong question (as, e.g., by mistaking means for ends), or to the influence of a hasty theory in falsifying immediate judgments. There is reason to hope, therefore, that a very large measure of agreement on ethical questions may be expected to result from clearer thinking; and this is probably the chief benefit to be ultimately derived from the study of ethics.

We may now sum up our whole discussion of ethics. The most fundamental notions in ethics, we agreed, are the notions of intrinsic good and evil. These are wholly independent of other notions, and the goodness or badness of a thing cannot be inferred from any of its other qualities, such as its existence or non-existence. Hence what actually occurs has no bearing on what ought to occur, and what ought to occur has no bearing on what does occur. The next pair of notions with which we were concerned were those of objective right and wrong. The objectively right act is the act which a man will hold that he ought to perform when he is not mistaken. This, we decided, is that one, of all the acts that are possible, which will probably produce the best results. Thus in judging what actions are *right* we need to know what results are *good*. When a man is mistaken as to what is objectively right, he may nevertheless act in a way which is subjectively right; thus we need a new pair of notions, which we called *moral* and *immoral*. A moral act is virtuous and deserves praise; an immoral act is sinful and deserves blame. A moral act, we decided, is one which the agent would have judged right after an appropriate amount of candid reflection,[6] where the appropriate amount of reflection depends upon the difficulty and importance of his decision. We then considered the bearing of determinism on morals, which we found to consist in a limitation of the acts which are *possible* under any circumstances. If determinism is true, there is a sense in which no act is possible except the one which in fact occurs; but there is another sense, which is the one relevant to ethics, in which any act is possible which is contemplated during deliberation (provided it is *physically* possible, i.e. will be performed if we will to perform it). We then discussed various forms of egoism, and decided that all of them are false. Finally, we considered some mistakes which are liable to be made in attempting to form an immediate judgment as to the goodness or badness of a thing, and we decided that, when these mistakes are avoided, people probably differ very little in their judgments of intrinsic value. The making of such judgments we did not undertake; for if the reader agrees, he could make them himself, and if he disagrees without falling into any of the possible confusions, there is no way of altering his opinion.

NOTES

1. What follows is largely based on Mr. G. E. Moore's *Principia Ethica,* to which the reader is referred for fuller discussions.

2. *Ethics,* pt. ii. df. vi.

3. The judgment of approval does not always coincide with the emotion of approval. For example, when a man has been led by his reason to reject a moral code which he formerly held, it will commonly happen, at least for a time, that his emotion of approval follows the old code, though his judgment has abandoned it. Thus he may have been brought up, like Mohammed's first disciples, to believe it a duty to avenge the murder of relations by murdering the murderer or his relations; and he may continue to *feel* approval of such vengeance after he has ceased to *judge* it approvingly. The *emotion* of approval will not be again in question in what follows.

4. A *motive* means merely a *cause of volition.*

5. I use *free-will* to mean the doctrine that not all volitions are determined by causes, which is the denial of determinism. Free-will is often used in senses compatible with determinism, but I am not concerned to affirm or deny it in such senses.

6. Or after a small amount in the case of acts which ought to be impulsive.

2

Science and Ethics

Originally published as chapter 9 of Religion and Science, *"Science and Ethics" contains Russell's clearest and most forceful exposition of his subjectivist ethic. It also offers a point-by-point denial of his earlier objectivist theory. "Good" and "bad" are no longer regarded as qualities that belong to objects. Instead, Russell explicitly distinguishes "good" and "bad" from such concepts as "square" and "sweet": "If two men differ about values, there is not disagreement as to any [objective] kind of truth, but a difference in taste." In this essay, as in later his writings on ethics, Russell argues for the concept of good as satisfaction of desire. Here, Russell expresses his belief that science cannot provide insight into the realm of values; it can only be applied to ethics with respect to questions of the means selected to achieve our chosen ends.*

Those who maintain the insufficiency of science appeal to the fact that science has nothing to say about "values." This I admit; but when it is inferred that ethics contains truths which cannot be proved or disproved by science, I disagree. The matter is one on which it is not altogether easy to think clearly, and my own views on it are quite different from what they were thirty years ago. But it is necessary to be clear about it if we are to appraise such arguments as those in support of Cosmic Purpose. As there is no consensus of opinion about ethics, it must be understood that what follows is my personal belief, not the dictum of science.

The study of ethics, traditionally, consists of two parts, one concerned with moral rules, the other with what is good on its own account. Rules of conduct, many of which have a ritual origin, play a great part in the lives of savages and primitive peoples. It is

From *Religion and Science* by Bertrand Russell (London: T. Butterworth-Nelson, 1935), pp. 234–255.

forbidden to eat out of the chief's dish, or to seethe the kid in its mother's milk; it is commanded to offer sacrifices to the gods, which, at a certain stage of development, are thought most acceptable if they are human beings. Other moral rules, such as the prohibition of murder and theft, have a more obvious social utility, and survive the decay of the primitive theological systems with which they were originally associated. But as men grew more reflective there is a tendency to lay less stress on rules and more on states of mind. This comes from two sources—philosophy and mystical religion. We are all familiar with passages in the prophets and the gospels, in which purity of heart is set above meticulous observance of the Law; and St. Paul's famous praise of charity, or love, teaches the same principle. The same thing will be found in all great mystics, Christian and non-Christian: what they value is a state of mind, out of which, as they hold, right conduct must ensue; rules seem to them external, and insufficiently adaptable to circumstances.

One of the ways in which the need of appealing to external rules of conduct has been avoided has been the belief in "conscience," which has been especially important in Protestant ethics. It has been supposed that God reveals to each human heart what is right and what is wrong, so that, in order to avoid sin, we have only to listen to the inner voice. There are, however, two difficulties in this theory: first, that conscience says different things to different people; secondly, that the study of the unconscious has given us an understanding of the mundane causes of conscientious feelings.

As to the different deliverances of conscience: George III's conscience told him that he must not grant Catholic Emancipation, as, if he did, he would have committed perjury in taking the Coronation Oath, but later monarchs have had no such scruples. Conscience leads some to condemn the spoliation of the rich by the poor, as advocated by Communists; and others to condemn exploitation of the poor by the rich, as practiced by capitalists. It tells one man that he ought to defend his country in case of invasion, while it tells another that all participation in warfare is wicked. During the [First World] War, the authorities, few of whom had studied ethics, found conscience very puzzling, and were led to some curious decisions, such as that a man might have conscientious scruples against fighting himself, but not against working on the fields so as to make possible the conscription of another man. They held also that, while conscience might disapprove of all war, it could not, failing that extreme position, disapprove of the war then in progress. Those who, for whatever reason, thought it wrong to fight, were compelled to state their position in terms of this somewhat primitive and unscientific conception of "conscience."

The diversity in the deliverances of conscience is what is to be expected when its origin is understood. In early youth, certain classes of acts meet with approval, and others with disapproval; and by the normal process of association, pleasure and discomfort gradually attach themselves to the acts, and not merely to the approval and disapproval respectively produced by them. As time goes on, we may forget all about our early moral training, but we shall feel uncomfortable about certain kinds of actions, while others will give us a glow of virtue. To introspection, these feelings are mysterious, since we no longer remember the circumstances which originally caused them; and therefore it is natural to attribute them to the voice of God in the heart. But in fact conscience is a product of education, and can be trained to approve or disapprove, in the great majority of mankind, as educators may see fit. While, therefore, it is right to wish to liberate ethics from external moral rules, this can hardly be satisfactorily achieved by means of the notion of "conscience."

Philosophers, by a different road, have arrived at a different position in which, also, moral rules of conduct have a subordinate place. They have framed the concept of the Good, by which they mean (roughly speaking) that which, in itself and apart from its consequences, we should wish to see existing—or, if they are theists, that which is pleasing to God. Most people would agree that happiness is preferable to unhappiness, friendliness to unfriendliness, and so on. Moral rules, according to this view, are justified if they promote the existence of what is good on its own account, but not otherwise. The prohibition of murder, in the vast majority of cases, can be justified by its effects, but the practice of burning widows on their husbands' funeral pyres cannot. The former rule, therefore, should be retained, but not the latter. Even the best moral rules, however, will have *some* exceptions, since no class of action *always* has bad results. We have thus three different senses in which an act may be ethically commendable: (1) it may be in accordance with the received moral code; (2) it may be sincerely intended to have good effects; (3) it may in fact have good effects. The third sense, however, is generally considered inadmissible in morals. According to orthodox theology, Judas Iscariot's act of betrayal had good consequences, since it was necessary for the Atonement; but it was not on this account laudable.

Different philosophers have formed different conceptions of the Good. Some hold that it consists in the knowledge and love of God; others in universal love; others in the enjoyment of beauty; and yet others in pleasure. The Good once defined, the rest of ethics follows: we ought to act in the way we believe most likely to create as much good as possible, and as little as possible of its correlative evil. The framing of moral rules, so long as the ultimate Good is supposed known, is matter for science. For example: Should capital punishment be inflicted for theft, or only for murder, or not at all? Jeremy Bentham, who considered pleasure to be the Good, devoted himself to working out what criminal code would most promote pleasure, and concluded that it ought to be much less severe than that prevailing in his day. All this, except the proposition that pleasure is the Good, comes within the sphere of science.

But when we try to be definite as to what we mean when we say that this or that is "the Good," we find ourselves involved in very great difficulties. Bentham's creed that pleasure is the Good roused furious opposition, and was said to be a pig's philosophy. Neither he nor his opponents could advance any argument. In a scientific question, evidence can be adduced on both sides, and in the end one side is seen to have the better case—or, if this does not happen, the question is left undecided. But in a question as to whether this or that is the ultimate Good, there is no evidence either way; each disputant can only appeal to his own emotions, and employ such rhetorical devices as shall rouse similar emotions in others.

Take, for example, a question which has come to be important in practical politics. Bentham held that one man's pleasure has the same ethical importance as another man's, provided the quantities are equal; and on this ground he was led to advocate democracy. Nietzsche, on the contrary, held that only the great man can be regarded as important on his own account, and that the bulk of mankind are only means to his well-being. He viewed ordinary men as many people view animals: he thought it justifiable to make use of them, not for their own good, but for that of the superman, and this view has since been adopted to justify the abandonment of democracy. We have here a sharp disagreement of great practical importance, but we have absolutely no means, of a scientific or intellectual kind, by which to persuade either party that the other is in the right. There are, it is true, ways of altering man's opinions on such subjects, but they are all emotional, not intellectual.

Questions as to "values"—that is to say, as to what is good or bad on its own acocunt, independently of its effects—lie outside the domain of science, as the defenders of religion emphatically assert. I think that in this they are right, but I draw the further conclusion, which they do not draw, that questions as to "values" lie wholly outside the domain of knowledge. That is to say, when we assert that this or that has "value," we are giving expression to our own emotions, not to a fact which would still be true if our personal feelings were different. To make this clear, we must try to analyze the conception of the Good.

It is obvious, to begin with, that the whole idea of good and bad has some connection with *desire*. *Prima facie,* anything that we all desire is "good," and anything that we all dread is "bad." If we all agreed in our desires, the matter could be left there, but unfortunately our desires conflict. If I say, "What I want is good," my neighbor will say, "No, what *I* want." Ethics is an attempt—though not, I think, a successful one—to escape from this subjectivity. I shall naturally try to show, in my dispute with my neighbor, that my desires have some quality which makes them more worthy of respect than his. If I want to preserve a right of way, I shall appeal to the landless inhabitants of the district; but he, on his side, will appeal to the landowners. I shall say: "What use is the beauty of the countryside if no one sees it?" He will retort: "What beauty will be left if trippers are allowed to spread devastation?" Each tries to enlist allies by showing that his own desires harmonize with those of other people. When this is obviously impossible, as in the case of a burglar, the man is condemned by public opinion, and his ethical status is that of a sinner.

Ethics is thus closely related to politics: it is an attempt to bring the collective desires of a group to bear upon individuals; or, conversely, it is an attempt by an individual to cause his desires to become those of his group. This latter is, of course, possible only if his desires are not too obviously opposed to the general interest: the burglar will hardly attempt to persuade people that he is doing them good, though plutocrats make similar attempts, and often succeed. When our desires are for things which all can enjoy in common, it seems not unreasonable to hope that others may concur; thus the philosopher who values Truth, Goodness and Beauty seems, to himself, to be not merely expressing his own desires, but pointing the way to the welfare of all mankind. Unlike the burglar, he is able to believe that his desires are for something that has value in an impersonal sense.

Ethics is an attempt to give universal, and not merely personal, importance to certain of our desires. I say "certain" of our desires, because in regard to some of them this is obviously impossible, as we saw in the case of the burglar. The man who makes money on the Stock Exchange by means of some secret knowledge does not wish others to be equally well informed: Truth (in so far as he values it) is for him a private possession, not the general human good that it is for the philosopher. The philosopher may, it is true, sink to the level of the stock-jobber, as when he claims priority for a discovery. But this is a lapse: in his purely philosophic capacity, he wants only to enjoy the contemplation of Truth, in doing which he in no way interferes with others who wish to do likewise.

To seem to give universal importance to our desires—which is the business of ethics—may be attempted from two points of view, that of the legislator, and that of the preacher. Let us take the legislator first.

I will assume, for the sake of argument, that the legislator is personally disinterested. That is to say, when he recognizes one of his desires as being concerned only with his own welfare, he does not let it influence him in framing the laws; for example, his code is not designed to increase his personal fortune. But he has other desires which seem to him impersonal. He may believe in an ordered hierarchy from king to peasant, or from mine-owner to black indentured laborer. He may believe that women should be submissive to men. He may hold that the spread of knowledge in the lower classes is dangerous. And so on and so on. He will then, if he can, so construct his code that conduct promoting the ends which he values shall, as far as possible, be in accordance with individual self-interest; and he will establish a system of moral instruction which will, where it succeeds, make men feel wicked if they pursue other purposes than his.[1] Thus "virtue" will come to be in fact, though not in subjective estimation, subservience to the desires of the legislator, in so far as he himself considers these desires worthy to be universalized.

The standpoint and method of the preacher are necessarily somewhat different, because he does not control the machinery of the State, and therefore cannot produce an artificial harmony between his desires and those of others. His only method is to try to rouse in others the same desires that he feels himself, and for this purpose his appeal must be to the emotions. Thus Ruskin caused people to like Gothic architecture, not by argument, but by the moving effect of rhythmical prose. *Uncle Tom's Cabin* helped to make people think slavery an evil by causing them to imagine themselves as slaves. Every attempt to persuade people that something is good (or bad) in itself, and not merely in its effects, depends upon the art of rousing feelings, not upon an appeal to evidence. In every case the preacher's skill consists in creating in others emotions similar to his own—or dissimilar, if he is a hypocrite. I am not saying this as a criticism of the preacher, but as an analysis of the essential character of his activity.

When a man says, "This is good in itself," he *seems* to be making a statement, just as much as if he said, "This is square," or, "This is sweet." I believe this to be a mistake. I think that what the man really means is: "I wish everybody to desire this," or rather, "Would that everybody desired this." If what he says is interpreted as a statement, it is merely an affirmation of his own personal wish; if, on the other hand, it is interpreted in a general way, it states nothing, but merely desires something. The wish, as an occurrence, is personal, but what it desires is universal. It is, I think, this curious interlocking of the particular and the universal which has caused so much confusion in ethics.

The matter may perhaps become clearer by contrasting an ethical sentence with one which makes a statement. If I say, "All Chinese are Buddhists," I can be refuted by the production of a Chinese Christian or Mohammedan. If I say, "I believe that all Chinese are Buddhists," I cannot be refuted by any evidence from China, but only by evidence that I do not believe what I say; for what I am asserting is only something about my own state of mind. If, now, a philosopher says "Beauty is good," I may interpret him as meaning either, "Would that everybody loved the beautiful" (which corresponds to "All Chinese are Buddhists") or, "I wish that everybody loved the beautiful" (which corresponds to "I believe that all Chinese are Buddhists"). The first of these makes no assertion, but expresses a wish; since it affirms nothing, it is logically impossible that there should be evidence for or against it, or for it to possess either truth or falsehood. The second sentence, instead of being merely optative, does not make a statement, but it is one about the philosopher's state of mind, and it could be refuted only by evidence that he does not have the wish that he says he has. This second sentence does not belong to ethics, but to psychology or biography. The first sentence, which does belong to ethics, expresses a desire for something, but asserts nothing.

Ethics, if the above analysis is correct, contains no statements, whether true or false, but consists of desires of a certain general kind, namely, such as are concerned with the desires of mankind in general—and of gods, angels, and devils, if they exist. Science can discuss the causes of desires, and the means for realizing them, but it cannot contain any genuinely ethical sentences, because it is concerned with what is true or false.

The theory which I have been advocating is a form of the doctrine which is called the "subjectivity" of values. This doctrine consists in maintaining that, if two men differ about values, there is not a disagreement as to any kind of truth, but a difference of taste. If one man says, "Oysters are good," and another says, "*I* think they are bad," we recognize that there is nothing to argue about. The theory in question holds that all differences as to values are of this sort, although we do not naturally think them so when we are dealing with matters that seem to us more exalted than oysters. The chief ground for adopting this view is the complete impossibility of finding any arguments to prove that this or that has intrinsic value. If we all agreed, we might hold that we know values by intuition. We cannot *prove,* to a color-blind man, that grass is green and not red. But there are various ways of proving to him that he lacks a power of discrimination which most men possess, whereas in the case of values there are no such ways, and disagreements are much more frequent than in the case of colors. Since no way can be even imagined for deciding a difference as to values, the conclusion is forced upon us that the difference is one of tastes, not one as to any objective truth.

The consequences of this doctrine are considerable. In the first place, there can be no such thing as "sin" in any absolute sense; what one man calls "sin" another may call "virtue," and though they may dislike each other on account of this difference, neither can convict the other of intellectual error. Punishment cannot be justified on the ground that the criminal is "wicked," but only on the ground that he has behaved in a way which others wish to discourage. Hell, as a place of punishment for sinners, becomes quite irrational.

In the second place, it is impossible to uphold the way of speaking about values which is common among those who believe in Cosmic Purpose. Their argument is that certain things which have been evolved are "good," and therefore the world must have had a purpose which was ethically admirable. In the language of subjective values, this argument becomes: "Some things in the world are to our liking, and therefore they must have been created by a Being with our tastes, Whom, therefore, we also like, and Who, consequently, is good." Now it seems fairly evident that, if creatures having likes and dislikes were to exist at all, they were pretty sure to like *some* things in their environment, since otherwise they would find life intolerable. Our values have been evolved along with the rest of our constitution, and nothing as to any original purpose can be inferred from the fact that they are what they are.

Those who believe in "objective" values often contend that the view which I have been advocating has immoral consequences. This seems to me to be due to faulty reasoning. There are, as has already been said, certain ethical consequences of the doctrine of subjective values, of which the most important is the rejection of vindictive punishment and the notion of "sin." But the more general consequences which are feared, such as the decay of all sense of moral obligation, are not to be logically deduced. Moral obligation, if it is to influence conduct, must consist not merely of a belief, but of a desire. The desire, I may be told, is the desire to be "good" in a sense which I no longer allow. But when we analyze the desire to be "good" it generally resolves itself into a desire to be approved, or, alternatively, to act so as to bring about certain general consequences which we desire. We have wishes which are not purely personal, and, if we had not, no amount of ethical teaching would influence our conduct except through fear of disapproval. The sort of life that most of us admire is one which is guided by large impersonal desires; now such desires can, no doubt, be encouraged by example, education, and knowledge, but they can hardly be created by the mere abstract belief that they are good, nor discouraged by an analysis of what is meant by the word "good."

When we contemplate the human race, we may desire that it should be happy, or healthy, or intelligent, or warlike, and so on. Any one of these desires, if it is strong, will produce its own morality; but if we have no such general desires, our conduct, whatever our ethic may be, will serve social purposes only in so far as self-interest and the interests of society are in harmony. It is the business of wise institutions to create such harmony as far as possible, and for the rest, whatever may be our theoretical definition of value, we must depend upon the existence of impersonal desires. When you meet a man with whom you have a fundamental ethical disagreement—for example, if you think that all men count equally, while he selects a class as alone important—you will find yourself no better able to cope with him if you believe in objective values than if you do not. In either case, you can influence his conduct only through influencing his desires: if you succeed in that, his ethic will change, and if not, not.

Some people feel that if a general desire, say, for the happiness of mankind, has not the sanction of absolute good, it is in some way irrational. This is due to a lingering belief in objective values. A desire cannot, in itself, be either rational or irrational. It may conflict with other desires, and therefore lead to unhappiness; it may rouse opposition in others, and therefore be incapable of gratification. But it cannot be considered "irrational" merely because no reason can be given for feeling it. We may desire A because it is a means to B, but in the end, when we have done with mere means, we must come to something which we desire for no reason, but not on that account "irrationally." All systems of ethics embody the desires of those who advocate them, but this fact is concealed in a mist of words. Our desires are, in fact, more general and less purely selfish than many moralists imagine; if it were not so, no theory of ethics would make moral improvement possible. It is, in fact, not by ethical theory, but by the cultivation of large and generous desires through intelligence, happiness, and freedom from fear, that men can be brought to act more than they do at present in a manner that is consistent with the general happiness of mankind. Whatever our definition of the "Good," and whether we believe it to be subjective or objective, those who do not desire the happiness of mankind will not endeavor to further it, while those who do desire it will do what they can to bring it about.

I conclude that, while it is true that science cannot decide questions of value, that is because they cannot be intellectually decided at all, and lie outside the realm of truth and falsehood. Whatever knowledge is attainable, must be attained by scientific methods; and what science cannot discover, mankind cannot know.

NOTES

1. Compare the following advice by a contemporary of Aristotle (Chinese, not Greek): "A ruler should not listen to those who believe in people

having opinions of their own and in the importance of the individual. Such teachings cause men to withdraw to quiet places and hide away in caves or on mountains, there to rail at the prevailing government, sneer at those in authority, belittle the importance of rank and emoluments, and despise all who hold official posts." Waley, *The Way and Its Power,* p. 37.

3

Power and Ethical Rules

This was Russell's last important ethical discussion before he published his book, Human Society in Ethics and Politics *in 1954. In this essay, Russell expands and elaborates upon the subjectivist ethic he had outlined in "Science and Ethics." Here he offers his most detailed analysis of an ethical doctrine and in what ways such doctrine can be tested. Russell outlines his main problem for discussion quite clearly at the beginning of the essay: What is the effect of power on moral rules, and can some objective basis other than power be found for justifying such rules?*

Russell begins his discussion of ethics with an analysis of utilitarianism as a characteristic moral philosophy that claims to have a "rational" foundation. He shows that the question of rationality in morality is a much more complex and difficult problem than the utilitarian realizes. Thus, this essay marks a decided change in Russell's outlook. Previously Russell had only committed himself to the utilitarian standard of justification for a moral rule, where right is always justified in terms of consequences. Although in this essay Russell does not reject utilitarian theory outright, he has begun to view this and other problems involved in ethics in a more penetrating fashion.

Morality, at any rate since the days of the Hebrew prophets, has had two divergent aspects. On the one hand, it has been a social institution analogous to law; on the other hand, it has been a matter for the individual conscience. In the former aspect, it is part of the apparatus of power; in the latter, it is often revolutionary. The kind which is analogous to law is called "positive" morality; the other

---

kind may be called "personal." I wish here to consider the relations of these two kinds of morality to each other and to power.

Positive morality is older than personal morality, and probably older than law and government. It consists originally of tribal customs, out of which law gradually develops. Consider the extraordinarily elaborate rules as to who may marry whom, which are found among very primitive savages. To us, these seem merely rules, but presumably to those who accept them they have the same moral compulsive force as we feel in our rules against incestuous unions. Their source is obscure, but is no doubt in some sense religious. This part of positive morality appears to have no relation to social inequalities; it neither confers exceptional power nor assumes its existence. There are still moral rules of this sort among civilized people. The Greek Church prohibits the marriage of godparents of the same child, a prohibition which fulfils no social purpose, either good or bad, but has its source solely in theology. It seems probable that many prohibitions which are now accepted on rational grounds were originally superstitious. Murder was objectionable because of the hostility of the ghost, which was not directed only against the murderer, but against his community. The community therefore had an interest in the matter, which they could deal with either by punishment or by ceremonies of purification. Gradually purification came to have a spiritual signification, and to be identified with repentance and absolution; but its original ceremonial character is still recalled by such phrases as "washed in the blood of the Lamb."

This aspect of positive morality, important as it is, is not the one with which I wish to deal. I wish to consider those aspects of accepted ethical codes in which they minister to power. One of the purposes—usually in large part unconscious—of a traditional morality is to make the existing social system work. It achieves this purpose, when it is successful, both more cheaply and more effectively than a police force does. But it is liable to be confronted with a revolutionary morality, inspired by the desire for a redistribution of power. I want, in this chapter, to consider, first, the effect of power on moral codes, and then the question whether some other basis can be found for morality.

The most obvious example of power-morality is the inculcation of obedience. It is (or rather was) the duty of children to submit to parents, wives to husbands, servants to masters, subjects to princes, and (in religious matters) laymen to priests; there were also more specialized duties of obedience in armies and religious orders. Each of these duties has a long history, running parallel with that of the institution concerned.

Let us begin with filial piety. There are savages at the present day who, when their parents grow too old for work, sell them to be eaten. At some stage in the development of civilization, it must have occurred to some man of unusual forethought that he could, while his children were still young, produce in them a state of mind which would lead them to keep him alive in old age; presumably he was a man whose own parents were already disposed of. In creating a party to support his subversive opinion, I doubt whether he appealed merely to motives of prudence; I suspect that he invoked the Rights of Man, the advantages of a mainly frugiferous diet, and the moral blamelessness of the old who have worn themselves out laboring for their children. Probably there was at the moment some emaciated but unusually wise elder, whose advice was felt to be more valuable than his flesh. However this may be, it came to be felt that one's parents should be honored rather than eaten. To us, the respect for fathers in early civilizations seems excessive, but we have to remember that a very powerful deterrent was needed to put an end to the lucrative practice of having them eaten. And so we find the Ten Commandments suggesting that if you fail to honor your father and mother you will die young, the Romans considering parricide the most atrocious of crimes, and Confucius making filial piety the very basis of morality. All this is a device, however instinctive and unconscious, for prolonging parental power beyond the early years when children are helpless. The authority of parents has of course been reinforced by their possession of property, but if filial piety had not existed young men would not have allowed their fathers to retain control of their flocks and herds after they had become feeble.

The same sort of thing happened in regard to the subjection of women. The superior strength of male animals does not, in most cases, lead to continual subjection of the females, because the males have not a sufficient constancy of purpose. Among human beings, the subjection of women is much more complete at a certain level of civilization than it is among savages. And the subjection is always reinforced by morality. A man, says St. Paul, "is the image and glory of God: but the woman is the glory of the man. For the man is not of the woman; but the woman of the man. Neither was the man created for the woman; but the woman for the man" (I Corinthians xi. 7-9). It follows that wives ought to obey their husbands, and that unfaithfulness is a worse sin in a wife than in a husband. Christianity, it is true, holds, in theory, that adultery is equally sinful in either sex, since it is a sin against God. But this view has not prevailed in practice, and was not held even theoretically in pre-Christian times. Adultery with a married woman was wicked, because it was an offense against her husband; but female slaves and war-captives were the legitimate property of their master, and no blame attached to intercourse with them. This view was held by pious Christian slave-owners, though not by their wives, even in nineteenth-century America.

The basis of the difference between morality for men and morality for women was obviously the superior power of men. Originally the superiority was only physical, but from this basis it gradually extended to economics, politics, and religion. The great advantage of morality over the police appears very clearly in this case, for women, until quite recently, genuinely believed the moral precepts which embodied male domination, and therefore required much less compulsion than would otherwise have been necessary.

The code of Hammurabi gives an interesting illustration of the unimportance of women in the eyes of the legislator. If a man strikes the daughter of a gentleman when she is pregnant, and she dies in consequence, it is decreed that the daughter of the striker shall be put to death. As between the gentleman and the striker, this is just; the daughter who is executed is merely a possession of the latter, and has no claim to life on her own account. And in killing the gentleman's daughter the striker is guilty of an offense, not against her, but against the gentleman. The daughters had no rights because they had no power.

Kings, until George I, were objects of religious veneration.

> There's such divinity doth hedge a king,
> That treason can but peep the thing it would,
> Acts little of his will.

The word "treason," even in republics, has still a flavor of impiety. In England, government profits much by the tradition of royalty. Victorian statesmen, even Mr. Gladstone, felt it their duty to the Queen to see to it that she was never left without a Prime Minister. The duty of obedience to authority is still felt by many as a duty towards the sovereign. This is a decaying sentiment, but as it decays government becomes less stable, and dictatorships of the Right or the Left become more possible.

Bagehot's *English Constitution*—a book still well worth reading—begins the discussion of the monarchy as follows:

The use of the Queen, in a dignified capacity, is incalculable. Without her in England, the present English Government would fail and pass away. Most people when they read that the Queen walked on the slopes at Windsor—that the Prince of Wales went to the Derby—have imagined that too much thought and prominence were given to little things. But they have been in error; and it is nice to trace how the actions of a retired widow and an unemployed youth become of such importance.

The best reason why Monarchy is a strong government is, that it is an intelligible government. The mass of mankind understand it, and they hardly anywhere in the world understand any other. It is often said that men are ruled by their imaginations; but it would be truer to say that they are governed by the weakness of their imaginations.

This is both true and important. Monarchy makes social cohesion easy, first, because it is not so difficult to feel loyalty to an individual as to an abstraction, and secondly, because kingship, in its long history, has accumulated sentiments of veneration which no new institution can inspire. Where hereditary monarchy has been abolished, it has usually been succeeded, after a longer or short time, by some other form of one-man rule: tyranny in Greece, the Empire in Rome, Cromwell in England, the Napoleons in France, Stalin and Hitler in our own day. Such men inherit a part of the feelings formerly attached to royalty. It is amusing to note, in the confessions of the accused in Russian trials, the acceptance of a morality of submission to the ruler such as would be appropriate in the most ancient and traditional of absolute monarchies. But a new dictator, unless he is a very extraordinary man, can hardly inspire *quite* the same religious veneration as hereditary monarchs enjoyed in the past.

In the case of kingship, the religious element, as we have seen, has often been carried so far as to interfere with power. Even then, however, it has helped to give stability to the social system of which the king is a symbol. This has happened in many semi-civilized countries, in Japan, and in England. In England, the doctrine that the king can do no wrong has been used as a weapon for depriving him of power, but it has enabled his Ministers to have more power than they would have if he did not exist. Wherever there is a traditional monarchy, rebellion against the government is an offense against the king, and is regarded by the orthodox as a sin and an impiety. Kingship acts therefore, broadly speaking, as a force on the side of the *status quo,* whatever that may be. Its most useful function, historically, has been the creation of a widely diffused sentiment favorable to social cohesion. Men are so little gregarious by nature that anarchy is a constant danger, which kingship has done much to prevent. Against this merit, however, must be set the demerit of perpetuating ancient evils and increasing the forces opposed to desirable change. This demerit has, in modern times, caused monarchy to disappear over the greater part of the earth's surface.

The power of priests is more obviously connected with morals than any other form of power. In Christian countries, virtue consists in obedience to the will of God, and it is priests who know what the will of God commands. The precept that we ought to obey God rather than man is, as we saw, capable of being revolutionary; it is so in two sets of circumstances, one, when the State is in opposition to the Church, the other, when it is held that God speaks directly to each individual conscience. The former state of affairs existed before Constantine, the latter among the Anabaptists and Independents. But in non-revolutionary periods, when there is an established and traditional Church, it is accepted by positive morality as the intermediary between God and the individual conscience. So long as this acceptance continues, its power is very great, and rebellion against the Church is thought more wicked than any other kind. The Church has its difficulties none the less for, if it uses its power too flagrantly men begin to doubt whether it is interpeting the will of God correctly; and when this doubt becomes common, the whole ecclesiastical edifice crumbles, as it did in Teutonic countries at the Reformation.

In the case of the Church, the relation between power and morals is, to some extent, the opposite of what it is in the cases we have hitherto considered. Positive morality enjoins submission to parents, husbands, and kings, because they are powerful; but the Church is powerful because of its moral authority. This, however, is only true up to a point. Where the Church is secure, a morality of submission to the Church grows up, just as a morality of submission to parents, husbands, and kings has grown up. And a revolutionary rejection of this morality of submission also grows up in the same way. Heresy and schism are specially abhorrent to the Church, and are therefore essential elements in revolutionary programmes. There are, however, more complicated results of opposition to priestly power. The Church being the official guardian of the moral code, its opponents are likely to revolt in morals as well as in doctrine and government. They may revolt, like the Puritans, into greater strictness, or, like the French Revolutionaries, into greater laxity; but in either case morals come to be a private matter, not, as before, the subject of official decisions by a public body.

It must not be supposed that personal morality is in general worse than official priestly morality, even when it is less severe. There is some evidence that when, in the sixth century B.C., Greek sentiment was becoming strongly averse from human sacrifice, the oracle at Delphi tried to retard this humanitarian reform, and to keep alive the old rigid practices. Similarly in our own day, when the State and public opinion consider it permissible to marry one's deceased wife's sister, the Church, in so far as it has power, maintains the old prohibition.

Morality, where the Church has lost power, has not become genuinely personal except for a few exceptional people. For the majority, it is represented by public opinion, both that of neighbors in general, and that of powerful groups such as employers. From the point of view of the sinner, the change may be slight, and may also be for the worse. Where the individual gains is not as sinner, but as judge: he becomes part of an informal democratic tribunal, whereas, where the Church is strong, he must accept the rulings of Authority. The Protestant whose moral feelings are strong usurps the ethical functions of the priest, and acquires a quasi-governmental attitude towards other people's virtues and vices, especially the latter:

> Ye've naught to do but mark and tell
> Your neighbors' faults and folly.

This is not anarchy; it is democracy.

The thesis that the moral code is an expression of power is, as we have seen, not wholly true. From the exogamous rules of savages onward, there are, at all stages of civilization, ethical principles which have no visible relation to power—among ourselves, the condemnation of homosexuality may serve as an example. The Marxist thesis, that the moral code is an expression of *economic* power, is even less adequate than the thesis that it is an expression of power in general. Nevertheless, the Marxist thesis is true in a very great many instances. For example: in the Middle Ages, when the most powerful of the laity were landowners, when bishoprics and monastic orders derived their income from land, and when the only

investors of money were Jews, the Church unhesitatingly condemned "usury," i.e. all lending of money at interest. This was a
debtor's morality. With the rise of the rich merchant class, it became
impossible to maintain the old prohibition: it was relaxed first by
Calvin, whose clientèle was mainly urban and prosperous, then by
the other Protestants, and last of all by the Catholic Church.[1] Credi-
tor's morality became the fashion, and nonpayment of debts a heinous sin. The Society of Friends, practically if not theoretically, excluded bankrupts until very recently.

The moral code towards enemies is a matter as to which different ages have differed greatly, largely because the profitable uses
of power have differed. On this subject, let us first hear the Old
Testament.

> When the Lord thy God shall bring thee into the land whither
> thou goest to possess it, and hath cast out many nations before thee,
> the Hittites, and the Girgashites, and the Amorites, and the Canaan-
> ites, and the Perizzites, and the Hivites, and the Jebusites, seven na-
> tions greater and mightier than thou;
> And when the Lord thy God shall deliver them before thee; thou
> shalt smite them, and utterly destroy them; thou shalt make no cove-
> nant with them, nor show mercy unto them;
> Neither shalt thou make marriages with them; thy daughter shalt
> thou not give unto his son, nor his daughter shalt thou take unto
> thy son.
> For they will turn away thy son from following me, that they may
> serve other gods: so will the anger of the Lord be kindled against you,
> and destroy thee suddenly.

If they do all this, "there shall not be male or female barren
among you, or among your cattle."[2]

As regards these seven nations, we are told in a later chapter
even more explicitly:

> Thou shalt save alive nothing that breatheth . . . that they teach
> you not to do after all their abominations.[3]

But towards "cities which are very far off from thee, and which
are not of these nations" it is permissible to be more merciful:

> Thou shalt smite every male thereof with the edge of the sword:
> but the women, and the little ones, and the cattle, and all that is in

the city, even all the spoil thereof, shalt thou take unto thyself.[4]

It will be remembered that when Saul smote the Amalekites he got into trouble for being insufficiently thorough:

> And he took Agag the king of the Amalekites alive, and utterly destroyed all the people with the edge of the sword.
>
> But Saul and the people spared Agag, and the best of the sheep, and of the oxen, and of the fatlings, and the lambs, and all that was good, and would not utterly destroy them: but everything that was vile and refuse, that they destroyed utterly.
>
> Then came the word of the Lord unto Samuel, saying,
>
> It repenteth me that I have set up Saul to be king: for he is turned back from following me, and hath not performed my commandments.[5]

It is obvious in these passages that the interests of the children of Israel were to prevail completely when they came into conflict with those of the Gentiles, but that internally the interests of religion, i.e., of the priests, were to prevail over the economic interests of the laity. The word of the Lord came unto Samuel, but it was the word of Samuel that came unto Saul, and the word was: "What meaneth then this bleating of sheep in mine ears, and the lowing of oxen to which I hear?" To which Saul could only reply by confessing his sin.

The Jews, from their horror of idolatry—of which the microbes apparently lurked even in sheep and cows—were led to exceptional thoroughness in the extermination of the vanquished. But no nation of antiquity recognized any legal or moral limits to what might be done with defeated populations. It was customary to exterminate some and sell the rest into slavery. Some Greeks—for instance, Euripides in the *Trojan Women*—tried to create a sentiment against this practice, but without success. The vanquished, having no power, had no claim to mercy. This view was not abandoned, even in theory, until the coming of Christianity.

Duty to enemies is a difficult conception. Clemency was recognized as a virtue in antiquity, but only when it was successful, that is to say, when it turned enemies into friends; otherwise, it was condemned as a weakness. When fear had been aroused, no one expected magnanimity: the Romans showed none towards Hannibal or the followers of Spartacus. In the days of chivalry, a knight was expected to show courtesy to a knightly captive. But the conflicts of knights were not very serious; not the faintest mercy was shown to the Albigenses. In our day, almost equal ferocity has been shown towards the victims of the white terrors in Finland, Hungary, Germany, and Spain, and hardly any protests have been aroused except among political opponents. The terror in Russia, likewise, has been condoned by most of the Left. Now, as in the days of the Old Testament, no duty to enemies is acknowledged in practice when they are sufficiently formidable to arouse fear. Positive morality, in effect, is still only operative within the social group concerned, and is therefore still, in effect, a department of government. Nothing short of a world government will cause people of pugnacious disposition to admit, except as a counsel of perfection, that moral obligations are not confined to a section of the human race.

I have been concerned hitherto, with positive morality, and, as has become evident, it is not enough. Broadly speaking, it is on the side of the powers that be, it does not allow a place for revolution, it does nothing to mitigate the fierceness of strife, and it can find no place for the prophet who proclaims some new moral insight. Certain difficult questions of theory are involved, but before considering them let us remind ourselves of some of the things that only opposition to positive morality could achieve.

The world owes something to the Gospels, though not so much as it would if they had had more influence. It owes something to those who denounced slavery and the subjection of women. We may hope that in time it will owe something to those who denounce war and economic injustice. In the eighteenth and nineteenth centuries, it owed much to the apostles of tolerance; perhaps it will again in some happier age than ours. Revolutions, against the medieval Church, the Renaissance monarchies, and the present power of plutocracy, are necessary for the avoidance of stagnation. Admitting, as we must, that mankind needs revolution and individual morality, the problem is to find a place for these things without plunging the world into anarchy.

There are two questions to be considered: First, what is the wisest attitude for positive morality, from its own standpoint, to take to personal morality? Second, what degree of respect does personal morality owe to positive morality? But before discussing either of these, something must be said as to what is meant by personal morality.

Personal morality may be considered as a historical phenomenon, or from the standpoint of the philosopher. Let us begin with the former.

Almost every individual that has ever existed, so far as history is aware, has had a profound horror of certain kinds of acts. As a rule, these acts are held in abhorrence, not only by one individual, but by a whole tribe or nation or sect or class. Sometimes the origin of the abhorrence is unknown, sometimes it can be traced to a historical personage who was a moral innovator. We know why Mohammedans will not make images of animals or human beings; it is because the Prophet forbade them to do so. We know why orthodox Jews will not eat hare; it is because the Mosaic Law declares that the hare is unclean. Such prohibitions, when accepted, belong to positive morality; but in their origins, at any rate when their origin is known, they belonged to private morality.

Morality, for us, however, has come to mean something more than ritual precepts, whether positive or negative. In the form in which it is familiar to us it is not primitive, but appears to have a number of independent sources—Chinese sages, Indian Buddhists, Hebrew prophets, and Greek philosophers. These men, whose importance in history it is difficult to overestimate, all lived within a few centuries of each other, and all shared certain characteristics which marked them out from their predecessors. Lao-Tse and Chuang-Tse deliver the doctrine of the Tao as what they know of their own knowledge, not through tradition or the wisdom of others; and the doctrine consists not of specific duties, but of a way of life, a manner of thinking and feeling, from which it will become plain, without the needs of rules, what must be done on each occasion. The same may be said of the early Buddhists. The Hebrew prophets, at their best, transcend the Law, and advocate a new and more inward kind of virtue, recommended not by tradition, but by the words "thus saith the Lord." Socrates acts as his daemon commands, not as the legally constituted authorities desire; he is prepared to suffer martyrdom rather than be untrue to the inner voice. All these men were rebels in their day, and all have come to be honored. Something of what was new in them has come to be taken as a matter of course. But it is not altogether easy to say what this something is.

The minimum that must be accepted by any thoughtful person who either adheres to a religion having a historical origin, or thinks that some such religion was an improvement on what went before, is this: that a way of life which was in some sense better than some previous way of life was first advocated by some individual or set of individuals, in opposition to the teaching of State and Church in their day. It follows that it cannot always be wrong for an individual to set himself up in moral questions, even against the judgment of all mankind up to his day. In science, everyone now admits the corresponding doctrine; but in science the ways of testing a new doctrine are known, and it soon comes to be generally accepted, or else rejected on other grounds than tradition. In ethics, no such obvious ways exist by which a new doctrine can be tested. A prophet may preface his teaching by "thus saith the Lord," which is sufficient for him; but how are other people to know that he has had a genuine revelation? Deuteronomy, oddly enough, proposes the same test as is often held to be conclusive in science, namely success in prediction: "And if thou say in thine heart, How shall we know the word which the Lord hath not spoken? When a prophet speaketh in the name of the Lord, if the thing follow not, nor come to pass, that is the thing which the Lord hath not spoken, but the prophet hath spoken it presumptuously."[6] But the modern mind can hardly accept this test of an ethical doctrine.

We must face the question: What is meant by an ethical doctrine, and in what ways, if any, can it be tested?

Historically, ethics is connected with religion. For most men, authority has sufficed: what is laid down as right or wrong by the Bible or the Church *is* right or wrong. But certain individuals have, from time to time, been divinely inspired: they have known what was right or wrong because God spoke directly to them. These individuals, according to orthodox opinion, all lived a long time ago, and if a modern man professes to be one of them it is best to put him in an asylum, unless, indeed, the Church sanctions his pronouncements. This, however, is merely the usual situation of the rebel become dictator, and does not help us to decide what are the legitimate functions of rebels.

Can we translate ethics into non-theological terms? Victorian freethinkers had no doubt that this was possible. The utilitarians, for instance, were highly moral men, and were convinced that their morality had a rational basis. The matter is, however, rather more difficult than it appeared to them.

Let us consider a question suggested by the mention of the utilitarians, namely: Can a rule of conduct ever be a self-subsistent proposition of ethics, or must it always be deduced from the good or bad effects of the conduct in question? The traditional view is that certain kinds of acts are sinful, and certain others virtuous, independently of their effects. Other kinds of acts are ethically neutral, and may be judged by their results. Whether euthanasia or marriage with a deceased wife's sister should be legalized is an ethical question, but the gold standard is not. There are two definitions of "ethical" questions, either of which will cover the cases to which this adjective is applied. A question is "ethical" (1) if it interested the ancient Hebrews, (2) if it is one on which the Archbishop of Canterbury is the official expert. It is obvious that this common use of the word "ethical" is wholly indefensible.

Nevertheless, I find, speaking personally, that there are kinds of conduct against which I feel a repugnance which seems to me to be moral, but to be not obviously based upon an estimate of consequences. I am informed by many people that the preservation of democracy, which I think important, can only be secured by gassing immense numbers of children and doing a number of other horrible things. I find that, at this point, I cannot acquiesce in the use of such means. I tell myself that they will not secure the end, or that, if they do, they will incidentally have other effects so evil as to outweigh any good that democracy might do. I am not quite sure how far this argument is honest: I think I should refuse to use such means even if I were persuaded that they would secure the end and that no others would. *Per contra,* psychological imagination assures me that nothing that I should think good can possibly be achieved by such means. On the whole, I think that, speaking philosophically, all acts ought to be judged by their effects; but as this is difficult and takes time, it is desirable, in practice, that some kinds of acts should be condemned and others praised without waiting to investigate consequences. I should say, therefore, with the utilitarians, that the right act, in any given circumstances, is that which, on the data, will probably produce the greatest balance of good over evil of all the acts that are possible; but that the performance of such acts may be promoted by the existence of a moral code.

Accepting this view, ethics is reduced to defining "good" and "bad," not as means, but as ends in themselves. The utilitarian says that the good is pleasure and the bad is pain. But if someone disagrees with him, what arguments can he produce?

Consider various views as to the ends of life. One man says "the good is pleasure"; another, "the good is pleasure for Aryans and pain for Jews"; another, "the good is to praise God and glorify Him for ever." What are these three men asserting, and what methods exist by which they can convince each other? They cannot, as men of science do, appeal to facts: no facts are relevant to the dispute. Their difference is in the realm of desire, not in the realm of statements about matters of fact. I do not assert that when I say "this is good" I mean "I desire this"; it is only a particular kind of desire that leads me to call a thing good. The desire must be in some degree impersonal; it must have to do with the sort of world that would content me, not only with my personal circumstances. A king might say: "Monarchy is good, and I am glad I am a monarch." The first part of this statement is indubitably ethical, but his pleasure in being a monarch only becomes ethical if a survey persuades him that no one else would make such a good king.

I have suggested on a former occasion (in "Religion and Ethics") that a judgment of intrinsic value is to be interpreted, not as an assertion, but as an expression of desire concerning the desires of mankind. When I say "hatred is bad," I am really saying: "Would that no one felt hatred." I make no assertion; I merely express a certain type of wish. The hearer can gather that I feel this wish, but that is the only *fact* that he can gather, and that is a fact of psychology. There are no facts of ethics.

The great ethical innovators have not been men who *knew* more than others; they have been men who *desired* more, or, to be more accurate, men whose desires were more impersonal and of larger scope than those of average men. Most men desire their own happiness; a considerable percentage desire the happiness of their children; not a few desire the happiness of their nation; some, genuinely and strongly, desire the happiness of all mankind. These men, seeing that many others have no such feeling, and that this is an obstacle to universal felicity, wish that others felt as they do; this wish can be expressed in the words "happiness is good."

All great moralists, from Buddha and the Stoics down to recent times, treated the good as something to be, if possible, enjoyed by all men equally. They did not think of themselves as princes or Jews or Greeks; they thought of themselves merely as human beings. Their ethic had always a twofold source: on the one hand, they valued certain elements in their own lives; on the other hand, sympathy made them desire for others what they desired for themselves. Sympathy is the universalizing force in ethics; I mean sympathy as an emotion, not as a theoretical principle. Sympathy is in some degree instinctive: a child may be made unhappy by another child's cry. But limitations of sympathy are also natural. The cat has no sympathy for the mouse; the Romans had no sympathy for any animals except elephants; the Nazis have none for Jews, and Stalin had none for kulaks. Where there is limitation of sympathy there is a corresponding limitation in the conception of the good: the good becomes something to be enjoyed only by the magnanimous man, or only by the superman, or the Aryan, or the proletarian, or the Christadelphian. All these are cat-and-mouse ethics.

The refutation of a cat-and-mouse ethic, where it is possible, is practical, not theoretical. Two adepts at such an ethic, like quarrelsome little boys, each begin: "Let's play I'm the cat and you're the mouse." "No, no," they each retort, "you shan't be the cat, I will." And so, more often than not, they become the Kilkenny cats. But if one of them succeeds completely, he may establish his ethic; we then get Kipling and the White Man's Burden, or the Nordic Race, or some such creed of inequality. Such creeds, inevitably, appeal only to the cat, not to the mouse; they are imposed on the mouse by naked power.

Ethical controversies are very often as to means, not ends. Slavery may be attacked by the argument that it is uneconomic; the subjection of women may be criticized by maintaining that the conversation of free women is more interesting; persecution may be deplored on the ground (wholly fallacious, incidentally) that the religious convictions produced by it are not genuine. Behind such arguments, however, there is generally a difference as to ends. Sometimes, as in Nietzsche's criticism of Christianity, the difference of ends becomes nakedly apparent. In Christian ethics, all men count alike; for Nietzsche, the majority are only a means to the hero. Controversies as to ends cannot be conducted, like scientific controversies, by appeals to facts; they must be conducted by an attempt to change men's feelings. The Christian may endeavor to rouse sympathy, the Nietzschean may stimulate pride. Economic and military power may reinforce propaganda. The contest is, in short, an ordinary contest for power. Any creed, even one which teaches universal equality, may be a means to the domination of a section; this happened, for instance, when the French Revolution set to work to spread democracy by force of arms.

Power is the means, in ethical contests as in those of politics. But with the ethical systems that have had most influence in the past, power is not the end. Although men hate one another, they have, until recently, given their reverence to those who preached a different way of life. The great religions that aimed at universality, replacing the tribal and national cults of earlier times, considered men as men, not as Jew or Gentile, bond or free. Their founders were men whose sympathy was universal, and who were felt, on this account, to be possessed of a wisdom surpassing that of temporary and passionate despots. The result was not all that the founders could have wished. At an *auto-da-fé*, the mob had to be prevented by the police from attacking the victims, and was furious if one whom it had hoped to see burnt alive succeeded, by a tardy recantation, in winning the privilege of being strangled first and burnt afterwards. Nevertheless, the principle of universal sympathy conquered first one province, then another. It is the analogue, in the realm of feeling, of impersonal curiosity in the realm of intellect; both alike are essential elements in mental growth. I do not think that the return to a tribal or aristocratic ethic can be of long duration; the whole history of man since the time of Buddha points in the opposite direction. However passionately power may be desired, it is not power that is thought good in moments of reflective meditation. This is proved by the characters of the men whom mankind have thought most nearly divine.

The traditional moral rules that we considered at the beginning of this essay—filial piety, wifely submission, loyalty to kings, and so on—have all decayed completely or partially. They may be succeeded, as in the Renaissance, by an absence of moral restraint, or, as in the Reformation, by a new code in many ways more strict than those that have become obsolete. Loyalty to the State plays a much larger part in positive morality in our time than it did formerly; this, of course, is the natural result of the increase in the power of the State. The parts of morals that are concerned with other groups, such as the family and the Church, have less control than they used to have; but I do not see any evidence that, on the balance, moral principles or moral sentiments have less influence over men's actions now than in the eighteenth century or the Middle Ages.

Let us end with a summary analysis. The moral codes of primitive societies are generally believed, in those societies, to have a supernatural origin; in part, we can see no reason for this belief, but to a considerable extent it represents the balance of power in the community concerned: the gods consider submission to the powerful a duty, but the powerful must not be so ruthless as to rouse rebellion. Under the influence of prophets and sages, however, a new morality arises, sometimes side by side with the old one, sometimes in place of it. Prophets and sages, with few exceptions, have valued things other than power—wisdom, justice, or universal love, for example—and have persuaded large sections of mankind that these are aims more worthy to be pursued than personal success. Those who suffer by some part of the social system which the prophet or sage wishes to alter have personal reasons for supporting his opinion; it is the union of their self-seeking with his impersonal ethic that makes the resulting revolutionary movement irresistible.

We can now arrive at some conclusion as to the place of rebellion in social life. Rebellion is of two sorts: it may be purely personal, or it may be inspired by desire for a different kind of community from that in which the rebel finds himself. In the latter case, his desire can be shared by others; in many instances, it has been shared by all except a small minority who profited by the existing system. This type of rebel is constructive, not archaic; even if his movement leads to temporary anarchy, it is intended to give rise, in the end, to a new stable community. It is the impersonal character of his aims that distinguishes him from the anarchic rebel. Only the event can decide, for the general public, whether a rebellion will come to be thought justified; when it is thought to have been justified, previously existing authority would have been wise, from its own point of view, in not offering a desperate resistance. An individual may perceive a way of life, or a method of social organization, by which more of the desires of mankind could be satisfied than under the existing method. If he perceives truly, and can persuade men to adopt his reform, he is justified. Without rebellion, mankind would stagnate, and injustice would be irremediable. The man who refuses to obey authority has, therefore, in certain circumstances, a legitimate function, provided his disobedience has motives which are social rather than personal. But the matter is one as to which, by its very nature, it is impossible to lay down rules.

NOTES

1. On this subject, cf. Tawney, *Religion and the Rise of Capitalism.*
2. Deuteronomy vii. 1-4 and 14.
3. Ibid., xx. 16, 18.
4. Ibid., 13-15.
5. I Samuel xv. 8-11.
6. Deuteronomy xviii. 21, 22.

4

Sources of Ethical Beliefs and Feelings

Ethics differs from science in the fact that its fundamental data are feelings and emotions, not percepts. This is to be understood strictly; that is to say, the data are the feelings and emotions themselves, not the fact that we have them. The fact that we have them is a scientific fact like another, and we become aware of it by perception, in the usual scientific way. But an ethical judgment does not state a fact; it states, though often in a disguised form, some hope or fear, some desire or aversion, some love or hate. It should be enunciated in the optative or imperative mood, not in the indicative. The Bible says, "Thou shalt love thy neighbor as thyself," and a modern man, oppressed with the spectacle of international discord, may say, "Would that all men loved one another"; these are pure ethical sentences, which clearly cannot be proved or disproved merely by amassing facts.

That feelings are relevant to ethics is easily seen by considering the hypothesis of a purely material universe, consisting of matter without sentience. Such a universe would be neither good nor bad, and nothing in it would be right or wrong. When, in Genesis, God "saw that it was good" before He had created life, we must suppose that the goodness depended either upon His emotions in contemplating His work, or upon the fitness of the inanimate world as an environment for sentient beings. If the sun were about to collide with another star, and the earth were about to be reduced to gas, we should judge the forthcoming cataclysm to be bad if we considered the existence of the human race good; but a similar cataclysm in a region without life would be merely interesting. Thus ethics is bound up with life, not as a physical process to be studied by the biochemist, but as made up of happiness and sorrow, hope and fear, and the other cognate pairs of opposites that make us prefer one sort of world to another.

But when the fundamental ethical importance of feeling and desire has been admitted, it still remains a question whether there is such a thing as ethical *knowledge*. "Thou shalt not kill" is imperative, but "murder is wicked" seems to be indicative, and to state something true or false. "Would that all men were happy" is optative, but "happiness is good" has the same grammatical form as "Socrates is mortal." Is this grammatical form misleading, or is there truth and falsehood in ethics as in science? If I say that Nero was a bad man, am I giving information, as I should be if I said that he was a Roman Emperor, or would what I say be more accurately expressed by the words, "Nero, Oh, fie!"? This question is not an easy one, and I do not think that any simple answer is possible.

There is another closely related question, and that is as to the subjectivity of ethical judgments. If I say that oysters are good, and you say they are nasty, we both understand that we are merely expressing our personal tastes, and that there is nothing to argue about. But when Nazis say that it is good to torture Jews, and we say that it is bad, we do not *feel* as if we were merely expressing a difference of taste; we are even willing to fight and die for our opinion, which we should not do to enforce our view about oysters. Whatever arguments may be advanced to show that the two cases are analogous, most people will remain convinced that there is a difference somewhere, though it may be difficult to say exactly what it is. I think this feeling, though not decisive, deserves respect, and should make us reluctant to accept at all readily the view that all ethical judgments are wholly subjective.

It may be said that if hopes and desires are fundamental in ethics, then everything in ethics must be subjective, since hopes and desires are so. But this argument is less conclusive than it sounds. The data of science are individual percepts, and these are far more subjective than common sense supposes; nevertheless, upon this basis the imposing edifice of impersonal science has been built up. This depends upon the fact that there are certain respects in which the percepts of the majority agree, and that the divergent percepts of the color blind and the victims of hallucinations can be ignored. It may be that there is some similar way of arriving at objectivity in ethics; if so, since it must involve appeal to the majority, it will take us from personal ethics into the sphere of politics, which is, in fact, very difficult to separate from ethics.

The separation of ethics from theology is more difficult than the analogous separation in the case of science. It is true that science has only emancipated itself after a long struggle. Until the latter half of the seventeenth century, it was commonly held that a man who did not believe in witchcraft must be an atheist, and there are still people who condemn evolution on theological grounds, but very many theologians now agree that nothing in science can shake the foundations of religious belief. In ethics the situation is different. Many traditional ethical concepts are difficult to interpret, and many traditional ethical beliefs are hard to justify, except on the assumption that there is a God or a World Spirit or at least an immanent cosmic Purpose. I do not say that these interpretations and justifications are *impossible* without a theological basis, but I do say that without such a basis they lose persuasive force and the power of psychological compulsion.

It has always been one of the favorite arguments of the orthodox that without religion men would become wicked. The nineteenth-century British freethinkers, from Bentham to Henry Sidgwick, vehemently repudiated this argument, and their repudiation gained force from the fact that they were among the most virtuous men that have ever existed. But in the modern world, which has been shocked by the excesses of totalitarians who professed themselves unbelievers, the virtues of Victorian agnostics seem less conclusive, and may even be attributed to imperfect emancipation from the Christian tradition. The whole question whether ethics, in any socially inadequate form, can be independent of theology, must therefore be re-examined, with more awareness of the deep possibilities of evil than was to be found among our grandfathers, who were kept cozy by their comfortable belief in rational progress.

Ethical beliefs, throughout recorded history, have had two very different sources, one political, the other concerned with personal religious and moral convictions. In the Old Testament the two appear quite separately, one as the Law, the other as the Prophets. In the Middle Ages there was the same kind of distinction between the official morality inculcated by the hierarchy and the personal holiness that was taught and practiced by the great mystics. In our own day the same duality persists. When Kropotkin, after the Russian Revolution, was able to return from his long exile, it was not the Russia of his dreams that he found being born. He had dreamed of a loosely knit community of free and self-respecting individuals, but what was being created was a powerful centralized State, in which the individual was regarded merely as a means. This duality of personal and civic morality is one of which any adequate ethical theory must take account. Without civic morality communities perish; without personal morality their survival has no value. Therefore civic and personal morality are equally necessary to a good world.

In all known human communities, even the most primitive, ethical beliefs and feelings exist. Some actions are praised, others are blamed; some are rewarded, others are punished. Some acts of individuals are thought to bring prosperity, not only to the individuals, but to the community; others are thought to bring disaster. The beliefs concerned are in part defensible on rational grounds, but in primitive communities there is a preponderance of purely superstitious beliefs, which often inspire, at first, even those prohibitions which, later, are found to be capable of a reasoned justification.

One of the chief sources of primitive morality is taboo. Certain objects, especially those belonging to the Chief, are imbued with *mana,* and if you touch them you will die. Certain things are dedicated to a Spirit, and must only be used by the medicine man. Some foods are lawful, others unlawful. Some individuals, until purified, are unclean; this applies especially to such as have some taint of blood, not only those who have committed suicide, but also women in childbirth and during menstruation (See Leviticus xv, 19-29). There are often elaborate rules of exogamy, making a large proportion of the tribe taboo to the opposite sex. All these taboos, if infringed, are liable to bring disaster upon the guilty, and indeed upon the whole community, unless appropriate purificatory ceremonies are performed.

There is no pretense of justice, as we understand it, in the punishment following an act forbidden by a taboo, which is rather to be conceived as analogous to death as the result of touching a live wire. When David was transporting the Ark on a cart, it jolted over a rough threshing floor, and Uzzah, who was in charge, thinking it would fall, stretched up his hand to steady it. For this impiety, in spite of his laudable motive, he was struck dead (II Samuel vi, 6-7). The same lack of justice appears in the fact that not only murder, but accidental homicide, calls for ritual purification.

Forms of morality based on taboo linger on into civilized communities to a greater extent than some people realize. Pythagoras forbade beans, and Empedocles thought it wicked to munch laurel leaves. Hindus shudder at the thought of eating beef; Mohammedans and orthodox Jews regard the flesh of the pig as unclean. St. Augustine, the missionary to Britain, wrote to Pope Gregory the Great to know whether married people might come to church if they had had intercourse the previous night, and the Pope ruled that they might only do so after a ceremonial washing. There was a law in Connecticut—I believe it is still formally unrepealed—making it illegal for a man to kiss his wife on Sunday. In 1916 a clergyman from Scotland wrote a letter to the press attributing our lack of success against the Germans to the fact that the Government had encouraged the planting of potatoes on Sundays. All these opinions can only be justified on a basis of taboo.

One of the best examples of taboo is the prevalence of laws or rules prohibiting various forms of endogamy. Sometimes a tribe is divided into a number of groups, and a man must take his wife from a group other than his own. In the Greek Church, godparents of the same child may not marry. In England, until recently, a man might not marry his deceased wife's sister. Such prohibitions are impossible to justify on the ground that the forbidden unions would do any harm; they are defended solely on the ground of ancient taboo. But further, those forms of incest which most of us still regard as not to be legally sanctioned are viewed, by most people, with a horror which is out of proportion to the harm that they would do, and which must be regarded as an effect of prerational taboo. Defoe's Moll Flanders is far from exemplary, and commits many crimes without a qualm; but when she finds that she has inadvertently married her brother she is appalled, and can no longer endure him as a husband although they had lived happily together for years. This is fiction, but it is certainly true to life.

Taboo has certain great advantages as a source of moral behavior. It is psychologically far more compelling than any merely rational rules; compare, for instance, the shuddering aversion from incest with the calm reprobation of such a crime as forgery, which is not viewed superstitiously because savages cannot commit it. Moreover, a taboo morality can be perfectly precise and perfectly definite. True, it may prohibit completely harmless acts such as eating beans, but it probably also prohibits genuinely harmful acts such as murder, and does so more successfully than any other ethical method open to primitive communities. It is useful also in promoting governmental stability.

> There's such divinity doth hedge a king,
> That treason can but peep the thing it would,
> Acts little of his will.

Since the assassination of a king usually leads to civil war, this "divinity" must be considered a beneficial effect of the taboos surrounding the Chief.

When the orthodox argue that rejection of theological dogmas must lead to a decay of morals, the strongest consideration on their side is the usefulness of taboo. When men cease to feel a superstitious reverence for ancient and venerable percepts, they may not be content with marrying their deceased wives' sisters and planting potatoes on Sundays; they may advance to even more heinous sins, such as murder, treachery, and treason. This happened in classical Greece and in Renaissance Italy, both of which, in consequence, suffered political disaster. In each case men whose grandfathers had been pious and orderly citizens became anarchic criminals under the influence of free thought. I do not wish to underestimate the weight of such considerations, more particularly in the present day, when dictatorships are largely an almost inevitable reaction against the diffused anarchic tendencies of men who have thrown off taboo morality without acquiring any other.

The arguments against reliance on taboo morality are, however, to my mind, considerably stronger than those in favor, and as I am engaged in the attempt to expound a rational ethic I must set forth these arguments in order to justify my purpose.

The first argument is that, in a modern educated and scientific society, it is difficult to preserve respect for what is merely traditional except by a tight control over education designed to destroy capacity for independent thought. If you are brought up as a Protestant, you must be kept from noticing that Saturday, not Sunday, is the day on which it is wicked to plant potatoes. If you are brought up as a Catholic, you must remain ignorant of the fact that, in spite of the indissolubility of marriage, dukes and duchesses can have their marriages annulled by the Church on evidence which would not be thought adequate for an obscure couple. The necessary degree of stupidity is socially harmful, and can only be secured by means of a rigidly obscurantist regime.

The second argument is that, if moral education has been confined to the inculcation of taboos, the man who throws over one taboo is likely to throw over all the rest. If you have been taught that all the Ten Commandments are equally binding, and you then come to the conclusion that work on the Sabbath is not wicked, you may decide that murder also is permissible, and that there is no reason why any one act should be thought worse than any other. The general moral collapse which often follows a sudden irruption of free thought is attributable to the absence of a rational basis for the traditional ethical code. There was no such collapse among freethinkers in nineteenth-century England, largely because they believed that utilitarianism afforded a nontheological ground for obedience to those moral precepts which it recognized as valid, which were in fact all those that contributed to the welfare of the community.

The third argument is that, in every taboo morality that has hitherto existed, there have been some precepts that were positively harmful, sometimes in a high degree. Consider, for example, the text: "Thou shalt not suffer a witch to live" (Exodus xxii, 18). As a result of this text, in Germany alone, some 100,000 witches were put to death during the century from 1450 to 1550. Belief in witchcraft was peculiarly prevalent in Scotland, and was encouraged in England by James I. It was to flatter him that *Macbeth* was written, and the witches are part of the flattery. Sir Thomas Browne maintained that those who deny witchcraft are a sort of atheists. It was not Christian charity, but the spread of the scientific outlook, that, from about the time of Newton, put an end to the burning of harmless women for imaginary crimes. The taboo elements in conventional morality are less fierce in our day than they were three hundred years ago, but they are still in part obstacles to humane feeling and practice, for example in the opposition to birth control and euthanasia.

As men begin to grow civilized, they cease to be satisfied with mere taboos, and substitute divine commands and prohibitions. The Decalogue begins: "God spake these words and said." Throughout the Books of the Law it is the Lord who speaks. To do what God forbids is wicked, and will also be punished; it would still be wicked even if it were not punished. Thus the essence of morality becomes obedience. The fundamental obedience is to the will of God, but there are many derivative forms which owe their sanction to the fact that social inequalities have been divinely instituted. Subjects must obey the king, slaves their master, wives their husbands, and children their parents. The king owes obedience only to God, but if he fails in this he or his people will be punished. When David took a census, the Lord, who disliked statistics, sent a plague, of which many thousands of the children of Israel died (I Chron. xxi). This shows how important it was for everybody that the king should be virtuous. The power of priests depended partly upon the fact that they could to some extent keep the king from sin, at any rate from the grosser sins such as worship of false gods.

Obedience as the fundamental precept of ethics works fairly well in a stable community where no one questions the established religion and the government is tolerable. But at various times these conditions have failed. In the opinion of the Prophets they failed when kings were idolators; in the opinion of the early Church they failed when rulers were pagan or Arian. They failed on a large scale at the Reformation, when no duty of allegiance was acknowledged by Protestants to Catholic sovereigns or by Catholics to Protestant sovereigns. But Protestants were faced with greater difficulties than those that beset Catholics, for Catholics still had the Church, whose ethical teaching was infallible, whereas Protestants had no official source of moral precepts in countries where the government opposed them. There was, of course, the Bible, but on some subjects the Bible was silent and on others it spoke with a divided voice. Was it lawful to lend money at interest? No answer was to be found in the Scriptures. Should a childless widow marry her deceased husband's brother? Leviticus says no, Deuteronomy says yes (Lev. xx, 21; Deut. xxv, 5).

Protestants were thus led to revive an opinion already to be found in the Prophets and the New Testament, to the effect that God instructs each man's conscience as to what is right and what is wrong. There is therefore no need of an external ethical authority; nay, more, it is sin to obey such an authority when its behests go against the individual conscience. No precept enjoining obedience to an earthly authority is absolute, or can be binding except insofar as conscience approves it. This doctrine has had a profound effect in transforming ethics and politics, even among those who by no means accept it. It has afforded a justification for religious toleration, revolution against bad governments, refusal of social inferiors to submit to their "betters," equality of women, and the decay of parental authority. But it has failed disastrously to supply a new moral basis for social coherence in place of the old basis which it has destroyed. Conscience, *per se,* is an anarchic force upon which no system of government can be built.

There has been from the first a quite different source of ethical

feeling and ethical precept, namely give-and-take, or social compromise. This is not dependent, like the kinds of morality that we
have been considering hitherto, either upon superstition or upon
religion; it arises, broadly speaking, from the desire for a quiet life.
When I want potatoes, I might go by night and dig up those of my
neighbor, but he might retaliate by stealing the fruit off my apple
trees. Each of us would then have to keep somebody on the watch all
night to guard against such depredations. This would be inconvenient and tiresome; in the end, we should find it less trouble to
respect each other's property—always supposing that neither of us
was dying of starvation. A morality of this sort, though it may in
early stages be helped by taboos or religious sanctions, can survive
their decay, since, at least in intention, it offers advantages to everyone. With the progress of civilization, it has come to play a larger
and larger part in legislation, government, and private morality,
and yet it has never succeeded in inspiring the intense emotions of
horror or veneration that are connected with religion or taboo.

Man is a gregarious animal, not, like the ants and bees, by instinct, but in the main from a more or less obscure sense of collective
self-interest. The largest social unit that has a firm instinctive basis
is the family, and the family has begun to be undermined by the
State since the State has come to consider it a duty to preserve the
lives of infants neglected by their parents. Ants and bees, one must
suppose, act on impulse in doing what is for the good of the nest or
the hive, and never reflect that they might better themselves as individuals by antisocial behavior. But human beings are not so fortunate. To cause their actions to be in accordance with the public
interest, vast forces of law, of religion, and of education in enlightened self-interest have had to be called into play, and their success
has been very limited. It may be presumed that the earliest communities were enlarged families, but the main source of all further
social cohesion has been war. In war a large community may be
expected to defeat a small one, and therefore any method of gene-
rating social cohesion in a large group is biologically advantageous.

In so far as war has been the motive force tending to increase
social cohesion, morality has had to consist of two very different
parts, duties toward members of one's own herd, and duties having
reference to individuals or groups outside the herd. Religions aiming
at universality, such as Buddhism and Christianity, have sought to
obliterate this distinction, and to treat all mankind as one single
herd. This point of view began, in the West, with the Stoics, as a

consequence of Alexander's conquests. But hitherto, in spite of all that religion could do, it has remained an aspiration of a few philosophers and saints.

It is only morality within the herd that I wish to consider at present, and this only in so far as its purpose is to facilitate social co-operation. It is obvious that what is most imperative is some method, other than individual force, by which it can be decided what is to belong to whom. The two institutions by which most civilized communities have set to work to solve this problem are *law* and *property*, and the moral principle supposed to regulate these institutions has been *justice*, or what public opinion could accept as such.

Law consists essentially of a set of rules governing the use of force by the State, together with a prohibition of the use of force by private individuals or groups except in certain specified circumstances, such as self-defense. In the absence of law there is anarchy, involving the use of naked force by muscular individuals, and, although laws may be bad, they can seldom be so bad as to be worse than anarchy. A sentiment of respect for law is therefore a rational one.

Private property is a device by means of which submission to law is rendered less unpalatable than it would otherwise be. Originally, when primitive communism broke down, a man had a right to the produce of his own labor and to the dwelling and plot of land where he had always lived; mcreover it appeared natural and right that he should be permitted to leave his property to his children. In a nomadic community his property would consist mainly of flocks and herds.

Where law and property exist, "theft" becomes a definable concept, and can be included in the Decalogue as one among the ten worst sins.

Laws are held to be good when they are "just," but "justice" is a concept which it is very difficult to make precise. Plato's *Republic* professes to be an attempt to define it, but it cannot be said that the attempt is very successful. Under the influence of democratic sentiment modern men tend to identify justice with equality, but even now there are limits to this view. If it were proposed that the Queen should have the same income as a bricklayer, most people, including bricklayers, would think the proposal shocking. Until recent times, this feeling in favor of inequality had a much wider scope. I think that in fact "justice" must be defined as "what most people think just," or rather, to avoid the vicious circle, "that system which gives

the least commonly recognized ground of complaint." To give concrete content to this definition, we must take account of the traditions and sentiments of the community to which it is to be applied.
What remains the same for every community is that the "just"
system is the one that causes the smallest amount of discontent.

It is clear that ethics considered as a matter of give-and-take is
scarcely distinguishable from politics. In this it differs from the
more personal ethic which consists in obedience to the will of God or
submission to the voice of conscience. One of the problems that an
ethical theory must consider is the relation of these two kinds of
moral system, and the delimitation of their respective spheres. Consider the kind of sentiment that makes an artist prefer to do good
work rather than potboilers; this must be allowed an ethical value
although it has nothing to do with justice. For such reasons, I do
not think that ethics can be *wholly* social. Each of the sources of
ethical feeling that we have been considering, however crude in its
beginnings, is capable of development into forms that can influence
highly civilized men. If we ignore any one of them, the resulting
ethic will be partial and inadequate.

5

Is There Ethical Knowledge?

Here Russell expresses with remarkable frankness his dissatisfaction with
subjectivist ethics. This essay marks Russell's last attempt to find some
objective foundation for ethical beliefs and to determine whether ethical
propositions could be either true or false in the same sense as propositions
of science.

Russell ultimately had to admit that he failed to discover any objective
knowledge in ethics. In his lifelong quest for the foundations of ethics he
had only discovered a few principles to guide practice. Later Russell was to
state in a radio broadcast: "Philosophers are fond of endless puzzles about
ultimate ethical values and the basis of morals. My own belief is that so
far as politics and practical living are concerned we can sweep aside all
these puzzles, and use common sense principles."*

We come now at last to the problem to which all our previous ethical
discussions have been leading. The question may be put in dry
technical language, or in language showing that it involves issues
of great emotional importance. Let us begin with the latter.

If we say, "Cruelty is wrong," or "You ought to love your neighbor as yourself," are we saying something which has impersonal
truth or falsehood, or are we merely expressing our own preferences?
If we say, "Pleasure is good and pain is bad," are we making a
statement, or are we merely expressing an emotion which would be
more correctly expressed in a different grammatical form, say, "Hur-

---

*Werner Martin. *Bertrand Russell: A Bibliography of His Writings* (Connecticut:
Linnet Books, 1981), p. 201.

rah for pleasure, and away dull care"? When men dispute or go to war about a political issue, is there any sense in which one side is more in the right than the other, or is there merely a trial of strength? What is meant, if anything, by saying that a world in which human beings are happy is better than one in which they are unhappy? I, for one, find it intolerable to suppose that when I say, "Cruelty is bad" I am merely saying, "I dislike cruelty," or something equally subjective. What I want to discuss is whether there is anything in ethics that is not, in the last analysis, subjective.

To put the same problem in more technical language: When we examine what purport to be ethical statements, we find that they differ from statements asserting matters of fact by the presence of one or both of two terms, "ought" and "good," or their synonyms. Are these terms, or equivalents of them, part of any minimum vocabulary of ethics? Or are they definable in terms of desires and emotions and feelings? And, if so, do they have essential reference to the desires and emotions and feelings of the person using the words, or have they a reference to the general desires and emotions and feelings of mankind? There are words such as "I," "here," "now," which have a different meaning for each different person who uses them, or even on each different occasion when they are used. Such words I call "egocentric." Our question is: Are ethical terms egocentric?

In discussing the above questions I shall repeat in abbreviated form arguments which have occurred elsewhere,* but this time we must arrive at decisions, and not, as before, leave many questions open.

One possible theory is that "ought" is indefinable, and that we know by ethical intuition one or more propositions about the kinds of acts that we ought, or ought not, to perform. There is no *logical* objection to this theory, and I am not prepared to reject it decisively. It has, however, a grave drawback, namely, that there is no general agreement as to what sorts of acts ought to be performed, and that the theory affords no means of deciding who is in the right where there is disagreement. It thus becomes, in practice though not in theory, an egocentric doctrine. If A says, "You ought to do this" and B says, "No, you ought to do that," you only know that these are their opinions, and you have no means of knowing which, if either, is right. You can only escape from this conclusion by saying dog-

---

[*I.e., earlier chapters of *Human Society in Ethics and Politics*—Ed.]

matically: "Whenever there is a dispute as to what ought to be done, I am in the right, and those who disagree with me are mistaken." But as those who disagree will make a similar claim, ethical controversy will become merely a clash of rival dogmas. These considerations lead us to abandon "ought" as the fundamental ethical term. Let us see whether we can do any better with the concept "good."

We shall call something "good" if it has value on its own account, independently of its effects. Perhaps, since the term "good" is ambiguous, we shall do well to substitute the term "intrinsic value." Thus the theory that we are now to examine is the theory that there is an indefinable which we are calling "intrinsic value," and that we know, by a different kind of ethical intuition from that considered in connection with "ought," that certain kinds of things possess intrinsic value. The term has a negative, to which we will give the name "disvalue." A possible ethical intuition of the sort appropriate to our present theory would be: "Pleasure has intrinsic value and pain has intrinsic disvalue." We shall now define "ought" in terms of intrinsic value: An act "ought" to be performed if, of those that are possible, it is the one having the most intrinsic value. To this definition we must add the principle: "The act having most intrinsic value is the one likely to produce the greatest balance of intrinsic value over intrinsic disvalue, or the smallest balance of intrinsic disvalue over intrinsic value." An intrinsic value and an intrinsic disvalue are defined as equal when the two together have zero intrinsic value.

This theory, like its predecessor, is not logically refutable. It has the advantage, over the theory which makes "ought" fundamental, that there are many fewer disagreements as to what has intrinsic value than as to what ought to be done. And when we examine disagreements as to what ought to be done, we find, usually, though perhaps not always, that they are derived from disagreements as to the effects of actions. A savage may believe that infringing a taboo causes death; some sabbatarians believe that working on Sunday leads to defeat in war. Such considerations suggest that moral rules are really based on an estimate of consequences even when they seem to be absolute. And if we judge the morality of an act by its consequences, we seem driven to adopt some such definition of "ought" as that suggested at the end of the last paragraph. Our present theory is, therefore, a definite improvement upon the theory which makes "ought" indefinable.

There are, however, still objections, some analogous to the former ones, and some of a new kind. Although there is more agreement as to intrinsic value than as to rules of conduct, there are still some disagreements that are serious. One of these is as to vindictive punishment. Is there intrinsic value in inflicting pain upon those whose acts have intrinsic disvalue? Believers in hell must answer in the affirmative, and so must all those who believe that the purpose of the criminal law should not be merely deterrent and reformatory. Some stern moralists have maintained that pleasure has no intrinsic value, but I do not think they were quite sincere in this, as they maintained at the same time that the virtuous will be happy in heaven. The question of vindictive punishment is more serious, because, as in the case of disagreement about moral rules, there is no way in which the matter can be argued: if you think it good and I think it bad, neither of us can advance any reasons whatever in support of our belief.

There is a consideration of quite another kind, which, while not conclusive, tends to throw doubt on the view that intrinsic value is indefinable. When we examine the things to which we are inclined to attach intrinsic value, we find that they are all things that are desired or enjoyed. It is difficult to believe that anything would have value in a universe devoid of sentience. This suggests that "intrinsic value" may be definable in terms of desire or pleasure or both.

If we say, "Pleasure is good and pain is bad," do we mean anything more than "We like pleasure and dislike pain"? It seems as if we must mean something more than this, but this is certainly a part of what we mean. We cannot attribute intrinsic value to everything that is desired, because desires conflict, for instance in a war, where each side desires its own victory. We could perhaps evade this difficulty by saying that only states of mind have intrinsic value. In that case, if A and B compete for something which only one of them can have, we shall say that there is intrinsic value in the pleasure of the victor, whichever he may be. There is now nothing which one of the two judges to have intrinsic value, while the other judges that the same thing has intrinsic disvalue. A may admit that the pleasure which B would derive from victory would have intrinsic value, but may argue that B's victory is nevertheless to be prevented if possible, on account of its effects. Thus we shall now consider the definition: "Intrinsic value" means "the property of being a state of mind desired by the person who experiences it." This differs very little from the view that the good is pleasure. We come even nearer to the good as pleasure if we substitute "enjoyed" for "desired" in the above definition.

I do not think the statement "The good is pleasure" is quite correct, but I think that most of the difficulties of ethics are the same when this statement is adopted as when we adopt one which seems to me more exact. I shall, therefore, for the sake of simplicity, adopt hypothetically, for the moment, the hedonistic definition of the good. It remains to examine how this definition can be connected with our ethical feelings and convictions.

Henry Sidgwick, in his *Methods of Ethics,* argued at length that all moral rules that are generally recognized can be deduced from the principle that we ought to aim at maximizing pleasure; he even contended that this principle accounts for the occasional exceptions that moral rules are admitted to have. There are occasions when most people would say that it is right to tell a lie, or to break a promise, or to steal or kill; all these the hedonist's principle explains. I think that, as regards the moral code of civilized communities, Sidgwick's contention is broadly true; at any rate, I am not prepared to argue against it, subject to these limitations.

What, on this theory, shall we say about praise and blame? Blame, when it is deliberate, is both an emotion and a judgment: I feel a dislike of the act that I blame, and I judge that I do right in feeling this dislike. The emotion is just a fact, and raises no theoretical issue, but the judgment is a more difficult matter. I certainly do not *mean,* when I judge an act to be right, that it is the act best calculated to maximize pleasure, for, if I did, it would be logically impossible to dispute hedonism, which it is not. Perhaps the judgment is not really a judgment, but another emotion, namely, an emotion of approval toward my likes or dislikes. According to this view, when I deliberately, and not impulsively, blame an act, I dislike the act, and feel toward my dislike an emotion of approval.

Another person, who disagrees with me about ethics, may disapprove of my approval; he will express his feeling in what *seems* to be a judgment, saying, "You ought not to have blamed that act," or something equivalent. But on our present theory he is still expressing an emotion; neither he nor I is making any assertion, and therefore our conflict is only practical, not theoretical.

If we define "right," the matter is different. We can then have a *judgment,* "This is right." If our definition is not to have paradoxical results, our definition of "right" must be such that usually, when an act is right according to our definition, it is one toward which we feel the emotion of approval, and when it is wrong, it is one toward which we feel disapproval. We are thus led to seek for some common property of as many as possible of the acts commonly approved (or disapproved). If *all* had such a common property, we should have no hesitation in defining this as "right." But we do not find anything quite so convenient as this. What we do find is that most of the acts toward which people feel the emotion of approval have a certain common property, and that the exceptional acts, which have not this property, tend to be no longer approved of when people have become clearly aware of their exceptional character. We may then say, in a sense, that approval of such acts is mistaken.

We can now set up a series of fundamental propositions and definitions in Ethics.

(1) Surveying the acts which arouse emotions of approval or disapproval, we find that, as a general rule, the acts which are approved of are those believed likely to have, on the balance, effects of certain kinds, while opposite effects are expected from acts that are disapproved of.

(2) Effects that lead to approval are defined as "good," and those leading to disapproval as "bad."

(3) An act of which, on the available evidence, the effects are likely to be better than those of any other act that is possible in the circumstances, is defined as "right"; any other act is "wrong." What we "ought" to do is, by definition, the act which is right.

(4) It is right to feel approval of a right act and disapproval of a wrong act.

These definitions and propositions, if accepted, provide a coherent body of ethical propositions, which are true (or false) in the same sense as if they were propositions of science.

It is clear that the difficulties are mainly concerned with the first proposition of the above series. We must therefore examine it more closely.

We have seen in previous chapters that different societies in different ages have given approval to a wide diversity of acts. Primitive communities, at a certain stage of development, approved of cannibalism and human sacrifice. Spartans approved of homosexuality, which to Jews and Christians was an abomination. Until the late seventeenth century, almost everybody approved of the burning of reputed witches, which we now regard as senseless cruelty. But these differences were rooted in differences of belief as to the effects of actions. Human sacrifice was supposed to promote fertility. The Spartans thought that homosexuality promoted courage in battle. We might still approve of the execution of witches, if we believed that they had the maleficent powers with which they were credited in the Middle Ages. The difference between ourselves and other ages in these respects is attributable to a difference between our beliefs and theirs as to the effects of actions. The actions which they condemned were such as, in their opinion, would have certain effects, and we agree with them in thinking that such effects are to be avoided if possible.

We are thus led to the conclusion that there is more agreement among mankind as to the effects at which we should aim than as to the kinds of acts that are approved. I think the contention of Henry Sidgwick, that the acts which are approved of are those that are likely to bring happiness or pleasure, is, broadly speaking, true. Not infrequently, an ancient taboo, which it was formerly thought disastrous to infringe, may survive, through the force of custom and tradition, long after the beliefs which gave rise to it have been forgotten. But in such cases the taboo has a precarious life, and is apt to be thrown over by those who come across, by travel or by study, customs different from those in which they have been brought up.

I do not think, however, that pleasure is quite the nearest that we can come to the common quality of the great majority of approved actions. I think we must include such things as intelligence and aesthetic sensibility. If we were really persuaded that pigs are happier than human beings, we should not on that account welcome the ministrations of Circe. If miracles were possible, most of us would prefer a life in which we could, at least part of the time, enjoy the delicate delights of art and intellect, to one consisting wholly of houris, wines, and hot baths—partly, no doubt, from fear of satiety, but not wholly. We do not, in fact, value pleasures in proportion to their intensity; some pleasures seem to us inherently preferable to others.

If it is admitted that the great majority of approved acts are such as are believed to have certain effects, and if it is found, further, that exceptional acts, which are approved without having this character, tend to be no longer approved when their exceptional character is realized, then it becomes possible, in a certain sense, to speak of ethical error. We may say that it is "wrong" to approve of such exceptional acts, meaning that such approval does not have the effects which mark the great majority of approved acts, and which we have agreed to take as the criterion of what is "right."

Although, on the above theory, ethics contains statements which are true or false, and not merely optative or imperative, its basis is still one of emotion and feeling, the emotion of approval and the feeling of enjoyment or satisfaction, the former being involved in the definition of "right" and "wrong," the latter in that of "intrinsic value." And the appeal upon which we depend for the acceptance of our ethical theory is not the appeal to the facts of perception, but to the emotions and feelings which have given rise to the concepts of "right" and "wrong," "good" and "bad."

Part Two

Moral Rules

Introduction

While it is obvious to anyone familiar with Russell's life and his extensive writings on social and political issues that he held very strong moral convictions, it is not at all obvious how he came to reconcile his ethical subjectivism with his life as a passionate moral critic and social reformer. Russell, of course, believed that the moral and social views he expressed, for example, in *Marriage and Morals* and *War Crimes in Vietnam* were, comparatively speaking, superior to the views advocated by his opponents. In fact, on many occasions, Russell argued that his opponents' positions were irrational, wrong, or unsupported by the evidence. Russell's biographer, Alan Wood, related one humorous example: "Once [Russell] was expounding to Lowes Dickinson his theory that 'good' and 'bad' had no objective validity. A few minutes afterwards Lowes Dickinson was laughing because the name of somebody Russell disliked had come up in conversation, Russell had declared in the fiercest tone of conviction: 'He is a scoundrel!'"[1]

It did not take long for some of Russell's more eager critics to point out an apparent inconsistency between his views on ethics and his strong moral pronouncements. After all, Russell had written in "Science and Ethics" that "It is logically impossible that there should be evidence for or against"[2] a moral judgment since it "makes no assertion"[3] and hence possesses neither truth nor falsity. Russell's response to his critics is worth quoting at length:

> I am accused of inconsistency, perhaps justly, because, although I hold ultimate ethical valuations to be subjective, I nevertheless allow myself emphatic opinions on ethical questions. If there is an inconsistency, it is one that I cannot get rid of without insincerity; more-

over, an inconsistent system may well contain less falsehood than a consistent one . . . .

In the first place, I am not prepared to forego my right to feel and express ethical passions; no amount of logic, even though it be my own, will persuade me that I ought to do so. There are some men whom I admire, and others whom I think vile; some political systems seem to me tolerable, others an abomination. Pleasure in the spectacle of cruelty horrifies me, and I am not ashamed of the fact that it does. I am no more prepared to give up all this than I am to give up the multiplication table.

The trouble arises through the subjectivity of ethical valuations. Let us see what this amounts to.

In practice, when two people disagree as to whether a certain kind of conduct is right, the difference of opinion can usually, though not always, be reduced to a difference as to means. This is a question in the realm of science. Suppose, for example, one person advocates capital punishment whereas another condemns it: they will probably argue as to its efficacy as a deterrent, which is a matter at least theoretically capable of being decided by statistics. Such cases raise no theoretical difficulty. But there are cases that are more difficult. Christianity, Kant, and Bentham maintain that all human beings are to count alike; Nietzsche says that most of them should be merely means to an aristocracy. He would not assent to the modern development of this doctrine, that good consists of pleasure to a German or pain to a Jew, and evil consists of pleasure to a Jew or pain to a German, but from the standpoint of ethical theory his doctrine raises the same problems as does that of the Nazis.

Let us consider two theories as to the good. One says, like Christianity, Kant, and democracy: whatever the good may be, any one man's enjoyment of it has the same value as any other man's. The other says: there is a certain sub-class of mankind—white men, Germans, gentiles, or what not—whose good or evil alone counts in an estimation of ends; other men are only to be considered as means. I shall suppose that A takes the first view, and B the second. What can either say to convict the other of error? I can only imagine arguments that would be strictly irrelevant. A might say: If you ignore the interests of a large part of mankind, they will rebel and murder you. B might say: The portion of mankind that I favor is so much superior to the rest in skill and courage that it is sure to rule in any case, so why not frankly acknowledge the true state of affairs? Each of these is an argument as to means, not as to ends. When such arguments are swept away, there remains, so far as I can see, nothing to be said except for each party to express moral disapproval of the other. Those who reject this conclusion advance no argument against it except that it is unpleasant.

The question arises: What am I to mean when I say that this or that is good as an end? To make the argument definite, let us take pleasure as the thing to be discussed. If one man affirms and another denies that pleasure is good *per se,* what is the difference between them? My contention is that the two men differ as to what they desire, but not as to what they assert, since they assert nothing. I maintain that neither asserts anything except derivatively, in the sense in which everything we say may be taken as affirming something about ourselves. If I say, "It will rain tomorrow," I mean to make a meteorological assertion, but to a skeptical listener I only convey that I believe something about tomorrow's weather. There is a similar difference between expressing a desire and stating that I feel the desire. An ethical judgment, according to me, expresses a desire, but only inferentially implies that I feel this desire, just as a statement in the indicative expresses a belief, but inferentially implies that I have this belief.

I do not think that an ethical judgment *merely* expresses a desire; I agree with Kant that it must have an element of universality. I should interpret, "A is good" as "Would that all men desired A." This *expresses* a wish, but does not *assert* one except by implication. . . .

I am quite at a loss to understand why any one should be surprised at my expressing vehement ethical judgments. By my own theory, I am, in doing so, expressing vehement desires as to the desires of mankind; I feel such desires, so why not express them?

What, I imagine, is mainly felt to be lacking in my ethical theory is the element of command, in fact the "categorical imperative." Ethics is a social force which helps a society to cohere, and every one who utters an ethical judgment feels himself in some sense a legislator or a judge, according to the degree of generality of the judgment in question. . . . The point is that an ethical judgment ought—so it is felt—to have the same kind of objectivity as a judgment of fact. A judgment of fact—so I hold—is capable of a property called "truth," which it has or does not have quite independently of what any one may think about it. Very many American philosophers, perhaps most, disagree with me about this, and hold that there is no such property as "truth." For them the problem that I am considering does not exist. But for me it is necessary to acknowledge that I see no property, analogous to "truth," that belongs or does not belong to an ethical judgment. This, it must be admitted, puts ethics in a different category from science.

I cannot see, however, that this difference is as important as it is sometimes thought to be. Take, for example, the question of persuasion. In science there is a technique of persuasion which is so effective that controversies seldom last very long. This technique consists of an appeal to evidence, not to the emotions. But as soon as a question becomes in any way entangled in politics, theoretical methods become inadequate. Are colored people congenitally less intelligent than white people? Are there national characteristics distinguishing individuals of the various nations? Is there any anatomical evidence that women's brains are inferior to men's? Such questions are normally decided by rhetoric, brass bands, and broken heads. Nevertheless, the detached scientist, if he exists, may, neglected and alone, persist in applying scientific methods even to questions that rouse passion.

In the matter of persuasion it is often overlooked that the advocate of scientific methods must—since persuading is a practical activity—base himself on the ethical principle that it is better to believe truth than falsehood. In my interpretation, this means that the advocate of scientific methods wishes that men believed truly, and wishes that others shared this wish. Clearly he will not, in fact, advocate scientific methods unless he has this wish. Propaganda agencies are different: they wish people to have certain beliefs, which they may themselves entertain, but which they seldom wish to see subjected to a scientific scrutiny.

Persuasion in ethical questions is necessarily different from persuasion in scientific matters. According to me, the person who judges that A is good is wishing others to feel certain desires. He will therefore, if not hindered by other activities, try to rouse these desires in other people if he thinks he knows how to do so. This is the purpose of preaching, and it was my purpose in the various books in which I expressed ethical opinions. The art of presenting one's desires persuasively is totally different from that of logical demonstration, but it is equally legitimate.

All of this may be true, I shall be told, *provided your desires are good:* if they are evil, rhetoric in their defense is an art of the devil. But what are "good" desires? Are they anything more than desires that you share? Certainly there *seems* to be something more. Suppose, for example, that someone were to advocate the introduction of bullfighting in this country. In opposing the proposal, I should *feel,* not only that I was expressing my desires, but that my desires in the matter are *right,* whatever that may mean. As a matter of argument, I can, I think, show that I am not guilty of any logical inconsistency in holding to the above interpretation of ethics and at the same time expressing strong ethical preferences.[4]

Although religious beliefs have traditionally been a source for moral values, Russell tried to find solutions without a religious framework. However, had no intention of rejecting all the moral values that were laid down by traditional religions. Russell saw himself much more as a reformer, in the sense that he wanted to keep what he considered good moral values and reform those values he believed to be bad.

In examining Russell's writings in the area of moral theory, we will find a gradual change and development of his view as his ideas on language, logic, and philosophy altered over the years.

NOTES

1. Alan Wood. *Bertrand Russell: The Passionate Skeptic* (New York: Simon and Schuster, 1958), p. 61.

2. "Science and Ethics," this volume p. 63

3. Ibid.

4. Paul Schlipp (ed.). *The Philosophy of Bertrand Russell* (La Salle, Ill.: Open Court, 1971) fourth edition, pp. 720-724.

6

What Makes a Social System
Good or Bad?

In 1920 Russell was invited to join a Labor delegation to the Soviet Union to see what was happening in the wake of the Bolshevik revolution that he had so ardently welcomed. He returned to England a few months later in a state of total disillusionment. Although admittedly sympathetic to the aims of Bolshevism, Russell could accept neither its methods nor the final submission to the state or its theoretical basis. He was also dismayed by those of his friends who "saw only what they wanted to see" and then tried to prevent him from publishing the truth because they felt that any criticism of the revolution would play into the hands of the reactionaries who wanted to reestablish the old order.

Then in 1921, Russell was invited for a one-year term to lecture at the University of Peking. He was able to observe the gentle culture and society of pre-revolutionary China, a climate that brought Russell fresh hope. However, he did not fail to see the dangers that were then threatening the then agreeable situation in China.

This essay and the one that follows ("Moral Standards and Social Well-being") were written by Russell shortly after these two excursions and draw upon his experiences from both visits.

"What Makes a Social System Good or Bad?" is a comprehensive attempt by Russell to examine some of the common mistakes that people make in judging social systems. He then suggests a more scientific way in which such judgments could be formed.

Originally published in *Century* 1014 (May 1922): 14–21.

I

Any man who desires, as I do, a fundamental change in the structure of society is forced sooner or later to ask himself the question: what is it that makes one social system seem to him good and another bad? This is undoubtedly very largely a matter of individual caprice. In history, for example, some prefer one epoch, some another. Some admire the polished and civilized ages, while others profess to admire the rude virtues of more barbarous times. One does not wish to think that one's political opinions result from mere fanciful preferences of this sort, yet I believe that an enormous proportion of political opinion comes, in the last analysis, from some untested, unexamined, almost unconscious love for a certain type of society actual or imagined. I think it is possible to arrive at something less subjective than such tastes and fancies, and I think the advocate of fundamental change, more obviously than anyone else, needs to find ways of judging a social system which do not embody merely his individual tastes.

Men's proximate political opinions are defended by arguments—arguments to the effect of this course or that: such a course will lead to war; such another to economic slavery; such another to starvation. But in choosing the danger we most wish to avoid or the advantage we most wish to secure, we are almost all of us dominated by some more or less vague picture of the sort of society we should like to see existing. One man is not afraid of war, because he has a picture of Homeric heroes whose fighting he finds it agreeable to contemplate. Another is not afraid of economic slavery, because he thinks that he himself and his friends will be the slave-drivers rather than the slaves. Another is not afraid of starvation, because he has a secret hoard and therefore believes that privation brings out the latent heroism in men. And so they differ as to the course which is best to be pursued, and the grounds of their differences remain obscure to themselves and others. Being obscure, they are suitable subjects for endless quarrels. The only way to make people's political judgments more conscious, more explicit, and therefore more scientific, is to bring to the light of day the conception of an ideal society which underlies each man's opinion, and to discover, if we can, some method of comparing such ideals in respect of the universality, or otherwise, of their appeal.

I propose first of all to examine some ways of judging a social system which are common but which I believe to be erroneous, and then to suggest the ways in which I think such judgments should be formed.

Among most people at most times, the commonest way of judging is simply by inherited prejudices. Any society which is not in a state of rapid transition has customs and beliefs which have been handed down from previous generations, which are unquestioned, and which it appears utterly monstrous to go against. Such are the customs connected with religion, the family, property and so on. The peculiar merit of the Greeks was due largely to the fact that, being a commercial and seafaring people, they came across the customs and beliefs of innumerable and widely differing nations, and were thus led to a skeptical examination of the basis of all such customs, including their own. If my memory serves me, there is somewhere in Herodotus a story of a conversation between some Greeks and a barbarian tribe, in which the Greeks expressed horror of the barbarians for the practice of eating their dead, but the barbarians expressed quite equal horror of the practice of burying the dead, which to them was just as shocking as the other to to the Greeks. Such experiences of intercourse with other nations diminish the hold which merely inherited beliefs have upon the man who lives in a fixed environment. In our age, this effect is produced not only by travel and commerce, but also by the changes in social custom inevitably caused by the growth of industrialism. Wherever industry is well developed and not very new, one finds that religion and the family, which are the twin props of every merely traditional social structure, lose their hold over men's minds. Consequently the force of tradition is less in the present age than it has ever been before. Nevertheless, it is even now as great probably as all other forces combined. Take, for example, the belief in the sacredness of private property—a belief bound up originally with the patriarchal family, the right which a man was supposed to have to the produce of his own labor, and the right which he was able to extort to what he had conquered by the sword. In spite of the antiquity and diminishing strength of these ancient grounds of belief in private property, and in spite of the fact that no new grounds are suggested, the enormous majority of mankind have a deep and unquestioning belief in its sacredness, due largely to the taboo effect of the words "thou shalt not steal." It is clear that private property is an inheritance from the pre-industrial era when an individual man or family could make an individual product. In an industrial system a man never makes the whole of anything, but makes the thousandth part of a million things. Under these circumstances, it is totally absurd to say that a man has a right to the produce of his own labor. Consider a porter on a railway whose business it is to shunt goods trains: what proportion of the goods carried can be said to represent the produce of his labor? The question is wholly insoluble. Therefore it is impossible to secure social justice by saying that each man shall have what he himself produces. Early socialists in the days before Marx were apt to suggest this as a cure for the injustices of capitalism, but their suggestions were both utopian and retrograde, since they were incompatible with large-scale industry. It is, therefore, evident that the injustice of capitalism cannot be cured so long as the sacredness of private property is recognized. The Bolsheviks have seen this and have, therefore, confiscated all private capital for the use of the State. It is because they have challenged man's belief in the sacredness of private property that the outcry against them has been so great. Even among professing socialists there are many who feel a thrill of horror at the thought of turning rich men out of their mansions in order to make room for overcrowded proletarians. Such instinctive feelings are difficult to overcome by mere reason. The few men who do so, like the leading Bolsheviks, have to face the hostility of the world. But by the actual creation of a social order which does not respect merely traditional prejudices, more is done to destroy such prejudices in ordinary minds than can be done by a century of theoretical propaganda. I believe it will appear, when time enables men to see things in due proportion, that the chief service of the Bolsheviks lies in their practical challenge to the belief in private property, a belief existing by no means only among the rich, and forming at the present time an obstacle to fundamental progress—so great an obstacle that only its destruction will make a better world possible.

Another thing which affects people's instinctive judgment of a social system, whether actual or imagined, is whether it would provide a career for the sort of person they think they are. One cannot imagine that Napoleon, even in youth, could have been very enthusiastic about dreams of universal peace; or that captains of industry would be attracted by Samuel Butler's *Erewhon,* where all machines were illegal. Similarly, the artist will not enjoy the thought of a society where no man is allowed to paint unless his pictures are pleasing to the town council. And on this ground many artists are opponents of socialism. Men of science struggled against the system which existed in the seventeenth century and compelled them to teach nothing contradictory to revealed religion; and in like manner intellectuals in Russia object to having to teach their subjects from a Marxian point of view. People who find a pleasure in ordering others about (and this includes most of the energetic people in the world) will not like anarchism, where every man can do as he pleases. They will be in rebellion against existing authority unless they are part of it, but will wish to replace it by their own authority, not to abolish it, because in a world where every man could do as he pleases, executive people would find no career. On the other hand, easy-going people will hate strenuous systems. They will oppose the setting-up of drill and severe educational methods. During the war, they called such things "Prussianism." If they were better informed about Russia, they would now call them "Bolshevism." I confess to a temperamental sympathy with this point of view, and my sympathy was confirmed by what I saw of China, the most easy-going country left in the world. But this is not an easy-going age, nor one in which such temperamental preferences can be allowed to weigh. It is an age in which we have to think less of the present than of the future, less of the lives of our own generation than of the lives they are preparing for the generations to come.

Another thing which influences people, more or less unconciously, in their judgment as to a suggested social system, is the question whether the activities involved in the creating of it would be agreeable to them. I fear that revolutionaries are not always exempt from this motive. There are certainly some in whom hatred of the possessing classes is stronger than love for the dispossessed; there are some to whom mere benevolent feeling appears to be repulsive humbug, and who derive the zeal of their revolutionary ardor mainly from the delight which they feel in the thought of punishing the bourgeoisie. Such men will, of course, always be found among the advocates of violent tactics, since without violence there is no satisfaction for their impulses. Patriotism and militarism have, in many men, a similar origin. The thought of fighting, or more probably, the thought of setting others to fight, is delightful to them, and patriotism recommends itself to them as a creed likely to produce fighting. I do not mean that men are conscious of these impulsive sources of their beliefs, but I do mean that such impulses operate in the kind of way studied by psycho-analysis, and I believe that it is of great importance to drag the operation of these impulses into the light of day, to be aware of their operation in ourselves and to do what we can to make others similarly aware; for an underground, unconscious force operates against reason, eludes discussion, and makes objectivity impossible while it remains undetected.

Among writers of sociology and political theorists generally, a very common way of judging the social structure is by whether it constitutes a pleasant pattern to contemplate. Many social theorists forget that a community is composed of individuals, and that what- ever of good or bad it may contain must be embodied in those individuals. They think of the State as something having a good of its own quite distinct from the good of the citizens; and what they call the good of the State is usually, unconsciously to themselves, what gives them a certain aesthetic or moral satisfaction. We know that when God created the world he saw that it was good, obviously not from the point of view of the unfortunates who have to live in it, but from a higher point of view, presumably that of aesthetic con- templation. In like manner, social theorists create worlds in their imagination which they also see to be good in spite of the fact that they would be intolerable to live in. Such worlds are neat and tidy; everybody does at each moment something which is in accordance with the central plan; they obey the will of the administrator as the universe obeys the will of God. The theorist, of course, is always in imagination himself the administrator. This kind of social theory was made popular among professors by Hegel; it was used by him to laud the Prussian State, and has been used by his academic followers to support the conservatisms of their several countries. Since the war, the Hegelian theory has been at a discount, having been supposed in some mysterious way to have inspired the inva- sion of Belgium; but in other forms a similar outlook remains com- mon. Much of the belief in industrialism, particularly as applied to backward countries, is of this sort; it is intolerable to the industrially minded to think of lazy populations sitting under banana-trees, eat- ing the fruit as it drops, and being happy in unproductive idleness. Some forms of socialism are not free from this defect: they aim rather at creating the kind of State which is pleasing to theoretical contemplation than the kind which will suit with the temperaments of its citizens. A very great deal of imperialism is also of this sort; it is pleasant to see much of one's natural color on the map, and it is unpleasant to see one's dominions jagged and scattered owing to the intrusion of foreign territories. The habit of judging the State as it is to contemplate, not as it is to live in, arises from giving more importance to the faint and transient sentiments of an observer (when that observer happens to be oneself) than to the vivid and continual experiences of those who have to live under the government of the State. It is certainly a very potent source of bad social theory. Whoever wishes to be a social theorist should daily remind himself of the very simple, but important, maxim that a State is something in which people have to live, and not merely something to be read about in books, or contemplated as we contemplate the view from a mountain-top.

II

So far we have been concerned with ways of judging a society which we believe to be mistaken. It is time to turn to those to which we can assent.

There are two elements in a good society, namely: first, the present well-being of those who compose it, and secondly, its capacity for developing into something better. These two do not, by any means, always go together. Sometimes a society in which there is little present well-being may contain within itself the seeds of something better than any previous system. Sometimes, on the other hand, a society in which there is much diffused well-being may be unprogressive, for a time static, and ultimately decadent. It is, therefore, necessary to take account of both elements as independent ingredients of the sort of society we should wish to see existing. If the science of social dynamics were more developed and the art of prophecy less insecure, progressiveness would be a much more important quality in a society than present well-being. But politics is so far from scientific and the social future so very uncertain, that present well-being, which is indubitable, must be allowed as much weight as an uncertain future good, although this future good, if realized, will outweigh anything merely present because of its longer extension in time. "A bird in hand is worth two in the bush"—and this is particularly true when we are not sure there are any birds in the bush at all. Let us therefore begin with what makes the present well-being of a community.

In judging of the present well-being of a community, there are two opposite fallacies to be avoided. We may call these, respectively, the fallacy of the aristocrat and the fallacy of the outside observer. We considered a moment ago the fallacy of the outside observer. The fallacy of the aristocrat consists in judging a society by the kind of

life it accords to a privileged minority. The ancient empires of Egypt
and Babylonia afforded a thoroughly agreeable existence for kings
and priests and nobles, but the rest of the community were mostly
slaves or sefs, and must have had an existence composed of unre-
mitting toil and hardship. Modern capitalism affords a delightful
existence for the captains of industry: for them there is adventure
and free initiative, luxury and the admiration of contemporaries.
But for the great mass of the workers there is merely a certain place
in the great machine. To that place they are confined by the need of
a livelihood, and no effective choice is open to them except the
collective stopping of the whole machine by strikes or revolutions,
which involve imminent risk of starvation. Defenders of the capitalist regime are apt to vaunt the liberty which it grants to men of
enterprise, but this is an example of the aristocratic fallacy. In new
countries, such as the United States used to be, and such as South
America still is, there may be some truth in it, and therefore in such
countries one sees capitalism at its best; but in older countries whose
resources are developed and whose population is nearly as great as
present methods of industry can support, the supposed freedom of
enterprise exists only for a few. The early history of railways in the
United States is full of bold piratical adventures; the railroad kings
of that period remind one of Elizabethan buccaneers. But a railway
in modern England is a very sober affair; its capital is held largely
by innumerable maiden ladies and orphans whose funds are administered by trustees, its directors are sleepy peers, its policy is
traditional, and it does nothing to encourage new men with bold
schemes. This is not due, as superficial observers suppose, to a difference between the British and American temperaments, but to a
difference in their geography and industrial antiquity. But even
taking the capitalist case at its best, even considering America as it
was forty years ago, it was only the men of unusual enterprise and
push and unscrupulousness who came to the top. Such men are, by
definition, the minority, and a society which suits only them cannot
be considered satisfactory except by one who commits the aristocratic fallacy. I am afraid there are many socialists who commit the
same fallacy; they imagine industry developed under State control,
and they visualize themselves in that future millennium as part of
the State control, not as part of the ordinary workaday labor. In a
system of centralized bureaucratic State socialism, those who direct
the machine will have all the advantages at present enjoyed by the
captains of industry, with the exception of enormous wealth, which

to a vigorous, executive and combative person is one of the smallest advantages of business success, being valued mainly as a tangible proof of ability and power and as a means of acquiring the respect of the herd. But it is not only the great captains of industry who will enjoy an exceptionally agreeable life under State socialism; it is also the whole army of officials. It is obvious that the man who sits in a government office, and spends his time interfering with other people, has a pleasanter life than the man who works in a mine or stokes a liner. Yet there are many forms of socialism which would do nothing to remedy this inequality. The industrial machine as it has been developed by capitalism is full of injustices other than the inequality of wealth. Unless these other injustices are also remedied, a socialistic society may be scarcely pleasanter to the average manual worker than the existing system. This is concealed from labor politicians and from men with bureaucratic minds, because they envisage themselves in the new order as leaders or officials, not as ordinary workers. Their judgment of the society they aim at creating is, in fact, vitiated by the aristocratic fallacy. It may be that the evils of the present world must be cured one by one, that inequality of wealth must be tackled first, leaving inequality of power for a later stage, and inequality in the pleasantness of labor for perhaps a still later stage. It may be that a bureaucratic centralized State socialism is the necessary first step. It is not this that I am denying. What I am denying is that such a society is good in itself, and I do not think that any one who imagines with equal vividness the lives of all the members of the community can remain contented with an ideal which confines initiative, power, and the use of intelligence to a few.

A society which is to bring diffused well-being not only to one class or to one type of character, but as far as possible to every member of the community, must not be too systematic or too orderly. It must not be the kind of society which a man of administrative temperament plans in his head and enforces by bayonets and the criminal law. Different individuals have different needs, and it is important to suit all needs that can be suited without damage to others. It is, of course, necessary to restrain predatory impulses. The insufficient amount of such restraint is one of the greatest evils of the world as it is. But it is at least equally disastrous to restrain creative impulses. This is the danger of what one may call tight systems. A military machine or an industrial machine treats men as all alike, with the exception of the privileged few who direct it; it has no room for other exceptions, no desire for the kind of work that would not be ordered from above, no toleration for the kind of person to whom it is difficult to become a mere cog in the machinery.

Perhaps the most important of all the qualities that a social system can possess, is that it must be such as people can *believe* in. Europe during the last five centuries has advanced with quite extraordinary rapidity in all that makes what we call civilization, but step by step with this advance has gone a progressive disintegration of belief. I do not mean merely belief in religious dogma, though this also has played its part. I mean belief in all the assumptions on which the social order is based; all the sources of authority have become suspect and all inherited institutions have ceased to command assent. The war and the Russian Revolution gave the *coup de grâce* to such beliefs as remained. At the beginning of the war, democracy was still a fighting creed, something for which men were willing to die. At the end, poor President Wilson was left its one remaining votary, proclaiming his gospel in pathetic isolation to a world which shrugged its shoulders and went about its business as if he had not spoken. It may be that some element of injustice is essential to the existence of a social order, at any rate for many ages to come. But in ages of faith, men believe in the social order even when it makes them suffer, even when they are the victims of what to a later age appears unmerited misfortune. Nowadays this is not the case. The only men nowadays who believe in injustice are those who profit by it, and even they in their hearts feel that their belief is not genuine, but merely an embodiment of self-interest. I except from this indictment the big capitalists of America, who are more naive, more untouched by modern thought than any other set of men, with the exception possibly of a few Central African negroes. American business men still believe in the capitalist system, but business men elsewhere merely hope it will last their lifetime, provided they can obtain sufficient machine guns and ships to shoot down or starve those who advocate systems which, in their hearts, they know to be better. Such half-hearted belief does not bring happiness. The capitalists tried to persuade themselves that their war against Russia was a holy crusade, but in this attempt they were very unsuccessful throughout Europe. And everybody except the capitalists is unable to create in himself even a semblance of belief in the old order, the order which made the war and blockaded Russia, the order which devastated Ireland, starves Germany and Austria, imprisons or kills socialists, and amid the tottering ruins of our old civilization, pursues the old diplomatic game of haggling for territories and arming against nominally friendly nations.. This old order is no longer capable of bringing happiness. It is not only its nominal victims who suffer, it is not only the defeated nations or the proletarians who find that life has lost its meaning. Even the well-to-do classes of Western Europe have no longer the sense of anything to live for. Having no purpose in life, they have plunged into a frantic pursuit of pleasure. But with every added pleasure comes added unhappiness; while the senses are gratified, the soul remains hungry—there is no inward sense of well-being, but only futility and despair.

There is only one cure for this despair, and that is a faith that a man can believe. No man can be happy unless he feels his life in some way important; so long as his life remains a futile round of pleasures or pains leading to no end, realizing no purpose that he can believe to be of value, so long it is impossible to escape despair. In most men at the present time this despair is dumb and unconscious, and because it is unconscious, it cannot be avoided. It is like a spectre always looking over a man's shoulder and whispering acid words into his ear, but never seen, never looked at face to face. Once acknowledged, once faced, this despair can be coped with, but it can be coped with only by a new belief, by something which supersedes the search for pleasure. Although it may sound old-fashioned to say so, I do not believe that a tolerable existence is possible for an individual or a society without some sense of duty.

There is only one kind of duty that the modern man can acknowledge without superstition, and that is a duty to the commumity. There was a time when such ideals as God, country, family, could move men. That time is past. All such ideals were used by elderly rulers throughout the war to drive the young to slaughter each other in futile carnage. Most of the young at the time believed that the war was about something important, but now that it is nominally over, they see their mistake. Nothing good has come out of it except revolt against the system which caused it; the vices of the vanquished have been acquired by the victors, and the only new hope has come from Russia, the most defeated of all the nations in the great war. Socialism is, I believe, the only faith which can restore happiness to the world, which can cure it of the sickness left by the war, which can give men the sense that their lives are capable of something better than pleasure and can end the despair that drives men to frivolous cruelty. The faith of the Russian communists

in the new thing they are endeavoring to create is rather crude,
rather ruthless, possibly rather premature, but it makes their lives
happy as hardly any Western life is happy; it enables them to endure privations and dangers, and preserves throughout a kind of joy
and freshness in the soul such as one does not find in the weary
West. If there were no other argument for socialism the fact that it
is a creative faith which the modern man can believe would be
alone enough to make it the hope of the world.

And this brings me to the second of the two characteristics
which a good society must have. It must be progressive; it must lead
on to something still better. Now fundamental progress seldom
comes from those who fit comfortably and easily into the existing
system. It is not, for example, from trust magnates that we expect
the inauguration of the new era. In like manner, if we imagine
socialism established, it will not be from those who administer it or
from those who have least difficulty in adapting themselves to it
that new growth will come. New growth will come from the creative
people, the men of science, the artists, the thinkers, many of whom
very probably will be critics of the new order. Under the influence of
commercialism, many men have come to think that the important
progress is progress in the technical methods of production, better
machinery, better means of communication, and so on. This has
been true, since in the past labor was not sufficiently productive to
provide a good life for all. But it is true no longer, and with our
existing technical knowledge, if we had a scientific socialist organization, every man could have enough without long hours of work.
When once men have enough of material commodities, there is no
great importance in providing them with a superfluity. It is only
commercialism, the competitive struggle for markets, as reinforced
by the luxury of the very rich, that has made mere quantity of
goods seem so important. We have reached the point where we could
organize our material resources in a way that would leave suffi-
ciency and leisure for all. Therefore the important progress now is
not in industrial production, but in ideas. One might hope that
under socialism the energy liberated from the production of luxuries
and armament would be employed in the pursuit of knowledge and
in the beautifying of life, bringing back for the many that artistic
excellence which existed in the pre-industrial era for the few. But if
this is to happen, there must be freedom for the creative people, the
men of science and the artists. They must not be controlled at every
point by State officials, or obliged to do work at every moment

which is pleasing to existing prejudices. Without freedom, the man who is ahead of his age is rendered impotent. All innovations are, to begin with, displeasing to the majority, yet without innovations no society can progress. Freedom for exceptional people, provided their work is creative and not predatory, is the most important condition of progress in any society. There is always a tendency for the administrator to think of himself as God Almighty and to imagine himself capable of judging the good or bad in every new idea. This tendency is dangerous, and would be particularly dangerous in the earlier phases of socialism, where the administrator may be expected to have more power than he has ever had before. The danger can only be met by acknowledging the importance of creative work and the fact that the best creative work often does not commend itself to contemporaries. It is not in the least necessary that the artists and men of science should be rewarded for their work, since the best of them are indifferent to rewards and do their work merely because they love it. But it is necessary that they should be free to do it and free to make it known—that, for example, a man of science should be able to print his work without having first to find favor in the eyes of officials. All this will come about of itself if socialism comes as a liberation for the many, not as a punishment for the few, if it is love for the good we are creating that inspires us, and not merely hatred for the evil we are destroying. It would be demanding the impossible to suggest that hatred should be wholly absent as a generator of energy in the time of transition, but it is important that it should not be the fundamental motive. If hatred is the fundamental motive, the regime created will be oppressive and restrictive, not only where it must be, but also in many directions where oppression and restriction must be avoided if progress is not to cease. It is a world full of hope and joy that we must seek to create, not a world mainly designed to restrain men's evil impulses. Evil impulses must be restrained, especially during the time of transition while they are still strong, but this is an incidental part of our task, not its main purpose or inspiration. The main purpose and inspiration of any reconstruction which is to make a better world must be the liberation of creative impulses, so that men may see that out of them a happier life can be built than out of the present frantic struggle to seize and hold what others desire. Socialism once established may so regulate the material side of existence as to enable men to take it for granted and to leave their minds free to employ their leisure in those things which make the true glory of man.

7

Moral Standards and Social Well-being

This essay expresses Russell's emerging distrust of industrial civilization, which he feared would endanger the worthwhile things in life: the promotion of instinctive happiness, friendly feelings and affection, a capacity for creating and enjoying beauty, and the intellectual curiosity that leads to the advancement and diffusion of knowledge.

I

To anyone who reflects upon industrialism it is clear that it requires, for its successful practice, somewhat different virtues from those that were required in a pre-industrial community. But there is, to my mind, widespread misapprehension as to the nature of those virtues, owing to the fact that moralists confine their survey to a short period of time, and are more interested in the success of the individual than in that of the race. There is also, in all conventional moralists, a gross ignorance of psychology, making them unable to realize that certain virtues imply certain correlated vices, so that in recommending a virtue the consideration which ought to weigh is: Does this virtue, with its correlative vice, outweigh the opposite virtue with its correlative vice? The fact that a virtue is good in itself is not enough; it is necessary to take account of the vices that it entails and the virtues that it excludes.

I shall define as virtues those mental and physical habits which tend to produce a good community, and as vices those that tend to produce a bad one. Different people have different conceptions of what makes a community good or bad, and it is difficult to find arguments by which to establish the preferability of one's own conception. I cannot hope, therefore, to appeal to those whose tastes are very different from my own, but I hope and believe that there is nothing very singular in my own tastes. For my part, I should judge a community to be in a good state if I found a great deal of instinctive happiness, a prevalence of feelings of friendship and affection rather than hatred and envy, a capacity for creating and enjoying beauty, and the intellectual curiosity which leads to the advancement and diffusion of knowledge. I should judge a community to be in a bad state if I found much unhappiness from thwarted instinct, much hatred and envy, little sense of beauty, and little intellectual curiosity. As between these different elements of excellence or the reverse, I do not pretend to judge. Suppose, for the sake of argument, that intellectual curiosity and artistic capacity were found to be in some degree incompatible, I should find it difficult to say which ought to be preferred. But I should certainly think better of a community which contained something of both than of one which contained more of the one and none of the other. I do not, however, believe that there is any incompatibility among the four ingredients I have mentioned as constituting a good community, namely: happiness, friendship, enjoyment of beauty, and love of knowledge.

It is to be observed that I do not define as a virtue merely what leads to these good things for its possessor, but what leads to them for the community to which he belongs. For different purposes, the community that has to be considered is different. In the case of acts which have little effect outside the family, the family will be the community concerned. In the official actions of a mayor, the community concerned will be the municipality; in internal politics it will be the nation, and in foreign politics the world. Theoretically, it is always the whole world that is concerned, but practically the effects outside some limited circle are often negligible.

However moralists may recommend altruism, all the moral exhortations that have had widespread effects have appealed to purely selfish desires. Buddhism urged virtue on the ground that it led to Nirvana; Christianity, on the ground that it led to heaven. In each of these great religions, virtue was that line of conduct which would be pursued by a prudent egoist. Neither of these, however, has much influence on the practical morality of our own time. For energetic people, the moral code of our time is that of "success"—the code which my generation learnt in childhood from Smiles's *Self-help,* and which modern young men learn from efficiency experts. In this code, "success" is defined as the acquisition of a large income. According to this code, it is wicked for a young man to be late at the office, even if what has delayed him is fetching the doctor for a sudden illness of his child; but it is not wicked to oust a competitor by well-timed tale-bearing. Competition, hard work, and rigid self-control are demanded by this code; its rewards are dyspepsia and unutterable boredom, in all who have not a quite exceptional physique. By comparison with its votaries, St. Simeon Stylites was a voluptuary; nevertheless they, like him, are pure egoists.

In sociology, we are concerned with men in the mass, not with rare and exceptional individuals. It is possible for a few saints to live a life which is in part unselfish, but it does not appear to be possible for the vast majority of mankind. The study of psychology, and more particularly of psycho-analysis, has torn aside the cloaks that our egoism wears, and has shown that when we think we are being unselfish, this is hardly ever in fact the case. It would therefore be useless to preach a morality which required unselfishness on the part of any large number of men. I do not think myself that there is any need to do so. Our natural impulses, properly directed and trained, are, I believe, capable of producing a good community, provided praise and blame are widely apportioned.

It is through the operation of praise and blame that the positive morality of a community becomes socially effective. We all like praise and dislike blame; moreover, rewards and punishments often accompany them. "Positive morality"—i.e. the habit of attaching praise to certain types of behavior and blame to certain other types— has enormous influence on conduct. In Somaliland, and formerly among the aborigines of Formosa, a man was not thought sufficiently manly to deserve a wife until he had killed someone; in fact, he was expected to bring the head of his victim to the wedding ceremony. The result was that even the mildest and gentlest of men, in obedience to the moral sense of the community, felt obliged to practice homicide. This custom is rapidly dying out among savages, but among the white races the same feeling persists as regards military service in war-time. Thus in spite of the egoism of human nature, the positive morality of neighbors forces men into conduct quite different from that which they would pursue if positive morality were different; they even often sacrifice their lives for fear of being blamed. Positive morality is therefore a very tremendous power. I believe that at present it is quite unadapted to industrialism, and that it will have to be radically changed if industrialism is to survive.

There is one point in which the definition of virtue and vice given above departs from tradition and from common practice. We defined a virtue as a habit which tends to produce a good community, and a vice as one which tends to produce a bad community. In thus judging by results, we agreed in one important respect with the utilitarian school of moralists, among whom Bentham and the two Mills were the most eminent. The traditional view is different; it holds that certain specified classes of actions are vicious, and that abstinence from all these is virtue. It is wicked to murder or steal (except on a large scale), it is wicked to speak ill of those in power, from the Deity to the policeman; above all, it is wicked to have sexual intercourse outside marriage. These prohibitions may, in our degenerate age, be defended by utilitarian arguments, but in some cases—e.g. refusal of divorce for insanity—the utilitarian arguments are very far-fetched, and are obviously not what is really influencing the minds of those who use them. What is influencing their minds is the view that certain classes of acts are "wicked," quite independently of their consequences. I regard this view as superstitious, but it would take us too far from our theme to argue the question here. I shall therefore assume, without more ado, that actions are to be judged by the results to be expected from actions of that kind, and not by some supposed *a priori* moral code. I do not mean—what would be obviously impracticable—that we should habitually calculate the effects of our actions. What I mean is that, in deciding what sort of moral instruction should be given to the young, or what sort of actions should be punished by the criminal law, we should do our best to consider what sort of actions will promote or hinder the general well-being. It might almost seem as if this were a platitude. Yet a tremendous change would be effected if this platitude were acted upon. Our education, our criminal law, and our standards of praise and blame, would become completely different from what they are at present. How they would be altered, I shall now try to show.

Let us consider one by one the four kinds of excellence which we mentioned, beginning with instinctive happiness.

II

Instinctive Happiness

I mean by this the sort of thing that is diminished by ill-health and destroyed by a bad liver, the kind of delight in life which one finds always more strongly developed in the young of any mammalian species than in the old. I doubt whether there is anything else that makes as much difference to the value of life from the point of view of the person who has to live it. Those who have instinctive delight in life are happy except when they have positive causes of unhappiness; those who do not have it are unhappy except when they have positive causes of happiness. Moreover, outward causes of happiness have more effect upon those who delight in life, while those who do not are more affected by outward causes of unhappiness. Of all personal goods, delight in life is therefore the greatest; and it is a condition for many others. I do not deny that it can be too dearly purchased, if it is obtained at the cost of injustice and stupidity. In the advanced industrial nations, apart from the agricultural population, I can think of only one small class that lives so as to preserve it, namely, the male portion of the British upper class. The public schools develop a boy's physique at the expense of his intelligence and sympathy; in this way, by the help of a good income, he often succeeds in preserving instinctive happiness. But the system is essentially aristocratic, so that it cannot be regarded as in any degree a contribution to the solution of our problem. Our problem is to preserve instinctive happiness for the many, not only for a privileged few.

The causes of instinctive happiness could best be set forth by a medical man, but without medical knowledge observation makes it easy to see broadly what they are. Physical health and vigor come first, but are obviously not alone sufficient. It is necessary to have scope for instinctive desires, and also for instinctive needs which often exist without corresponding explicit desires. Very few adults, whether men or women, can preserve instinctive happiness in a state of celibacy; this applies even to those women who have no conscious desire for sexual satisfaction. On this point, the evidence of psycho-analysis may be taken as conclusive. Many women and some men need also to have children sooner or later. To most men, some kind of progressive career is important; both to men and women, a certain amount of occupation imposed by necessity, not chosen for its pleasurable quality, is necessary for the avoidance of boredom. But too much work and too little leisure are more destructive of instinctive happiness than too little work and too much leisure. Another essential is the right amount of human companionship, neither too much nor too little; but as to what is the right amount, people vary greatly. Our instinctive nature seems to be fairly adapted to the hunting stage, as may be seen from the passion of rich men for shooting big game, killing birds, and careering after foxes. In the hunting stage, men had periods of violent exertion alternating with complete quiescence, while women had activities which were more continuous but less strenuous and less exciting. This probably accounts for the fact that men are more prone to gambling than women. One result of adaptation to the hunting stage is that most people like loud noise at times of excitement, alternating with silence at other times. In modern industrial life the noise is continuous, and this certainly has a debilitating nervous effect. I believe that almost everyone has a need (though often not a desire) for the sights and smells of the country. The delight of slum children on a country holiday is of a kind that points to the satisfaction of an instinctive need which urban life cannot supply. In recovering from a dangerous illness, the pleasure of being still alive consists mainly in joy in sunshine and the smell of rain and other such sensations familiar to primitive man.

The difference between needs and desires is important in the consideration of instinctive happiness. Our desires are mainly for things which primitive man did not get without difficulty: food and drink (especially the latter), leadership of the tribe, improvements in the methods of hunting and fighting. But we have many needs which are not associated with desires, because under primitive conditions these needs were always satisfied. Such are the needs of country sensations, of occasional silence and occasional solitude, of alternations of excitement and quiescence. To some extent, sex and maternity in women come under this head, because in a primitive community men see to the satisfaction of these feminine needs without any necessity for female co-operation. *Per contra,* there are desires which do not correspond to instinctive needs. The most important of these are the desires for drugs, including alcohol and tobacco. The fact that these desires are so readily stimulated by habit is an example of natural maladjustment from a Darwinian point of view. They differ from instinctive needs in two ways. First, from the point of view of survival, their satisfaction is not biologically useful; drugs do not help a man either to survive himself or to have a numerous progeny. Secondly, from the psychological point of view, the craving that they satisfy depends upon the habit of taking them, not upon a pre-existent need. The instinctive dissatisfaction which leads a man to take to drink is usually something wholly unconnected with alcohol, such as business worries or disappointment in love. Drugs are a substitute for the thing instinctively needed, but an unsatisfactory substitute, because they never bring full instinctive satisfaction.[1]

With the advance of what is called civilization, our social and material environment has changed faster than our instincts, so that there has been an increasing discrepancy between the acts to which we are impelled by instinct and those to which we are constrained by prudence. Up to a point, this is quite unavoidable. Murder, robbery and rape are actions which may be prompted by instinct, but an orderly society must repress them. Work, especially when many are employed in one undertaking, requires regularity which is utterly contrary to our untrained nature. And although a man who followed his impulses in a state of nature would (at least in a cold climate) do a good deal of work in the course of an average day, yet it is very rare indeed that a man has any spontaneous impulse to the work which he has to do in a modern industrial community. He works for the sake of the pay, not because he likes the work. There are, of course, exceptions: artists, inventors, men of learning, healthy mothers who have few children and strong maternal instincts, people in positions of authority, a small percentage of sailors and peasants. But the exceptions are not sufficiently numerous to be an important section of the whole. The irksomeness of work has no doubt always existed since men took to agriculture; it is mentioned in Genesis as a curse, and heaven has always been imagined as a place where no one does any work. But industrial methods have certainly made work more remote from instinct, and have destroyed the joy in craftsmanship which gave handicraftsmen something of the satisfaction of the artist. I do not think that, if industrial methods survive, we can hope to make the bulk of necessary work pleasant. The best we can hope is to diminish its amount, but there is no doubt that its amount could be diminished very greatly. It is chiefly in this direction that we must look for a lessening of the instinctive dissatisfaction involved in work.

A "return to nature," such as Rousseau's disciples dreamt of, is not possible without a complete break-up of our civilization. Regimentation, especially, is of the very essence of industrialism, which would necessarily perish without it. If this is an evil, and is unavoidable, our aim must be to have as little of it as is possible. This aim will be realized by making the hours of industrial labor as short as is compatible with the production of necessaries, and leaving the remaining hours of the day entirely untrammelled. Four hours' boredom a day is a thing which most people could endure without damage; and this is probably about what would be required.

In many other respects, the restraints upon instinct which now exist could be greatly diminished. Production at present has two correlative defects: that it is competitive, and that it is thought important to produce as much as possible. A great deal less work is required now to produce a given amount of goods than was required before the industrial revolution, and yet people live at higher pressure than they did then. This is chiefly due to competition. An immense amount of labor is wasted in getting orders and securing markets. At times when there is a great deal of unemployment, those who are not unemployed are overworked, because otherwise employers could not make a profit. The competitive management of industry for profit is the source of the trouble. For the same reason there is a desire to maximize production, because, with industrial methods, the production of immense quantities of a commodity is more capable of yielding a profit than the production of moderate quantities.[2] The whole urgency of the modern business world is towards speeding up, greater efficiency, more intense international competition, when it ought to be towards more ease, less hurry, and combination to produce goods for use rather than profit. Competition, since the industrial revolution, is an anachronism, leading inevitably to all the evils of the modern world.

The sense of strain, which is characteristic of all grades in an industrial community from the highest to the lowest, is due to instinctive maladjustment. Every kind of failure to satisfy deep instinctive needs produces strain, but the manifestations are somewhat different according to the instinct which is thwarted. The chief needs thwarted by industrialism, as at present conducted, are: the need of spontaneous and variable activities, the need of occasional quiet and solitude, and the need of contact with the earth. This applies to the working classes, but in the middle classes the thwarting of instinct is much more serious. A man who has any ambition cannot marry young, must be very careful how he has children, must if possible marry a girl whose father will help him professionally rather than a girl he likes, and when married must avoid infidelity, except so furtively as not to be found out. Our society is so imbued with the belief that happiness consists of financial success that men do not realize how much they are losing, and how much richer their lives might be if they cared less for money. But the results of their instinctive dissatisfaction are all the worse for being unconscious. Middle-class men, when they are no longer quite young, are generally filled with envy: envy of their more successful colleagues, envy of the young, and (strange as it may seem) envy of working-men. The result of the first kind of envy is to make them hostile to all intellectual or artistic eminence until it is so well-established that they dare not challenge it; of the second, to make them rejoice in war because it gives them a chance to thwart the young who have to do the fighting; of the third, to make them politically opposed to everything calculated to benefit wage-earners, such as education, sanitation, maintenance during unemployment, knowledge of birth control (which the middle class practice as a matter of course), housing reform, and so on. They believe that their opposition to these measures is based on economy and a desire to keep down the taxes, but in this they deceive themselves, because they do not object to the spending of vastly greater sums on armaments and wars. The same man often will object to the education rate on the ground that the poor have larger families than the well-to-do, and to birth control on the ground that it is immoral and unnatural except for those whose income is fairly uncomfortable. Men are strangely unconscious of their passions, and the envy which dominates most middle-aged professional men is a thing of which they know nothing, though the methods of psycho-analysis reveal it unerringly.

The failure of instinctive satisfaction in the wage-earning classes is less profound than in the professional classes, because, whatever Marxians may say, they have more freedom in the really important matters, such as marriage. Of course this greater freedom is being rapidly diminished by improvement in police methods, and by the continual tightening up of the "moral" standard through the activities of thwarted middle-class busybodies. This has gone so far that at present, in English law the penalty for deserting a vindictive wife, if you are a wage-earner, is imprisonment for life.[3] In spite of this tendency, wage-earners, as yet, in good times, suffer less instinctive repression than professionals, because they are less dominated by respectability and snobbery. Nevertheless, the failure to satisfy instinctive needs is serious, particularly as regards spontaneity. The effect shows itself in love of excitement, thoughtless sentimentalism, and (in the more intelligent) hatred of richer people or of foreign nations.

It is evident that the first steps towards a cure for these evils are being taken by the trade unions, in those parts of their policy which are most criticized, such as restriction of output, refusal to believe that the only necessity is more production, shortening of hours, and so on. It is only by these methods that industrialism can be humanized and can realize the possibilities of good which are latent in it. It could be used to lighten physical labor and to set men free for more agreeable activities. Hitherto, the competitive system has prevented its being so used. It should have made life more leisurely, but it has made it more hustling. Instead of leisure, diminution of hustle, are the ends to be sought, not mere quantitative increase of production. The trade unions have clearly perceived this, and have persisted in spite of lectures from every kind of middle- and upper-class pundit. This is one reason why there is more hope from self-government in industry than from State Socialism. The Bolsheviks, when they had established State Socialism, ranged themselves on the side of the worst capitalists on all the matters we have been considering. It is obvious that this must always be the case when conditions of work are determined bureaucratically by officials, instead of by the workers themselves.

III

Friendly Feeling

It is impossible to find any single phrase to describe adequately the whole of what I wish to include under this head. I can, I think, best explain by avoiding hackneyed words which *seem* to convey the correct meaning but in fact fail to do so. An average human being is indifferent to the good or evil fortune of most other human beings, but has an emotional interest in a certain number of his fellow-creatures. This interest may involve pleasure in their good fortune and pain in their evil fortune; or it may involve pain in their good fortune and pleasure in their evil fortune; or it may involve one of these attitudes in certain respects and the other in certain other respects. I shall call these three attitudes friendly, hostile, and mixed, respectively. Broadly speaking, the second of the four goods which we wished to see realized in a community is the friendly attitude combined with as little as possible of the hostile attitude. But this is only a rough preliminary characterization of what I mean.

Biologically speaking, the purpose of life is to leave a large number of descendants. Our instincts, in the main, are such as would be likely to achieve this result in a rather uncivilized community. Biological success, in such a community, is achieved partly by co-operation, partly by competition. The former is promoted by friendly feeling, the latter by hostile feeling. Thus on the whole, we feel friendly towards those with whom it would be biologically advantageous to co-operate if we lived in uncivilized conditions, and hostile towards those with whom, in like conditions, it would pay us to compete. In all *genuine* friendship and hostility there is an instinctive basis connected with biological egoism (which includes the survival of descendants). Some religious teachers and moralists preach friendly feeling as a duty, but this only leads to hypocrisy. A great deal of morality is a cloak for hostility posing as "true kindness," and enabling the virtuous to think that in persecuting others out of their "vices" they are conferring a benefit. When I speak of friendly feeling I do not mean the sort that can be produced by preaching; I mean the sort which is instinctive and spontaneous. There are two methods of increasing the amount of this kind of feeling. One is physiological, by regulating the action of the glands and the liver; everyone knows that regular exercise makes one think better of other people. The other is economic and political, by producing a community in which the interests of different people harmonize as much as possible and as obviously as possible. Moral and religious teaching is supposed to be a third method, but this view seems to rest on a faulty psychology.

The stock instance of the friendly attitude is the feeling of a maternal mother for a young child. As the most obvious example of the unfriendly attitude we may take jealousy. Sex love is, of course, a good example of instinctive co-operation, since no one can have descendants without another's help. But in practice it is so hedged about by jealousy that, as a rule, it affords a less adequate example of friendly feeling than maternal affection. Paternal affection involves, as a rule, a mixed attitude. There is usually some genuine affection, but also much love of power, and much desire that children should reflect credit on their parents. A man will be pleased if

his boy wins a prize at school, but displeased if he inherits money
from his grandfather, so as to become independent of the paternal
authority as soon as he is twenty-one. There is (in some) a melancholy satisfaction when one's boy dies for his country, of a sort not
calculated to increase filial affection in those young men who witness it.

> Snug at the club two fathers sat,
> Cross, goggle-eyed, and full of chat.
> One of them said: "My eldest lad
> Writes cheery letters from Bagdad.
> But Arthur's getting all the fun
> At Arras with his nine-inch gun."
>
> "Yes," wheezed the other, "that's the luck!
> My boy's quite broken-hearted, stuck
> In England training all this year.
> Still, if there's truth in what we hear,
> The Huns intend to ask for more
>   Before they bolt across the Rhine."
> I watched them toddle through the door—
>   These impotent old friends of mine.[4]

Of course, war affords the supreme example of instinctive co-
operation and hostility. In war, the instinctive prime mover is hostility; the friendly feeling towards our own side is derivative from
hatred of the enemy. If we hear that some compatriot with whom
we are acquainted has been captured by the enemy and brutally
ill-used, we shall be full of sympathy, whereas if his brother dies a
lingering death from cancer we shall take it as a mere statistical
fact. If we hear that the enemy underfeed their prisoners, we shall
feel genuine indignation, even if we are ourselves large employers
paying wages which compel underfeeding. The formula is: sympathy with compatriots in all that they suffer through the common
enemy, but indifference to all that they suffer from other causes.
This shows that, as we asserted, the friendly feelings arising during
war are derivative from the hostile ones, and could not exist in the
same form or with the same widespread intensity if hatred did not
exist to stimulate them. Those who see in national co-operation during war an instinctive mechanism which could be applied to international co-operation during peace have failed to understand the
nature of the mechanism which war brings into play, or the fact

that without enmity there is no stimulus to set it in motion.

There is, it is true, in addition to sex and parenthood, a form of instinctive co-operation which involves no enemy, and looks at first sight very hopeful as a social incentive. I mean that kind of co-operation in work which, so far as human beings are concerned, one finds most developed among uncivilized peoples, and which is carried to its highest perfection by ants and bees. Rivers, in his book on *Instinct and the Unconscious* (p. 94 ff.) describes how the Melanesians carry out collective work apparently without any need of previous arrangements, by the help of the gregarious instinct. I do not believe, however, that much use can be made of this mechanism by civilized communities. The instinct involved appears to be very much weakened by civilization, and is probably incompatible with even the average degree of intellectual development that exists where school education is common. Moreover, even when it exists most strongly, it is not such as to make complicated large organizations possible. It seems also that with the progress of intelligence the individual grows more self-contained, less receptive to immediate impressions from other personalities, which survive chiefly in fragmentary and sporadic forms such as hypnotism. The primitive instinct for collective work is certainly one to be borne in mind, but I do not think it has any very important contribution to make to the solution of industrial problems.

In order to stimulate friendly feeling and diminish hostile feeling, the things that seem most important are: physical well-being, instinctive satisfaction, and absence of obvious conflict between the interests of different individuals or groups. On the first two heads, we have already said enough in considering instinctive happiness. The last head, however, raises some interesting points. Our present society, under the influence of liberal ideals, has become one which, while it retains immense social inequalities, leaves it open to any man to rise or sink in the social scale. This has resulted from combining capitalism with a measure of "equality of opportunity." In medieval society the inequalities were as great as they are now, but they were stereotyped, and accepted by almost everybody as ordained by God. They did not therefore cause much envy, or much conflict between different classes. In the society that socialists aim at, there will not be inequality in material goods, and therefore economic competition and economic envy will be non-existent. But at present we have the evils of the medieval system without its advantages: we have retained the injustices, while destroying the conception of life which made men tolerate them. It is evident that, if the prevalence of competition and envy is to be overcome, an economically stereotyped society is essential. It is also evident that in the absence of the medieval belief that hereditary social grades are of divine ordinance, the only stereotyped society in which people can acquiesce is one which secures economic justice in an obvious form—that is to say, economic equality for all who are willing to work. Until that is secured, our economic system will continue to grind out hatred and ill-will. What is called "equality of opportunity" is, of course, not real equality, even of opportunity, so long as we retain inheritance of private property and better education for the children of the well-to-do. Inequality must breed strife unless it is supported by a philosophy or religion which even the unfortunate accept. At present, no such doctrine is conceivable. Therefore equality in material goods is an essential condition for the prevalence of friendly feelings between different classes, and even between the more fortunate and the less fortunate members of the same class, or between rivals who hope in time to outdistance each other. A society will not produce much in the way of mental goods unless it is materially stereotyped. I believe that this applies to all kinds of mental goods, but for the present it is only friendliness that concerns us.

In preaching the advantages of a materially stereotyped society, I am conscious of running counter to the real religion of our age—the religion of material progress. We think that it would be a great misfortune if the rate at which new mechanical inventions are made were to slacken, or if people were to grow lazy and easy-going. For my part, since I came to know China, I have come to regard "progress" and "efficiency" as the great misfortunes of the Western world. I do not think it is worth while to preach difficult virtues or extremes of self-denial, because the response is not likely to be great. But I have hopes of laziness as a gospel. I think that if our education were strenuously directed to that end, by men with all the fierce energy produced by our present creed and way of life, it might be possible to induce people to be lazy. I do not mean that no one should work at all, but that few people should work more than is necessary for getting a living. At present, the leisure hours of a man's life are on the whole innocent, but his working hours, those for which he is paid (especially if he is highly paid), are as a rule harmful. If we were all lazy, and only worked under the spur of hunger, our whole society would be much happier. Think of a man like the late Lord Northcliffe, working like a galley-slave to produce bloodshed and misery on a scale hitherto unknown in human history. How admirable it would have been if he could have been persuaded to lie in the sun, or play bridge, or study chess-problems, or even take to drink. But, alas, such men have no such vices.

IV

Enjoyment of Beauty

On this subject it is not necessary to say much, as the defects of industrial civilization in this respect are generally recognized. It may, I think, be taken as agreed that industrialism, as it exists now, destroys beauty, creates ugliness, and tends to destroy artistic capacity. None of these are essential characteristics of industrialism. They spring from two sources: first, that industrialism is new and revolutionary; secondly, that it is competitive and commercial. The result of the first is that people do not aim at permanence in industrial products, and are loath to lavish much care on something that may be superseded by tomorrow. The result of the second is that manufacturers value their wares, not for their intrinsic excellence, but for the profit to be made out of them, which is (roughly) the excess of their apparent value above what they are really worth, so that every defect not evident at first sight is advantageous to the producer. It is obvious that both these causes of ugliness might be expected to be absent from an industrialism which was stereotyped and socialistic, since it would be neither revolutionary nor worked for profit. It therefore remains only to consider the third point, namely, artistic capacity.

It would seem, from the history of art, that nine-tenths of artistic capacity, at least, depends upon tradition, and one-tenth, at most, upon individual merit. All the great flowering periods of art have come at the end of a slowly maturing tradition. There has, of course, been no time for industrialism to generate a tradition, and perhaps, if the absence of tradition were the only thing at fault, we could wait calmly for the operation of time. But I fear that the other element, individual artistic merit, without which no good tradition can be created, can hardly exist in an atmosphere of industrialized commercialism. Commerce which is not industrial is often extraordinarily favorable to art: Athens, Venice, Florence are noteworthy examples. But commerce which is industrial seems to have quite different artistic results. This comes probably from the utilitarian attitude which it generates. An artist is by temperament a person who sees things as they are in themselves, not in those rough convenient categories which serve for the business life. To the ordinary man, grass is always green, but to the artist it is all sorts of different colors according to circumstances. This sort of thing, in anybody who is not already a famous artist, strikes the practical business man as a waste of time—it interferes with standardizing and cataloguing. The result is that, although eminent artists are fêted and highly-paid, the artistic attitude of mind is not tolerated in the young. A modern industrial community, when it wants an artist, has to import him from abroad; it then pays him such vast sums that his head is turned and he begins to like money better than art. When the whole world has adopted commercial industrialism, the artistic habit of mind will everywhere be stamped out in youth by people who cannot see any value in it unless its possessor is already labelled as a celebrity. This points to the same requirements as we found before: a society which is stable as regards the material side of life and the methods of production, where industrialism has ceased to be competitive and is used to make life more leisurely instead of more strenuous. And the first step towards this end is the general diffusion of a less energetic conception of the good life.

Knowledge

The strongest case for commercial industrialism can be made out under the head of scientific knowledge. Since the industrial revolution there has been an enormous increase both in the general level of education and in the number of men devoted to learning and research. The importance of science for industrial progress is very evident, and all industrial States encourage scientific research. But even in this sphere the utilitarian habit of mind inseparable from our present system has deleterious effects, which are only beginning to be evident. Unless some people love knowledge for its own sake, quite independently of its possible uses, the new discoveries will only concern the working-out of ideas inherited from disinterested investigators. Mendelism is now studied by hosts of agriculturists and stock-breeders, but Mendel was a monk who spent his leisure enjoying his peas-blossoms. A million years of practical agriculturists would never have discovered Mendelism. Wireless is of great practical importance: it facilitates slaughter in war, the dissemination of journalistic falsehood in time of peace, and the broadcasting of trivialities to relieve the tedium of evening hours not devoted to success. But the men who made it possible—Faraday, Maxwell and Hertz—were none of them the least interested in furthering this remarkable enrichment of human life; they were men solely interested in trying to understand physical processes, and it can hardly be said that the existence of industrialism helped them even indirectly. The modern study of the structure of the atom may have a profound effect upon industrial processes, but those who are engaged upon it are very little interested in this possible future effect of their work. It seems likely that the utilitarianism of commercial industry must ultimately kill the pure desire for knowledge, just as it kills the very analogous artistic impulse. In America, where the more utilitarian aspects of science are keenly appreciated, no great advance in pure theory has been made. None of the fundamental discoveries upon which practical applications depend have been made in America. It seems probable that, as the point of view appropriate to commercial industry spreads, utilitarianism will make such fundamental discoveries more and more rare, until at last those who love knowledge for its own sake come to be classified in youth as "morons" and kept in institutions for harmless lunatics.

This, however, is not one of the main points I wish to make. There are, in fact, two such points: first, that pure science is infinitely more valuable than its applications; secondly, that its applications, so far, have been in the main immeasurably harmful, and will only cease to be so when men have a less strenuous outlook on life.

To take the second point first: Science, hitherto, has been used for three purposes: to increase the total production of commodities; to make wars more destructive; and to substitute trivial amusements for those that had some artistic or hygienic value. Increase in total production, though it had its importance a hundred years ago, has now become far less important than increase of leisure and the wise direction of production. On this point it is not necessary to enlarge further. The increasing destructiveness of wars also needs no comment. As for trivial amusements, think of the substitution of the cinema for the theatre; think of the difference between the gramophone and the really beautiful songs of Russian peasants; think of the difference between watching a great football match and playing in a small one. Owing to our belief that WORK is what matters, we have become unable to make our amusements anything but trivial. This is part of the price we had to pay for Puritanism; it is no accident that the only great industrial countries are Protestant. People whose outlook on life is more leisurely have a higher standard for their amusements; they like good plays, good music, and so on, not merely something that enables them to pass the time vacuously. So far, however, science has only intruded into the world of amusement in ways that have made it more trivial and less artistic. Nor can this be prevented so long as men think that only work is important.

As for the greater value of pure rather than applied science, that is a matter which goes deeper, but which it is difficult to argue. Applied science, while men retain their present ideals, has the sort of effects we have been considering, which I for my part find it very difficult to admire. Pure science—the understanding of natural processes, and the discovery of how the universe is constructed—seems to me the most god-like thing that men do. When I am tempted (as I often am) to wish the human race wiped out by some passing comet, I think of scientific knowledge and of art; these two things seem to make our existence not wholly futile. But the *uses* of science, even at the best, are on a lower plane. A philosophy which values them more than science itself is gross, and cannot in the long run be otherwise than destructive of science.

On all four heads, therefore, we are led to the conclusion that our social system, our prevailing habits of mind, and our so-called moral ideals, are destructive of what is excellent. If excellence is to survive, we must become more leisurely, more just, less utilitarian, and less "progressive."

NOTES

1. I do not wish this to be regarded as an argument for prohibition, to which, on the whole, I am opposed.

2. Cf. R. Austin Freeman, *Social Decay and Regeneration* (Constable, 1921), esp. pp. 105-27.

3. This fact is not generally known. The mechanism is as follows: The Court makes an order for maintenance, the wife makes a scandal where the man is employed, he is dismissed, cannot pay the maintenance, and is imprisoned for contempt of Court. He is legally liable for maintenance even while in prison; therefore on the very day he comes out his wife can have him put back for not paying maintenance during the period of his first

imprisonment. And so it goes on until he dies or she is glutted with vengeance. This is not a fancy picture, as any one who knows prisoners can testify.

4. *Fathers,* by Siegfried Sassoon. *(Counter-Attack,* p. 24, Heinemann, 1918.)

8

New Morals for Old

In this essay, Russell follows two lines of argument: that morality has varied much like economic systems, and that it needs to lay down ends to be sought in life rather than offering up useless rules of conduct.

In all ages and nations positive morality has consisted almost wholly of prohibitions of various classes of actions, with the addition of a small number of commands to perform certain other actions. The Jews, for example, prohibited murder and theft, adultery and incest, the eating of pork and seething the kid in its mother's milk. To us the last two precepts may seem less important than the others, but religious Jews have observed them far more scrupulously than what seems to us fundamental principles of morality. South Sea Islanders could imagine nothing more utterly wicked than eating out of a vessel reserved for the use of the chief. My friend Dr. Brogan made a statistical investigation into the ethical valuations of undergraduates in certain American colleges. Most considered Sabbath-breaking more wicked than lying, and extra-conjugal sexual relations more wicked than murder. The Japanese consider disobedience to parents the most atrocious of crimes. I was once at a charming spot on the outskirts of Kioto with several Japanese socialists, men who were among the most advanced thinkers in the country. They told me that a certain well beside which we were standing was a favorite spot for suicides, which were very frequent.

Originally published as "Styles in Ethics" in *Our Changing Morality: A Symposium,* edited by Freda Kirchwey (New York: Albert and Charles Boni, 1924), pp. 3-16.

When I asked why so many occured they replied that most were those of young people in love whose parents had forbidden them to marry. To my suggestion that perhaps it would be better if parents had less power they all returned an emphatic negative. To Dr. Brogan's undergraduates this power of Japanese parents to forbid love would seem monstrous, but the similar power of husbands or wives would seem a matter of course. Neither they nor the Japanese would examine the question rationally; both would decide unthinkingly on the basis of moral precepts learned in youth.

When we study in the works of anthropologists the moral precepts which men have considered binding in different times and places we find the most bewildering variety. It is quite obvious to any modern reader that most of these customs are absurd. The Aztecs held that it was a duty to sacrifice and eat enemies captured in war, since otherwise the light of the sun would go out. The Book of Leviticus enjoins that when a married man dies without children his brother shall marry the widow, and the first born son shall count as the dead man's son. The Romans, the Chinese, and many other nations secured a similar result by adoption. This custom originated in ancestor-worship; it was thought that the ghost would make himself a nuisance unless he had descendants (real or putative) to worship him. In India the remarriage of widows is traditionally considered something too horrible to contemplate. Many primitive races feel horror at the thought of marrying anyone belonging to one's own totem, though there may be only the most distant blood-relationship. After studying these various customs it begins at last to occur to the reader that possibly the customs of his own age and nation are not eternal, divine ordinances, but are susceptible of change, and even, in some respects, of improvement. Books such as Westermarck's *History of Human Marriage* or Müller-Lyer's *Phasen der Liebe,* which relate in a scientific spirit the marriage customs that have existed and the reasons which have led to their growth and decay, produce evidence which must convince any rational mind that our own customs are sure to change and that there is no reason to expect a change to be harmful. It thus becomes impossible to cling to the position of many who are earnest advocates of *political* reform and yet hold that reform in our moral precepts is not needed. Moral precepts, like everything else, can be improved, and the true reformer will be as open-minded in regard to them as in regard to other matters.

Müller-Lyer, from the point of view of family institutions, divides the history of civilization into three periods—the clan period, the family period, and the personal period. Of these the last is only now beginning; the other two are each divided into three stages— early, middle and late. He shows that sexual and family ethics have at all times been dominated by economic considerations; hunting, pastoral, agricultural and industrial tribes or nations have each their own special kinds of institutions. Economic causes determine whether a tribe will practice polygamy, polyandry, group marriage, or monogamy, and whether monogamy will be lifelong or dissoluble. Whatever the prevailing practice in a tribe it is thought to be the only one compatible with virtue, and all departures from it are regarded with moral horror. Owing to the force of custom it may take a long time for institutions to adapt themselves to economic circumstances; the process of adaptation may take centuries. Christian sexual ethics, according to this author, belong to the middle-family period; the personal period, now beginning, has not yet been embodied in the laws of most Christian countries, and even the late-family period, since it admits divorce under certain circumstances, involves an ethic to which the Church is usually opposed.

Müller-Lyer suggests a general law to the effect that where the state is strong the family is weak and the position of women is good, whereas where the state is weak the family is strong and the position of women is bad. It is of course obvious that where the family is strong the position of women must be bad, and vice versa, but the connection of these with the strength or weakness of the state is less obvious though probably in the main no less true. Traditional China and Japan afforded good instances. In both the state was much weaker than in modern Europe, the family much stronger, and the position of women much worse. It is true that in modern Japan the state is very strong, yet the family also is strong and the position of women is bad; but this is a transitional condition. The whole tendency in Japan is for the family to grow weaker and the position of women to grow better. This tendency encounters grave difficulties. I met in Japan only one woman who appeared to be what we should consider emancipated in the West—she was charming, beautiful, high-minded, and prepared to make any sacrifice for her principles. After the earthquake in Tokyo the officer in charge of the forces concerned in keeping order in the district where she lived, seized her and the man with whom she lived in a free union and her twelve-year-old nephew, whom he believed to be her son; he took them to the police station and there murdered them by slow strangulation, taking about ten minutes over each except the boy. In his account of the matter he stated that he had not had much difficulty with the boy, because he had succeeded in making friends with him on the way to the police station. The boy was an American citizen. At the funeral, the remains of all three were seized by armed reactionaries and destroyed, with the passive acquiescence of the police. The question whether the murderer deserved well of his country is now set in schools, half the children answering affirmatively. We have here a dramatic confrontation of middle-family ethics with personal ethics. The officer's views were those of feudalism, which is a middle-family system; his victims' views were those of the nascent personal period. The Japanese state, which belongs to the late-family period, disapproved of both.

The middle-family system involves cruelty and persecution. The indissolubility of marriage results in appalling misery for the wives of drunkards, sadists and brutes of all kinds, as well as great unhappiness for many men and the unedifying spectacle of daily quarrels for the unfortunate children of ill-assorted couples. It involves also an immense amount of prostitution, with its inevitable consequence of widespread venereal disease. It makes marriage, in most cases, a matter of financial bargain between parents, and virtually proscribes love. It considers sexual intercourse always justifiable within marriage, even if no mutual affection exists. It is impossible to be too thankful that this system is nearly extinct in the Western nations (except France). But it is foolish to pretend that this ideal held by the Catholic church and in some degree by most Protestant churches is a lofty one. It is intolerant, gross, cruel and hostile to all the best potentialities of human nature. Nothing is gained by continuing to pay lip-service to this musty Moloch.

The American attitude on marriage is curious. America, in the main, does not object to easy divorce laws, and is tolerant of those who avail themselves of them. But it holds that those who live in countries where divorce is difficult or impossible ought to submit to hardships from which Americans are exempt, and deserve to be held up to obloquy if they do not do so. An interesting example of this attitude was afforded by the treatment of Gorki when he visited the United States.

There are two different lines of argument by which it is possible to attack the general belief that there are universal absolute rules of moral conduct, and that anyone who infringes them is wicked. One line of argument emerges from the anthropological facts which we have already considered. Broadly speaking, the view of the average man on sexual ethics are those appropriate to the economic system existing in the time of his great-grandfather. Morality has varied as economic systems have varied, lagging always about three generations behind. As soon as people realize this they find it impossible to suppose that the particular brand of marriage customs prevailing in their own age and nation represents eternal verities, whereas all earlier and later marriage customs, and all those prevailing in other latitudes and longitudes, are vicious and degraded. This shows that we ought to be prepared for changes in marriage customs, but does not tell us what changes we ought to desire.

The second line of argument is more positive and more important. Popular morality—including that of the churches, though not that of the great mystics—lays down rules of conduct rather than ends of life. The morality that ought to exist would lay down ends of life rather than rules of conduct. Christ says: "Thou shalt love thy neighbor as thyself"; this lays down one of the ends of life. The Decalogue says: "Remember that thou keep holy the Sabbath Day"; this lays down a rule of action. Christ's conduct to the woman taken in adultery showed the conflict between love and moral rules. All His priests, down to our own day, have gone directly contrary to His teachings on this point, and have shown themselves invariably willing to cast the first stone. The belief in the importance of rules of conduct is superstitious; what is important is to care for good ends. A good man is a man who cares for the happiness of his relations and friends, and, if possible, for that of mankind in general, or, again, a man who cares for art and science. Whether such a man obeys the moral rules laid down by the Jews thousands of years ago is quite unimportant. Moreover a man may obey all these rules and yet be extremely bad.

Let us take some illustrations. I have a friend, a high-minded man, who has taken part in arduous and dangerous enterprises of great public importance and is almost unbelievably kind in all his private relations. This man has a wife who is a dipsomaniac, who has become imbecile, and has to be kept in an institution. She cannot divorce him because she is imbecile; he cannot divorce her because she affords him no ground for divorce. He does not consider himself morally bound to her and is therefore, from a conventional point of view, a wicked man. On the other hand a man who is perpetually drunk, who kicks his wife when she is pregnant, and begets ten imbecile children, is not generally regarded as particularly wicked. A business man who is generous to all his employees but falls in love with his stenographer is wicked; another who bullies his employees but is faithful to his wife is virtuous. This attitude is rank superstition, and it is high time that it was got rid of.

Sexual morality, freed from superstition, is a simple matter. Fraud and deceit, assault, seduction of persons under age, are proper matters for the criminal law. Relations between adults who are free agents are a private matter, and should not be interfered with either by the law or by public opinion, because no outsider can know whether they are good or bad. When children are involved the state becomes interested to the extent of seeing that they are properly educated and cared for, and it ought to ensure that the father does his duty by them in the way of maintenance. But neither the state nor public opinion ought to insist on the parents living together if they are incompatible; the spectacle of parents' quarrels is far worse for children than the separation of the parents could possibly be.

The ideal to be aimed at is not lifelong monogamy enforced by legal or social penalties. The ideal to be aimed at is that all sexual intercourse should spring from the free impulse of both parties, based upon mutual inclination and nothing else. At present a woman who sells herself successfuly to different men is branded as a prostitute, whereas a woman who sells herself for life to one rich man whom she does not love becomes a respected society leader. The one is exactly as bad as the other. The individual should not be condemned in either case; but the institutions producing the individual's action should be condemned equally in both cases. The cramping of love by institutions is one of the major evils of the world. Every person who allows himself to think that an adulterer must be wicked adds his stone to the prison in which the source of poetry and beauty and life is incarcerated by "priests in black gowns."

Perhaps there is not, strictly speaking, any such thing as "scientific" ethics. It is not the province of science to decide on the ends of life. Science can show that an ethic is unscientific, in the sense that it does not minister to any desired end. Science also can show how to bring the interest of the individual into harmony with that of society. We make laws against theft, in order that theft may become contrary to self-interest. We might, on the same ground, make laws to diminish the number of imbecile children born into the world. There is no evidence that existing marriage laws, particularly where they are very strict, serve any social purpose; in this sense we may say that they are unscientific. But to proclaim the ends of life, and make men conscious of their value, is not the business of science; it is the business of the mystic, the artist and the poet.

9

How Will Science Change Morals?

Science has already affected our ethics profoundly, and is likely to affect them still more profoundly before the end of the present century. The effects of science are of three kinds:

1. The direct intellectual effects of scientific knowledge and method;

2. The influence of the changed outlook on life produced by scientific technique;

3. The influences of the changes in the pressure of public opinion owing to new opportunities.

Of these three kinds, the first is more commonly discussed than the other two, but is by no means more important. Nevertheless, as it was historically the first, we will begin with it.

I

The direct intellectual effects of science upon morals have hitherto been almost wholly negative, though whether they will remain so may be doubted. Science thrust its way with difficulty into a world dominated by authority and tradition; by substituting a little genuine knowledge for a great deal of unfounded belief, it greatly diminished the amount that men thought they knew, while at the same time giving them new hopes of progress. The conception of progress, which seems to us a commonplace, is very modern, and almost wholly a result of the rise of science. The ancients looked

Originally published in the *Menorah Journal* 14 (April 1928): 321-329.

back to a golden age; Lao-tze, in the sixth century B.C., deplored the hurry of modern life and the multiplicity of artificial contrivances. The Ages of Faith are full of laments concerning the corruption of morals in these latter days; almost all their ecclesiastical writers look back longingly to a time when the faith was purer and conduct was less depraved. In the Renaissance, men looked back to ancient Greece and Rome, and did not suppose it possible to surpass them. This attitude still existed in the eighteenth century. It was only the fructification of science in industrial technique that led men of active disposition to regard the present as better than any previous age, and the future as almost sure to be better than the present. Progress, though it existed as an idea in the eighteenth century, did not become a widespread popular creed till the nineteenth, and even then had to combat the romantic movement and the medieval revival in art and theology. For this combat, it found a powerful weapon in the philosophy of evolution.

The general effect of science in the nineteenth century was to substitute mundane hopes for hopes of heaven, with the result that morals became philanthropic rather than theological. The change is exemplified by the difference between Wesley and Lord Shaftesbury—both profoundly religious, but the latter devoting his activity to promoting human happiness here on earth. Although few men agreed explicitly with Bentham, that virtue consists in promoting the greatest happiness of the greatest number, yet in practice this idea increasingly prevailed. At present, although many men's morality is in fact derived from traditional codes, yet none of their adherents would frankly confess that obedience to these codes does not lead to happiness in this world. This practical Benthamism is an effect of science. It depends upon science in two ways: first, because science has diminished the intensity of men's theological convictions, so that they are less willing to surrender the joys of this life on the off chance of compensation in the next; secondly, because science has shown that it is possible to be hopeful about existence on this planet, and has therefore diminished the need of the emotional compensation of contemplating the joys of heaven.

It is a mistake to suppose, as many do, that there is such a thing as a scientific ethic, though there are such things as unscientific ethics. I mean by this that science alone cannot determine the ends of life, though it can determine means when the ends are given. An ethic is unscientific when it proposes means which will not realize the desired end. When the means which it proposes are in accordance with science, an ethic is as nearly scientific as it can hope to be, whatever end it may endeavor to achieve. An example will make clear what I mean. Let us imagine some modern scientific Caligula, who conceives that the sole purpose of human life is his own glory. He may invent a death-ray by means of which he becomes Emperor of the world; he may devote his power to causing vast monuments to be erected in his honor, and finally, as he dies, exterminate the human race, for fear lest some successor should surpass him. Such a person would be mad, but not unscientific. Science alone cannot prove that we ought to consider the welfare of others. Thus many ethics are compatible with science, and none can be proved true by scientific arguments alone.

It is evident that the life of a civilized community is impossible unless men, on the whole, abstain from acts which are very harmful to their neighbors. There are three traditional methods for securing this result. One is the criminal law, which attaches unpleasant consequences to certain forms of anti-social behavior. Forgery, for example, is contrary to self-interest if it is discovered; given an efficient system of crime detection, no sensible person, however selfish, will become a forger. The second method is that of theology: it is taught that certain kinds of conduct, whether detected by other human beings or not, have unpleasant consequences in a future life, and will therefore be avoided by a prudent egoist. The third method is that of pointing out that anti-social behavior tends to have unpleasant consequences through the natural resentment that it arouses. Science affects these three methods in different ways. It makes the criminal law more effective, by making it harder for criminals to escape and easier to collect evidence against them. Largely for this reason, there is less definite crime in a modern scientific community than in any community of former times, or in the unscientific communities of the present day.

The theological method, on the contrary, has been weakened by science. People do not believe in hell fire as firmly as they did formerly, and certainly few people think that they themselves are in imminent danger of it. This has had considerable effect upon behavior, more especially in matters of sex. There are various causes for the change in this respect, but certainly one of them is the decay of the belief in eternal damnation. While theologians may deplore this, there is another side to it. The duties inculcated by theologians were largely fantastic, and such as were calculated to diminish human happiness. Take, for example, the view that marriage to a partner who is insane or syphilitic is a sacrament which should be indissoluble, and, moreover, should not be artificially prevented from being fruitful. Such a doctrine demands the belief that the world is governed by a God who rejoices in human suffering, more particularly the suffering of little children, and who closes heaven to those who have adopted the most obvious methods of avoiding the infliction of such suffering. It is clear that, if God is good, he will not punish acts which promote happiness or avert misery. Therefore, whenever theology has to be invoked to prove an act wrong which would otherwise be right, it is implied that God is not good. The decay of the purely theological motive to virtue, accordingly, however it may have promoted conduct contrary to traditional notions of morality, is not in itself a thing to be regretted.

The argument that anti-social behavior causes resentment, and is therefore contrary to self-interest, is one which has a large measure of truth, but is subject to very important limitations. There are certain kinds of anti-social behavior which are admired; most of the men to whom equestrian statues have been set up were malefactors. And any man who acquires enormous wealth is respected, whatever the methods by which he acquired it. If the desire for admiration is to be a source of conduct calculated to promote human happiness, there will be need of a considerable education of public opinion.

The outcome of this is that anti-social conduct, in its grosser forms, can be prevented by an efficient police, provided the law forbids only harmful acts and not (as at present) a number of useful acts also; and that certain types of bad behavior can be prevented by the cultivation of enlightened self-interest. But there remains an important residue which will only be prevented by genuine good will or affection towards other people. For this emotion, no substitute can be found either in theology or in science; without kindly feeling, no genuinely good conduct is possible.

Will science promote kindly feeling? It can do so, by applying itself to such questions as diet and early education; but there is nothing in a scientific outlook as such to make people kindly. I think, however, that the effect of science in clearing away superstitious ethics tends to make men see more clearly that intelligent kindliness is the essence of morality. The systems of morality which old-fashioned theologians have inherited from the dark ages are impregnated with cruelty and persecution, so that anything which weakens them removes an excuse for the infliction of pain upon our neighbors and dependents. To this extent, science has a good effect:

but it may have a very much more potent and direct good effect if applied to the formation of character in the early years of life. Also, by promoting prosperity, it diminishes cruelty; for cruelty is, in the main, an outcome of fear and the struggle for life. This is, I think, the main reason for the very marked diminution of cruelty during the last three centuries, as shown, for example, in the mitigation of the criminal law, and in the lessening severity of the education of children, in which corporal punishment was formerly the chief engine of moral discipline.

II

The economic effects of science have had more influence upon morals than the direct intellectual effects, and I think the economic effects have been almost wholly beneficial from an ethical point of view. I have already mentioned the effect of increased prosperity in diminishing fear and ferocity. The effect of education, also, has been no doubt good on the whole, though there is a considerable item on the adverse side in balancing this account more particularly the increased power of the press to promote savagery in time of war. A considerable moral improvement has come from the diminution of boredom. Winter in the Middle Ages was appalling from this point of view. Most people could not read, and if they could the light was too bad after sunset. Roads were impassable, so that there was practically no social life. Meat was killed in the autumn and salted; there was no tea or coffee or tobacco. I think boredom accounts for the fact that large populations in the Middle Ages were subject to fits of collective insanity; also for the prevalence of incest and every kind of brutality in family life. The same kind of thing may still be seen among backward peasant communities; but good roads, automobiles, adequate lighting and heating are rapidly causing it to disappear.

Moralists are apt to complain of the love of excitement in modern urban life, and we are perpetually told of the harm done to children by the movies. All this is due to our ingrained habit of thinking that what people like must be bad for them, which has as a rule no better basis than sadism. Excitement, up to a point, is one of our needs, and if we cannot get it in any other way we get it by quarrels with our neighbors or relatives. No doubt the movies do not always supply the ideal form of excitement for children; no doubt, also, it is easy to overdo excitement. But a certain minimum is necessary for mental health. And from the introduction of agriculture until modern times, most people had less than their needs required, because tilling the soil is less exciting than hunting. In this respect, therefore, I regard the effects of science as beneficial.

But the most important effect of scientific technique upon the average man has been an increase in his sense of power over nature and a consequent diminution of fear as an element in life. Wells in *The War of the Worlds* describes admirably the change produced in man when he became a hunted animal living in fear of the Martians as other animals now live in fear of us. Primitive men must have lived in a constant dread of wild animals, whereas to the modern European a man-eating tiger is a pleasant object in a landscape. I remember when I was in Hong Kong a few years ago, all the British in that town were rejoicing in what they regarded as a very pleasant recent incident—a misguided tiger had swum across from the mainland and started to walk about the streets. All the British turned out with guns and found great pleasure in the sport. What applies to tigers, applies also to a large number of other natural phenomena; snowstorms in the Alps were formerly a cause of terror, now they create an opportunity for winter sports; earthquakes are still a source of fear—after the Tokyo earthquake the mentality of many Japanese seems to have temporarily reverted to something quite medieval—but the time will come when all houses in earthquake districts will be balanced upon air cushions and earthquakes will be regarded merely as pleasant amusements for children. The changes in ethics which are to be expected from science are almost wholly connected with the elimination of fear.

Originally, great disasters, like plagues, famines, hurricanes, floods and earthquakes, descended upon communities in ways that were not at all understood, and were attributed to the anger of the gods. As it gradually became to be known that certain kinds of acts were apt to have painful consequences, it was inferred, since the laws of natural causation were unknown, that such acts were displeasing to the gods; consequently they were labeled "sin." Often nowadays science knows of means by which the painful consequences of such acts can be averted, but the religious conscience still insists that these acts are sin and infers that it is impious to attempt any escape from their painful consequences. One striking example of this is the religious attitude toward venereal diseases, which is, as a rule, that cure is permissible but prevention is not. In this and in various other matters the original utilitarianism of religious morals has been lost sight of. Originally men said "this act is sinful because it produces misfortune"; now the religious conscience says "this act shall produce misfortune because it is sinful, and if science shows us ways by which the misfortune can be prevented, we must do our best to prevent such ways from becoming known." Thus, as a result of scientific discoveries, traditional morals have, in various not unimportant respects, become inimical to human happiness.

As people come to realize this fact, and as they become increasingly aware of the possibilities which science is opening up, they tend more and more to ignore the teachings of traditional dogmatists. There is a grave danger lest this should lead to a shallow and unsatisfactory hedonism. If all those who preach the necessity of moral restraint combine this preaching with what appears to modern-minded men to be superstition and obscurantism, there is a danger lest all those who are neither superstitious nor obscurantists may come to feel that life can be successfully conducted without any kind of moral discipline. This is, of course, not possible, but the source of the discipline must be hope rather than fear. If a man is to "scorn delights and live laborious days," it must be with a view to some positive achievement, not with a view to escaping starvation in this world or hell-fire in the next. Morality, in a word, will have to be positive rather than negative; it will have to occupy itself rather with what is to be done than with what is to be left undone. This transformation is coming about already and is attributable almost wholly to the influence of science.

In old days Nature, personified as the gods, was dreaded and worshiped: nowadays, owing to our greater powers of physical manipulation, nature is studied and utilized, but not respected or feared. For the first time in the history of this planet one of the animals to which it has given rise has succeeded, to a certain limited extent, in mastering the environment and, consequently, substituting exploitation for reverence. The moral changes which this is likely to produce are so vast that we can as yet only faintly guess at them.

It is to be feared, however, that these moral changes will come about with extreme slowness owing to the fact already mentioned, that mankind remain divided, on the whole, into ascetics and voluptuaries, both equally irrational. Men will make great efforts under the stress of fear, but the majority of mankind are too lazy to make equal efforts from the incentive of hope. Probably wholesale

destruction of the lazier races of mankind by the ruthless and energetic may be necessary before a morality not based upon fear can
acquire a hold over the average man. The possibilities of science
divorced from humanitarianism are somewhat terrible to contemplate, yet I fear there will be a time of transition in which very dark
and terrible deeds may be done in the name of a scientific civilization. All this, however, is in the highest degree speculative.

III

The incidence of the pressure of public opinion has been changed in
various ways owing to the development of a scientific civilization,
and this change has had a great deal of influence in modifying
moral standards, or at any rate in changing their intensity.

In some ways people are more subject to the pressure of public
opinion than they used to be, and in other ways less. Very few
people in a modern industrial community are as completely under
the thumb of their neighbors as people formerly were in villages
and small towns. But in former times there was a considerable
population that was not strictly confined to one place, and these
wanderers were much more able than they are now to escape from
the penalities of their crimes. Highwaymen, soldiers of fortune, even
ordinary sailors, could indulge in lawless actions in one place and
easily escape to another. Nothing could travel faster than a horse,
and therefore a man with a good mount could always escape from
the police. The prevalence of the highwaymen in the eighteenth
century was due to this fact, together with the practice of carrying
cash on a journey instead of a check-book. Crime altogether has
become far more difficult than it used to be, and this is mainly
attributable to science.

On the other hand, the decay of morals among the young, which
our older generation are continually deploring, is, I am afraid, due
as much to the automobile as to the decay of theological belief. If
our moralists were in earnest, they would conduct a compaign to
forbid the use of automobiles to all but elderly citizens whose virtue
could be vouched for by at least two ministers of religion. But few of
our traditional moralists would carry their principles so far as to
inflict damage upon a highly profitable industry. This is part of the
wider fact that all except the very poor are not now confined within
one small locality as the majority formerly were. In matters which

concern the police, escape from a locality is nowadays of little use, but in those branches of morals with which the police do not concern themselves, it is easy to be respectable at home and quite the reverse elsewhere. Any offense against morals which is frequently committed with impunity comes in time to be viewed leniently by the majority; consequently the offenses which are visited by severe moral condemnation are not now the same as they were in former times. Certain kinds of offenses are viewed with much greater disfavor than they used to be. In one of Smollett's novels the hero, who is an Englishman, takes service in the French Army during a war with England; when he has had enough of it he quietly returns to Dover, where he is deeply and sincerely shocked by the pro-French sentiments of certain eminent men whom he encounters. The whole of this is utterly remote from modern possibilities.

Our sense of obligation to the community is enormously greater than it formerly was; this is due to various causes, all of which have their root in science. The power of the State over the individual is greater than it used to be owing to the closer organization of society and the better machinery for the detection of crime. Education is a potent means of propaganda for the State, enabling people in later life to read the newspapers and thus become susceptible to any point of view which the holders of power desire to promote. Society is, in a word, more organic than it used to be, and a man's professional activities are consequently less anarchic than they were in former times. For the moment we do not reap the full benefit of this owing to the division of the powerful sections of mankind into mutually suspicious nations, but if, as seems probable, a world government is ultimately achieved, the increased possibilities of direction from the center will become highly beneficial. I think one must expect that the Government will continue to acquire an increasing control over the lives of individuals as it has done during the past century. The result may possibly be a dwarfing of the individual in comparison with the community. This in itself might be regrettable, but scientific technique undoubtedly makes anarchic conduct more dangerous to the community than it used to be, and therefore makes some diminution of individual liberty inevitable.

I have said nothing of the more sensational possibilities with which some writers have concerned themselves, possibilities connected largely with scientific breeding and early education. Given a greater knowledge of heredity than we at present possess, it would, of course, be possible to improve the breed almost indefinitely. The best 25 per cent of each generation of women might be set apart for maternity, and the best 1 percent of each generation of men; this would require, of course, a complete revolution in all our moral ideas as regards marriage and the family. It does not seem likely that the western nations would adopt any such plan except in some great emergency, but one could imagine it adopted by Japan, with the result that in a century the Japanese race would become physically and intellectually so enormously superior to all others as to be able to acquire world dominion. Fear then might terrify the western nations into imitation.

It is sometimes thought that all such schemes would be impossible because they would be contrary to what is called "human nature." This I believe to be a delusion. Human nature is much more plastic than it was formerly supposed to be, but it has to be molded in the early years of life if it is to take on a new shape. As a matter of fact economic motives have always played a larger part in matters of population and the family than is generally recognized. They operate slowly and more or less subconsciously, but in the long run their power is almost irresistible. The ordinary redblooded he-man would say that the Tibetan system of polyandry is contrary to human nature; nevertheless the poverty of that country, by promoting female infanticide and by making it difficult for one man to support the expenses of a wife and family, has become strong enough to overcome natural jealousy. I do not doubt that if a powerful State were to pay a certain percentage of the population to breed and the remainder to be sterilized, the system would in time come to seem perfectly natural and the only one consonant with human nature. People would wonder how in former ages those who had no reason to believe that their offspring would be healthy and secure as to their economic support could have been induced to undertake the responsibilities of a family. A new morality would grow up, doubtless just as rigid as that of the Catholic Church, based upon the view that not marriage but procreation is a sacrament, and that sexual intercourse not leading to procreation is a purely private affair. I am not saying that all this will come about, I am merely suggesting it as a possibility.

Science is a comparatively new and very explosive force in human affairs, and it is not to be supposed that it has as yet done a hundredth part of its work in transforming society: it has had as yet to cope with traditions and beliefs dating in their essence from the beginnings of agriculture. As these traditions and beliefs grow weaker, the influence of science over men's thoughts and feelings will increase. I do not feel by any means certain that the world produced by science will be better than the world in which we live, for, after all, science will have to be embodied in scientists, in whom love of system may easily lead to repression of much that is good but not easy to organize. But for good or evil the scientific world is pretty sure to come about, and any resistance that we may offer to it is not likely to make it better when it comes.

10

Morality and Instinct

This essay has not previously appeared in print. It was written in 1926 and contains themes and remarks that were later incorporated into Russell's book Marriage and Morals.

Those who advocate any ethical innovation are invariably accused, like Socrates, of being corrupters of youth; nor is this accusation always wholly unfounded, even when in fact the new ethic which they preach would, if accepted in its entirety, lead to a better life than the old ethic which they seek to amend. Probably to the Jew in the time of St. Paul the most noteworthy thing about Christianity must have been that it held it lawful to eat pork. On this ground it would have been held to have been an immoral doctrine. It is even possible that it may, in certain cases, have had demoralizing effects, since those who had hitherto restrained a passionate desire to eat pork would, if told that this desire might be indulged, infer, consciously or unconsciously, that the same was true of all their other passionate desires, and would therefore allow themselves to abandon self-control for a life of unregulated impulses. Everyone who knows the Mohammedan cast asserts that those who have ceased to think it necessary to pray five times a day have also ceased to respect other moral rules which we consider more important. The man who proposes any change in sexual morality is especially liable to be misinterpreted in this way, and I am conscious myself of having said things which some readers may have misinterpreted.

The general principle upon which the newer morality differs

from the traditional morality of puritanism is this: We believe that instinct should be trained rather than thwarted. Put in those general terms, the view is one which would win very wide acceptance among modern men and women, but it is one which is only valid when accepted with its full implications and applied from the earliest years. If in childhood instinct is thwarted rather than trained, the result may be that it has to be to some extent thwarted throughout later life, because it will have taken on highly undesirable forms as a result of thwarting in early years. The morality which I should advocate does not consist simply of saying to grown-up people or to adolescents: "Follow your impulses and do as you like." There has to be consistency in life; there has to be continuous effort directed to ends that are not immediately beneficial and not at every moment attractive; there has to be consideration for others; and there should be certain standards of rectitude. All these elements of conventional morality I should accept and even emphasize, and wherever they involve self-control, I should preach self-control as whole-heartedly as the strictest old-fashioned moralist. I should not, however, regard self-control as an end in itself, and I should wish our institutions and our moral conventions to be such as to make the need for self-control a minimum rather than a maximum. The use of self-control is like the use of brakes on a train. It is useful when you find yourself going in the wrong direction, but merely harmful when the direction is right. No one would maintain that a train ought always to be run with the brakes on, yet the habit of difficult self-control has a very similar injurious effect upon the energies available for useful activity. Self-control causes these energies to be largely wasted on internal friction instead of external activity; and on this account it is always regrettable, though sometimes necessary.

The degree to which self-control is necessary in life depends upon the early treatment of instinct. Instincts, as they exist in children, may lead to useful activities or harmful ones, just as the steam in a locomotive may take it towards its destination, or into a siding where it is smashed by an accident. The function of education is to guide instinct in the directions in which it will develop useful rather than harmful activities. If this task has been adequately performed in early years, a man or woman will, as a rule, be able to live a useful life without the need of severe self-control except, perhaps, at a few rare crises. If, on the other hand, early education has consisted in a mere thwarting of instinct, the acts to which instinct prompts in later life will be mainly harmful, and will therefore have to be continually restrained by self-control.

These general considerations apply with peculiar force to sexual impulses, both because of their great strength and because of the fact that traditional morality has made them its peculiar concern. Most traditional moralists appear to think that, if our sexual impulses were not severely checked, they would become trivial, anarchic, and gross. I believe this view to be derived from observation of those who have acquired the usual inhibitions from their early years and have subsequently attempted to ignore them. But in such men the early prohibitions are still operative even when they do not succeed in prohibiting. What is called conscience, that is to say the unreasoning and more or less unconscious acceptance of precepts learnt in early youth, causes man still to feel that whatever the conventions prohibit is wrong, and this feeling may persist in spite of intellectual convictions to the contrary. It thus produces a personality divided against itself; one in which instinct and reason no longer go hand in hand, but instinct has become trivial and reason has become anemic. One finds in the modern world various different degrees of revolt against conventional teaching. The commonest of all is the revolt of the man who intellectually acknowledges the ethical truth of the morality he was taught in youth, but confesses with a more or less unreal regret that he is not sufficiently heroic to live up to it. For such a man there is little to be said. It would be better that he should alter either his practice or his beliefs in such a way as to bring harmony between them. Next comes the man whose conscious reason has rejected much that he learnt in the nursery, but whose unconscious still accepts it in its entirety. Such a man will suddenly change his line of conduct under the stress of any strong emotion, especially fear. A serious illness or an earthquake may cause him to repent and to abandon his intellectual convictions as the result of an uprush of infantile beliefs. Even at ordinary times his behavior will be inhibited and the inhibition will take a peculiarly undesirable form. They will not prevent him from acting in ways that are condemned by traditional morals, but they will prevent him from doing so in a whole-hearted way and will thus eliminate from his actions everything that might have justified them, causing them to be just as bad as the rigid moralist maintains that they are. The substitution of a new moral code for the old one can never be satisfactory unless the new one is accepted with the whole personality, not only with that top layer which constitutes our conscious thought. To most people this is very difficult if throughout their early years they have been exposed to the old morality. It is therefore impossible to judge a new morality fairly until it has been applied in early education.

Sex morality has to be derived from certain general principles, as to which there is perhaps a fairly wide measure of agreement, in spite of the wide disagreement as to the consequences to be drawn from them. The first thing to be secured is that there should be as much as possible of that deep, serious love between man and woman which embraces the whole personality of both and leads to a fusion by which each is enriched and enhanced. The second thing of importance is that there should be adequate care of children, physical and psychological. Neither of these principles in itself can be considered in any way shocking, yet it is as consequences of these two principles that I should advocate certain modifications of the conventional code. Most men and women, as things stand, are incapable of being as whole-hearted and as generous in the love that they bring to marriage as they would be if their early years had been less hedged about with taboos. They either lack the necessary experience, or they have gained it in furtive or undesirable ways. Moreover, since jealousy has the sanction of moralists, they feel justified in keeping each other in a mutual prison. It is of course a very good thing when a husband and wife love each other so completely that neither is ever tempted to unfaithfulness; it is not, however, a good thing that unfaithfulness, if it does occur, should be treated as something terrible, nor is it desirable to go so far as to make all friendship with persons of the other sex impossible. A good life cannot be founded upon fear, prohibition, and mutual interference with freedom. Where faithfulness is achieved without these, it is good, but where all this is necessary it may well be that too high a price has been paid, and that a little mutual toleration of occasional lapses would be better. There can be no doubt that mutual jealousy, even where there is physical faithfulness, often causes more unhappiness in a marriage than would be caused if there were more confidence in the ultimate strength of a deep and permanent affection.

The obligations of parents towards children are treated far more lightly than seems to me right by many persons who consider themselves virtuous. As soon as there are children it is the duty of both parties to a marriage to do everything that they can to preserve harmonious relations, even if this requires considerable self-control. But the control required is not merely, as conventional moralists pretend, that involved in restraining every impulse to unfaithfulness; it is just as important to control impulses to jealousy, ill-temper, masterfulness, and so on. There can be no doubt that serious quarrels between parents are a very frequent cause of nervous disorders in children; therefore whatever can be done to prevent such quarrels should be done. At the same time, where one or both of the parties has not sufficient self-control to prevent disagreements from coming to the knowledge of the children, it may well be better that the marriage should be dissolved. It is by no means the case that the dissolution of a marriage is invariably the worst thing possible from the point of view of the children; indeed it is not nearly so bad as the spectacle of raised voices, furious accusations, perhaps even violence, to which many children are exposed in bad homes.

It must not be supposed that the sort of thing which a sane advocate of greater freedom desires is to be achieved by leaving adults, or even adolescents, who have been brought up under the old severe, restrictive maxims, to the unaided promptings of the damaged impulses which are all that the moralist has left to them. It is necessary that sane and self-disciplined freedom should have been learnt from the earliest years, since otherwise the only freedom possible will be a frivolous, superficial freedom, not freedom of the soul. Trivial impulses will lead to physical excesses, while the spirit remains in fetters. Instinct rightly trained from the first can produce something much better than what results from an education inspired by a Calvinist belief in original sin, but when such an education has been allowed to do its evil work, it is exceedingly difficult to undo the effect in later years. One of the most important benefits which psycho-analysis has conferred upon the world is its discovery of the bad effect of violent prohibitions and threats in early childhood; to undo this effect may require all the time and technique of a psycho-analytic treatment. This is true not only of those obvious neurotics who have suffered damage obvious to everyone; it is true also of most apparently normal people. I believe that nine out of ten of those who have had a conventional upbringing in their early years have become incapable of a decent and sane attitude towards marriage and sex generally. The kind of attitude and behavior that I should regard as the best has been rendered impossible for such people; the best that can be done is to make them aware of the damage that they have sustained and to persuade them to abstain from maiming their children in the same way in which they have been maimed.

The doctrine that I wish to preach is not one of license. It involves exactly as much self-control as is involved in the conventional doctrine, but self-control will be applied more to abstaining from the interference of the freedom of others than to restraining one's own freedom. It may, I think, be hoped that with the right education from the start this respect for the personality and the freedom of others may become comparatively easy, but for those of us who have been brought up to believe that we have a right to place a veto upon the actions of others in the name of virtue, it is undoubtedly difficult to forgo the exercise of this agreeable form of persecution. It may even be impossible. But it is not to be inferred that it would be impossible to those who had been taught from the first a less restrictive morality. The essence of a good marriage is respect for each other's personality combined with that deep intimacy, physical, mental and spiritual, which makes a serious love between man and woman the most fructifying of all human experiences. Such love, like everything that is great and precious, demands its own morality, and frequently entails a sacrifice of the less to the greater, but such sacrifice must be voluntary, for, where it is not, it will destroy the very basis of the love for the sake of which it is made.

11

Moral Codes

This essay contains an overview of the subjectivity of moral codes through-out societies and cultures and the hypocrisy that inevitably follows.

In every community, even the crew of a pirate ship, there are acts that are enjoined and acts that are forbidden, acts that are applauded and acts that are reprobated. A pirate must show courage in attack and justice in the distribution of the spoils; if he fails in these respects, he is not a "good" pirate. When a man belongs to a larger community, the scope of his duties and possible sins becomes greater, and the considerations involved become more complex, but there is still a code to which he must conform on pain of public obloquy. Most acts, it is true, are considered morally indifferent, provided a man is not a slave or in a semiservile condition. A man of independent means may get up when he likes and go to bed when he likes; he may eat and drink whatever he chooses, provided he avoids excess; he may marry the lady of his choice if she is willing. But he must perform his military duty when called upon by the State to do so, and he must abstain from crime, as well as from kinds of behavior that make a man unpopular. Men without independent means have much less freedom.

Moral codes have differed in different times and places to an almost incredible extent. The Aztecs considered it their painful duty to eat the flesh of enemies on ceremonial occasions; it was held that if they neglected to perform this service to the State the light of the sun would go out. The head-hunters of Borneo, before the Dutch

From *Human Society in Ethics and Politics* by Bertrand Russell, pp. 17-22. Copyright © 1954 by George Allen and Unwin. Reprinted by permission of the publisher.

government deprived them of the right of self-determination, could not marry until they brought a dowry of a certain number of heads; any young man who failed incurred the contempt which, in America, is bestowed upon a "sissy." Confucius laid it down that a man whose parents are living is guilty of a lack of filial piety if he refuses a lucrative government post, since the salary and perquisites should be devoted to making his father and mother comfortable in their old age. Hammurabi decreed that if the daughter of a gentleman dies as a result of being struck when pregnant, the daughter of the striker should be killed. The Jewish law laid it down that a woman taken in adultery should be stoned to death.

In view of this diversity of moral codes, we cannot say that acts of one kind are right or acts of another kind wrong, unless we have first found a way of deciding that some codes are better than others. The natural impulse of every untraveled person is to settle this question very simply: the code of his own community is the right one, and other codes, where they differ from his, are to be condemned. It is especially easy to maintain this position when one's own code is supposed to have a supernatural origin. This belief enabled the missionaries to hold that in Ceylon "only man is vile" and not to notice the "vileness" of British cotton manufacturers who grew rich on child labor and supported missions in the hope that "natives" would adopt cotton clothing. But when a number of divergent codes all claim an equally august origin, the philosopher can hardly accept any one unless it has some argument in its favor which the others lack.

It might be maintained that a man should obey the moral code of his own community whatever it may be. I should be inclined to concede that he cannot be blamed for doing so, but I think he should often be praised for not doing so. The practice of cannibalism was once almost universal, and in most cases it was connected with religion. It cannot be supposed that it died out of itself; there must have been moral pioneers who maintained that it was an evil practice. We read in the Bible that Samuel thought it wicked not to slaughter the cattle of conquered enemies, and that Saul, perhaps not from the noblest motives, opposed this view. Those who first advocated religious toleration were thought wicked, and so were the early opponents of slavery. The Gospels tell how Christ opposed the stricter forms of the Sabbath taboo. It cannot, in view of such instances, be denied that some actions which we all think highly laudable consist in criticizing or infringing the moral code of one's own community. Of course this only applies to past ages or to foreigners; nothing of the sort could occur among ourselves, since our moral code is perfect.

"Right" and "wrong" are not on a level in the general estimation; "wrong" is more primitive, and remains the more emphatic conception. In order to be a "good" man it is only necessary to abstain from sin; nothing in the way of positive action is necessary. This, however, is not wholly the case even in the most negative view; you must, for instance, save a child from drowning if you can do so without too great risk. But this is not the sort of thing upon which most conventional moralists insist. Nine of the Ten Commandments are negative. If throughout your life you abstain from murder, theft, fornication, perjury, blasphemy, and disrespect toward your parents, your Church, and your King, you are conventionally held to deserve moral admiration even if you have never done a single kind or generous or useful action. This very inadequate notion of virtue is an outcome of taboo morality, and has done untold harm.

Traditional morality is too much concerned with the avoidance of "sin" and with the ritual of purification when "sin" has occurred. This point of view, though prevalent in Christian ethics, antedates Christianity; it existed among the Orphics, and an account of it is to be found at the beginning of Plato's *Republic*. "Sin," as it appears in the teaching of the Church, consists in acts of certain specified kinds, some socially harmful, some neutral, some positively useful (e.g., euthanasia under proper safeguards). Sins incur Divine punishment unless there is sincere penitence; if there is, they can be forgiven, even if it is possible to undo any harm they may have caused. The sense of sin, and the fear of falling into sin, produce, where they are strong, an introspective and self-centered frame of mind, which interferes with spontaneous affection and breadth of outlook, and is apt to generate a timorous and somewhat disagreeable kind of humility. It is not by such a state of mind that the best lives are inspired.

"Right," as opposed to "wrong," is originally a conception connected with power, and having to do with the initiative of those who are not bound to obedience. Kings should "do right in the sight of the Lord." There is something of the same kind of positive duty in the case of every kind of office or profession, and indeed of every position that gives power. Soldiers must fight, firemen must risk their lives in saving people from burning houses, lifeboatmen must put to sea in a storm, doctors must risk infection in an epidemic, fathers must do everything lawful to provide food for their children.

In this way each profession comes to have its own ethical code, in part different from that of ordinary citizens, and in the main more positive. Doctors are bound by the Hippocratic oath, soldiers by the laws of military discipline, priests by a number of rules from which other men are exempt. Kings must marry as the interests of the State direct, and not according to the promptings of their own inclinations. The positive duties belonging to each profession are in part prescribed by law, in part enforced by the opinion of the profession or of the general public.

It is possible for two contradictory ethical codes to be simultaneously accepted by the same community. The most remarkable example of this is the contrast between Christian morality, as taught by the Church, and the code of honor formulated in the age of chivalry and by no means extinct in our own day. The Church condemned homicide, except in war or by due process of law, but honor demanded that a gentleman should at all times be ready to fight a duel to avenge an insult. The Church condemns suicide, but a German naval commander is expected to commit suicide if he loses his ship. The Church condemns adultery, but the code of honor, while not positively commanding it, nevertheless respected a man more when he had many amatory conquests to his credit, especially if the ladies concerned were highborn, and still more if he had slain their husbands in fair fight.

The code of honor is, of course, only binding upon "gentlemen," and in part only in their dealings with other "gentlemen." But where it is applicable it is utterly imperative, and is unhesitatingly obeyed at all costs. It is set forth in all its glorious absurdity in Corneille's *Cid.* The father of the Cid has been insulted by the father of the Cid's lady, but is too old to fight himself; therefore honor demands that the Cid shall fight, though it means disaster to his love. After a soliloquy in the grand manner, he makes his decision:

> *Allons, mon bras, sauvons du moins l'honneur,*
> *Puisqu' après tout il faut perdre Chimène.*

The same code, now degenerate and laughable, appears in Tom Moore's first dealings with Byron. Moore began by challenging Byron to a duel, but before the matter came to a head he wrote again, saying that he had remembered that he had a wife and children, whom his death would render destitute, and suggesting that they should make friends rather than fight. Byron, now quite secure, and afraid, as always, of being thought no gentleman, was very slow to accept Moore's apologies, and gave himself the appearance of a swashbuckling fire-eater. But in the end it was happily agreed that Moore should write his life instead of causing his death.

Although its manifestations were often absurd and sometimes tragic, belief in the importance of personal honor had important merits, and its decay is far from being an unmixed gain. It involved courage and truthfulness, unwillingness to betray a trust, and chivalry toward those who were weak without being social inferiors. If you wake up in the night and find that your house is on fire, it is clearly your duty, if you can, to wake sleepers before saving yourself; this is an obligation of honor. You will not be thought well of if you leave others to their fate on the ground that you are an important citizen while they are people of no account, though there are circumstances in which such a defense would have a kind of validity—for instance, if you were Winston Churchill in 1940. Another thing that honor forbids is abjectness in submission to unjust authority, for example in currying favor with an invading enemy. To come to smaller matters, betraying secrets and reading other people's letters are felt to be dishonorable actions. When the conception of honor is freed from aristocratic insolence and from proneness to violence, something remains which helps to preserve personal integrity and to promote mutual trust in social relations. I should not wish this legacy of the age of chivalry to be wholly lost to the world.

12

Taboo Morality

"Taboo Morality" was originally one of thirteen television interviews between Bertrand Russell and television commentator and member of Parliament Woodrow Wyatt. These interviews, filmed in the spring of 1959, were later collected together and published as Bertrand Russell Speaks His Mind.

WOODROW WYATT

Lord Russell, what do you mean by taboo morality?

LORD RUSSELL

Well, I mean the sort of morality that consists in giving a set of rules mainly as to things you must not do, without giving any reasons for those rules. Sometimes reasons cannot be found, other times they can, but in any case the rules are considered absolute and these things you must not do.

WYATT

What sort of things?

RUSSELL

Well, now, it depends on the level of civilization. Taboo morality is characteristic of the primitive mind. It is the only kind, I think, in

From *Bertrand Russell Speaks His Mind* (Cleveland and New York: World Publishing Co., 1960), pp. 61-70.

primitive tribes where, for example, it would be a rule you must not eat out of one of the chief's dishes. If you did you'd probably die, so they say, and there are all sorts of rules of that sort. I remember the King of Dahomey had a rule that he must not look long in any one direction because if he did, there would be tempests in that part of his dominions, and so there was a rule that he must always be looking around.

WYATT

Well, those are the sorts of taboos from what we would, I suppose, consider primitive societies. What about our own?

RUSSELL

Well, our own morality is just as full of taboos. There are all sorts, even in the most august things. Now there is one sin definitely recognized to be a sin, which I've never committed. It says, "Thou shalt not covet thy neighbor's ox." Now I never have.

WYATT

Yes, but what about more matter-of-fact everyday rules than that? Are there examples of taboo morality you can give us?

RUSSELL

Oh, yes. Of course a great deal of taboo morality is entirely compatible with what one might call rational morality. For instance, that you shouldn't steal or that you shouldn't murder. Those are precepts which are entirely in accord with reason, but they are set forth as taboos; they have consequences that they ought not to have. For instance, in the case of murder it is considered that it forbids euthanasia, which I think a rational person would be in favor of.

WYATT

Do you put into the category of taboo morality things like Hindus saying you shouldn't eat beef?

RUSSELL

Yes, it is typical of Hindu morality that Hindus shouldn't eat beef. The Mohammedans and the Jews say you mustn't eat pork, and there is no reason for that, it's just taboo.

WYATT

Well, you don't think these taboos serve any useful purpose?

RUSSELL

Some do and some don't, it all depends. I mean, if you get a rational basis for your ethic you can then look into the taboos and see which are useful, but the prohibition of beef, I should say, doesn't do any good at all.

WYATT

Well, if you don't believe in religion, and you don't, and if you don't think much of the unthinking rules of taboo morality, do you believe in any general system of ethics?

RUSSELL

Yes, but it's very difficult to separate ethics altogether from politics. Ethics, it seems to me, arise in this way. A man is inclined to do something which benefits him and harms his neighbors. Well, if it harms a good many of his neighbors they will combine together and say, "Look, we don't like this sort of thing, we will see to it that it doesn't benefit the man," and that leads to the criminal law, which is perfectly rational. It's a method of harmonizing the general and private interest.

WYATT

But now isn't it thought rather inconvenient if everybody goes about with his own kind of private system of ethics instead of accepting a general one?

RUSSELL

It would be if that were so, but in fact they're not so private as all that because, as I was saying a moment ago, they get embodied in the criminal law and, apart from the criminal law, in public approval and disapproval. People don't like to incur public disapproval and in that way the accepted code of morality becomes a very potent thing.

WYATT

Is there such a thing as sin?

RUSSELL

No. I think sin is difficult to define. If you mean merely undesirable actions, of course there are undesirable actions. When I say "undesirable" I mean that they are actions which I suppose do more harm than good, and of course there are. But I don't think sin is a useful conception. I think sin is something that it is positively good to punish, such as murder, not only because you want to prevent murder, but because the murderer deserves to suffer.

WYATT

Are you saying that the idea of sin is really an excuse for cruelty in many cases?

RUSSELL

I think very largely. I mean, I think only cruel people could have invented hell. People with humane feelings would not have liked the thought that those who do things on earth which are condemned by the morality of their tribe will suffer eternally without any chance of amendment. I don't think decent people would have ever adopted that view.

WYATT

Then, you mean the concept of sin is really a chance to get one's aggressive feelings out?

RUSSELL

Yes, I think so. It's the essence of what you might call a stern morality. It's to enable you to inflict suffering without a bad conscience, and therefore it is a bad thing.

WYATT

How are we to disapprove of things if we do not accept the proposition that there is such a thing as sin?

RUSSELL

Well, the disapproval in itself combined with the criminal law does, I think, all that you can do. You have to have a certain kind of public opinion. Now you see how important that is if you read the histories of the Italian Renaissance—the sort of histories that produced the Machiavellian theories. Public opinion tolerated things then which, in most times, public opinion would not tolerate.

WYATT

Would you agree, though, that some things are wicked?

RUSSELL

I shouldn't like to use that word. I should say some things do more harm than good; and if you know that they're going to do more harm than good, well, you'd better not do them. If you like to use the word "wicked," you can, but I don't think it's a useful word.

WYATT

A large part of taboo morality affects sexual relations. And a very large part of your output in writing has been about sexual relations. What advice would you give now to people who want to conduct themselves sensibly so far as sex is concerned?

RUSSELL

Well, I should like to say, by way of preface, that only about one per cent of my writings are concerned with sex, but the conventional public is so obsessed with sex that it hasn't noticed the other ninety-nine per cent of my writings. I should like to say that to begin with, and I think one percent is a reasonable proportion of human interest to assign that subject. But I should deal with sexual morality exactly as I should with everything else. I should say that if what you're doing does no harm to anybody there's no reason to condemn it. And you shouldn't condemn it merely because some ancient taboo has said that it is wrong. You should look into whether it does any harm or not, and that's the basis of sexual morality as of all other.

WYATT

Would you say that rape is to be condemned, but that ordinary fornication, provided it doesn't hurt anybody, isn't necessarily to be condemned?

RUSSELL

Yes, I should certainly say that rape is just like any other bodily violence. As for fornication, well, you'd have to look into the circumstances to see whether there was on this occasion a reason against it or whether there wasn't. But you shouldn't block condemnation always and under all circumstances.

WYATT

Do you think it's right to have rules about what can and can't be published?

RUSSELL

Well, that's a question on which I feel in rather an extreme position. A position which I'm afraid very few people agree with. I think there ought to be no rules whatever prohibiting improper publications. I think that partly because if there are rules stupid magistrates will condemn really valuable work because it happens to shock them. That's one of the reasons; another reason is that I think prohibitions immensely increase people's interest in pornography, as in anything else. I used often to go to America during Prohibition, and there was far more drunkenness than there was before, far more, and I think that prohibition of pornography has much the same effect. Now, I'll give you an illustration of what I mean about prohibitions. The philosopher Empedocles thought it was very very wicked to munch laurel leaves, and he laments that he will have to spend ten thousand years in outer darkness because he munched laurel leaves. Now nobody's ever told me not to munch laurel leaves and I've never done it, but Empedocles who was told not to, did it. And I think the same applies to pornography.

WYATT

Do you think that if everything that everybody wrote of an obscene nature were published, then it wouldn't increase people's interest at all?

RUSSELL

I think it would diminish it. Suppose, for instance, filthy post cards were permitted, I think for the first year or two there would be a great demand for them, and then people would get bored and nobody would look at them again.

WYATT

And this would apply to writing and so on as well?

RUSSELL

I think so, within the limits of what is sensible. I mean, if it was a fine piece of art, a fine piece of work, the people would read it, but not because it was pornographic.

WYATT

To come back to the basis of what we've just been talking about—the unthinking rules of taboo morality. What damage do you think they are doing now?

RUSSELL

Well, they do two different sorts of harm. One sort of harm is that they are usually ancient and come down from a different sort of society from that in which we live, where really a different ethic was appropriate, and very often they are not appropriate to modern times. I think that applies in particular to artificial insemination, which is a thing that the moralists of the past hadn't thought of. That is one sort of harm. Another is that taboo moralities tend to perpetuate ancient cruelties. I can give several examples of that. Take, for instance, human sacrifice. The Greeks, at a very early period in their history, began to turn against human sacrifice, which they had practiced, and they wanted to abolish it; but there was one institution which did not want it abolished, and stuck up for it, and that was the Oracle at Delphi. It made its living out of superstition, and it didn't want superstition diminished; so it stood up for human sacrifice long after other Greeks had given it up. That is one example. I can give you another example of some importance. It had always been held that to cut up a corpse was extraordinarily wicked; Vesalius, who was a very eminent doctor in the time of Emperor Charles V, realized that you couldn't really do a great many valuable medical things until you dissected corpses, and he used to dissect them. Now Emperor Charles V was a valetudinarian, and as this was the only doctor who could keep him well, he protected him. But after the Emperor had abdicated, there was nobody to protect Vesalius, and he was condemned for having dissected a body which they said was not quite dead; as a penalty he had to go on a pilgrimage to the Holy Land. On the way he got shipwrecked and died of hardship and that was the end of him. All this because there was this taboo against cutting up corpses. Taboo morality certainly is doing harm today. Take, for example, the question of birth control. There is a very powerful taboo by certain sections of the community which is calculated to do very enormous harm. Very enormous harm. It is calculated to promote poverty and war and to make the solution of many social problems impossible. That is, I think, perhaps the most important, and I think there are a number of others. Indissolubility of marriage is definitely harmful; it is based solely upon ancient tradition and not upon examination of present circumstances.

13

Chinese Morals

While lecturing at the University of Peking in 1921, Russell was very impressed by the fact that the Chinese were not subject to the commandments of any dogmatic religion, and that they were free to practice the virtues of dignity, self-control, and politeness insisted upon by Chinese culture. In this essay, Russell offers a brief survey of Chinese history after which he contrasts the moral outlook of Chinese and Western civilization.

A European who goes to New York and Chicago sees the future, the future to which Europe is likely to come if it escapes economic disaster. On the other hand, when he goes to Asia he sees the past. In India, I am told, he sees the Middle Ages; in China, he can see the eighteenth century. If George Washington were to return to earth, the country which he created would puzzle him dreadfully. He would feel a little less strange in England, still less strange in France; but he would not feel really at home until he reached China.

There, for the first time in his ghostly wanderings, he would find men who still believe in "life, liberty, and the pursuit of happiness," and who conceive these things more or less as Americans of the War of Independence conceived them. And I think it would not be long before he felt completely at home in the environment.

Western civilization embraces North and South America, Europe, excluding Russia, and the British self-governing dominions. In this civilization the United States leads the van; all the characteristics that distinguish the West from the East are most marked and farthest developed in America. We were accustomed to take

Originally published in *The Modern Thinker and Author's Review* (April 1932): 105-11.

progress for granted; to assume without hesitation that the changes which have happened during the last hundred years were unquestionably for the better, and that further changes for the better are certain to follow indefinitely.

On the continent of Europe, the depression and its results have administered a blow to this confident belief, and men have begun to look back to the time before 1929 as a golden age, not likely to recur for centuries. In England there has been much less of this shock to optimism, and in America still less.

For those of us who have been accustomed to take progress for granted, it is especially interesting to visit a country like China, which has remained where we were 150 years ago, and to ask ourselves whether on the balance, the changes which have happened to us have brought any real or valuable improvement.

The civilization of China, as everyone knows, is based upon the teaching of Confucius, who flourished 500 years before Christ. Like the Greeks and Romans, he did not think of human society as naturally progressive. On the contrary, he believed that in remote antiquity rulers had been wise and the people had been happy to a degree which the degenerate present could admire but hardly achieve. This, of course, was a delusion. But the practical result was that Confucius, like other teachers of antiquity, aimed at creating a stable society, but not always striving after new successes. In this he was more successful than any other man who ever lived.

His personality has been stamped on Chinese civilization from his day to our own. During his lifetime, the Chinese occupied only a small part of present-day China, and were divided into a number of warring states. During the next 300 years, they established themselves throughout what is now China proper, and founded an empire exceeding in territory and population any other that existed until the last 50 years. In spite of barbarian invasions, Mongol and Manchu dynasties, and occasional longer or shorter periods of chaos and civil war, the Confucian system survived, bringing with it art and literature and a civilized way of life.

It is only in our own day, through contact with the West and with the westernized Japanese, that this system has begun to break down.

A system which has had this extraordinary power of survival must have great merits, and certainly deserves our respect and consideration. It is not a religion, as we understand the word, because it is not associated with the supernatural or with mystical beliefs. It is a purely ethical system, but its ethics, unlike those of Christianity, are not too exalted for ordinary men to practice.

In essence, what Confucius teaches is something very like the old-fashioned ideal of a "gentleman" as it existed in the eighteenth century. One of his sayings will illustrate this (I quote from Lionel Gilais's *Sayings of Confucius*):

> The true gentleman is never contentious. If a spirit of rivalry is any-where unavoidable, it is at a shooting-match. Yet even here, he cour-teously salutes his opponents before taking up his position, and again, when having lost, he retires to drink the forfeit-cup. So that even when competing he remains a true gentleman.

He speaks much, as a moral teacher is bound to do, about duty and virtue and such matters, but he never exacts anything contrary to nature and the natural affections. This is shown in the following conversation:

The Duke of She addressed Confucius, saying: "We have an upright man in our country. His father stole a sheep, and the son bore witness against him."

"In our country," Confucius replied, "uprightness is something different from this. A father hides the guilt of his son, and a son hides the guilt of his father. It is in such conduct that true upright-ness is to be found."

Confucius was in all things moderate, even in virtue. He did not believe that we ought to return good for evil. He was asked on one occasion: "How do you regard the principle of returning good for evil?" And he replied: "What, then, is to be the return for good? Rather should you return justice for injustice, and good for good."

The principle of returning good for evil was being taught in his day in China by the Taoists, whose teaching is much more akin to that of Christianity than is the teaching of Confucius. The founder of Taoism, Lao-Tze (supposed to have been an older contemporary of Confucius) says:

> To the good I would be good; to the not-good I would also be good, in order to make them good. With the faithful I would keep faith; with the unfaithful I would also keep faith, in order that they may become faithful. Even if a man is bad, how can it be right to cast him off? Requite injury with kindness.

Some of Lao-Tze's words are amazingly like parts of the Sermon on the Mount. For instance, he says:

> He that humbles himself shall be preserved entire. He that bends shall be made straight. He that is empty shall be filled. He that is worn out shall be renewed. He who has little shall succeed. He who has much shall go astray.

It is characteristic of China that it was not Lao-Tze but Confucius who became the recognized national sage. Taoism has survived, but chiefly as magic and among the uneducated. Its doctrines have appeared visionary to the practical men who administered the Empire, while the doctrines of Confucius were eminently calculated to avoid friction. Lao-Tze preached a doctrine of inaction: "The Empire," he said, "has ever been won by letting things take their course. He who must always be doing is unfit to obtain the Empire."

But Chinese governors naturally preferred the Confucian maxims of self-control, benevolence and courtesy, combined with a great emphasis upon the good that could be done by wise government. The influence of these maxims has existed even to the present day.

It never occurred to the Chinese, as it has to all modern white nations, to have one system of ethics in theory and another in practice. I do not mean that they always live up to their own theories, but that they attempt to do so and are expected to do so, whereas there are large parts of the Christian ethic which are universally admitted to be too good for this wicked world.

We have, in fact, two kinds of morality side by side; one which we preach but do not practice and another which we practice but seldom preach. Christianity, like all religions, except Mormonism, is Asiatic in origin; it had in the early centuries that emphasis on individualism and other-worldliness which is characteristic of Asiatic mysticism. From this point of view, the doctrine of non-resistance was intelligible.

But when Christianity became the nominal religion of energetic European princes, it was found necessary to maintain that some texts must not be taken literally, while others, such as "Render unto Caesar the things that be Caesar's," acquired great popularity.

In our own day, under the influence of competitive industrialism, the slightest approach to non-resistance is despised, and men are expected to be able to keep their end up. In practice, our effective morality is that of material success achieved by means of a struggle; and this applies to nations as well as to individuals.

Anything else seems to us soft and foolish.

The Chinese do not adopt either our theoretical or our practical ethic. They admit in theory that there are occasions when it is proper to fight, and in practice that these occasions are rare; whereas we hold that in theory there are no occasions when it is proper to fight and in practice that such occasions are very frequent.

The Chinese sometimes fight, but are not a combative race, and do not greatly admire success in war or in business. Traditionally, they admire learning more than anything else; next to that, and usually in combination with it, they admire urbanity, courtesy.

For ages past, administrative posts have been awarded in China on the results of competitive examinations. As there has been no hereditary aristocracy for 2,000 years—with the sole exception of the family of Confucius, the head of which is a Duke—learning has drawn to itself the kind of respect which, in feudal Europe, was given to powerful nobles, as well as the respect which it inspired on its own account.

The old learning, however, was very narrow, consisting merely in an uncritical study of the Chinese classics and their recognized commentators. Under the influence of the West, it has come to be known that geography, economics, geology, chemistry, and so on, are of more practical use than the moralizings of former ages.

Young China—that is to say, the students who have been educated on European lines—recognize modern needs, and have perhaps hardly enough respect for the old tradition. Nevertheless, even the worst moderns, with few exceptions, retain the traditional virtues of moderation, politeness, and a pacific temper. Whether these virtues will survive a few more decades of Western tuition is perhaps doubtful.

If I were to try to sum up in a phrase the main difference between the Chinese and ourselves, I should say that they, in the main, aim at enjoyment, while we, in the main, aim at power. We like power over our fellowmen, and we like power over nature. For the sake of the former we have built up strong states, and for the sake of the latter we have built up science.

The Chinese are too lazy and too good-natured for such pursuits. To say that they are lazy is, however, only true in a certain sense. They are not lazy in the way of tropical peoples; that is to say, the Chinese will work hard for their living. Employers of labor find them extraordinarily industrious. But they will not work, as Americans and Western Europeans do, simply because they would be bored if they did not continue doing their daily work.

Nor do they love hustle for its own sake. When they have enough to live on, they live on it, instead of trying to augment it by hard work. They have an infinite capacity for leisurely amusements—going to the theatre, talking while they drink tea, admiring the Chinese art of earlier times, walking in beautiful scenery, or playing games.

To our way of thinking, there is something unduly mild about such a way of spending one's life; we respect more a man who goes to his office every day, even if all that he does in his office is harmful to himself or, possibly, to society as a whole.

Living in the East has, perhaps, a corrupting influence upon a white man, but I must confess that, since I was in China, I have regarded laziness as one of the best qualities of which men in the mass are capable.

We develop wonderful skill in manufacture, part of which we devote to making ships, automobiles, telephones, and other means of living luxuriously at high pressure, while another part is devoted to making guns, poison-gases and airplanes for the purpose of killing each other wholesale.

We have a first-class system of administration and taxation, part of which is devoted to education, sanitation and such useful objects, while the rest is devoted to war. In England at the present day, three-quarters of the national revenue is spent on past and future wars, and only one-quarter on useful objects.

On the Continent, in most countries, the proportion is even worse. We have a police system of unexampled efficiency, part of which is devoted to the detection and prevention of crime, and part to imprisoning anybody who has any new, constructive political ideas.

In China, they have none of these things. Industry is too inefficient to catch either bandits or Bolsheviks. The result is that in China, as compared to any white man's country, there is freedom for all, and a degree of diffused happiness which is amazing in view of the poverty of all but a tiny minority.

Comparing the actual outlook of the average Chinese with that of the average Westerner, two differences strike one: first, that the Chinese do not admire activity unless it serves some useful purpose; secondly, that they do not regard morality as consisting in checking our own impulses and interfering with those of others.

The first of these differences has been already discussed, but the second is perhaps equally important. Profesor Giles, an eminent

Chinese scholar, maintains that the chief obstacle to the success of Christian missions in China has been the doctrine of original sin. The traditional doctrine of orthodox Christianity—still preached by most Christian missionaries in the Far East—is that we are all born wicked, so wicked as to deserve eternal punishment. The Chinese might have no difficulty in accepting this doctrine if it applied only to white men; but when they are told that their own parents and grandparents are in hell-fire, they grow indignant.

Confucius taught that men are born good and that, if they become wicked, it is through the force of evil example of corrupting manners. This difference from traditional Western orthodoxy has a profound influence on the Chinese.

Among ourselves, the people who are regarded as moral luminaries are those who forgo ordinary pleasure themselves, and find compensation in interfering with the pleasure of others. There is an element of the busybody in our conception of virtue: unless a man makes himself a nuisance to a great many people, we do not think he can be an exceptionally good man. This attitude comes from our notion of sin. It leads not only to interference with freedom, but also to hypocrisy, since the conventional standard is too difficult for most people to live up to.

In China, this is not the case. Moral precepts are positive rather than negative. A man is expected to be respectful to his parents, kind to his children, generous to his poor relations, and courteous to all. These are not very difficult duties, but most men actually fulfill them, and the result is perhaps better than that of our higher standard from which most people fall short, and soon, forgetting them, withdraw.

Another result of the absence of the notion of sin is that men are much more willing to submit their differences to reason.

In China, although there are military men who are ready to appeal to force, no one takes them seriously, not even their own soldiers. They fight battles which are nearly bloodless, and they do much less harm than we should expect from our experience of the fiercer conflicts of the West. The great bulk of the population, including the civil administration, goes about its business as though generals and armies do not exist. The recent difficulties with Japan indicate how unprepared they are for the calamities of warfare and destruction.

In ordinary life, disputes are usually adjusted by the friendly mediation of some third party. Compromise is the accepted principle because it is necessary to save the face of both parties. Saving face, though in some forms it makes foreigners smile, is a most valuable national institution, making social and political life far less ruthless than it is with us.

There is one serious defect, and only one, in the Chinese system, and that is, that it does not enable China to resist more pugnacious nations. If the whole world were like China, the whole world could be happy; but so long as others are warlike and energetic, the Chinese, now that they are no longer isolated, have been compelled to copy our vices to some degree to preserve their national independence. But let us not flatter ourselves that this imitation is an improvement.

Part Three

Sexual Morality

Introduction

Although the sum total of Russell's writings on sexual morality form only a small segment of his published works, they attracted more public attention, and had more immediate influence than most of his greatest achievements in philosophical thought. More than anyone else, Russell influenced future generations to adopt a saner and more tolerant attitude toward marriage and sexual morality.

For the most part, Russell aimed his writings on sexual morality at a general audience; for this reason he did not always trouble his readers with the minutia of philosophical argument, although in the essays collected here Russell never loses sight of the theoretical problems that need to be addressed.

It is, of course, on the topic of sexual morality that Russell also encountered the most unfavorable opposition to his views. Along with this opposition came a widespread and fierce public campaign by both the clergy and the media to distort his ideas. The public soon came to the erroneous opinion (an opinion that still survives) that Russell's views on sexual morality amounted to nothing more than a simple advocacy of unrestricted sexual license. On the contrary, Russell's sexual ethic was heavily grounded in social responsibility. He wrote: "The doctrine that I wish to preach is not one of license; it involves nearly as much self-control as is involved in the conventional doctrine."[1] He went on to say: "Sexual morality, freed from superstition, is a simple matter. Fraud and deceit, assault, and seduction of persons under age are proper matters for the criminal law. Relations between adults who are free agents are a private matter, and should not be interfered with either by the law or by

199

public opinion, because no outsider can know whether they are good or bad."[2]

It must not be forgotten that at the time Russell was voicing his views on sexual morality the world was in a state where sexual ignorance was deliberately fostered, so that a boy or girl might think that the changes of puberty were signs of some dreadful disease, and a woman might marry without knowing anything of what lay ahead of her on her wedding night; where women were taught to look on sex, not as a source of joy, but as a painful matrimonial duty; where prudery extended to covering the legs of pianos; where no escape was possible from the misery of an unhappy marriage except by elaborate legal proof of adultery; where a rigid sexual code was accompanied by the tacit acceptance of prostitution; and where sex was considered synonymous with sin.

Russell labored hard to reform this cruel state of affairs. He wrote: "The doctrine that there is something sinful about sex is one which has done untold harm to individual character—a harm beginning in early childhood and continuing throughout life. By keeping sex love in a prison, conventional morality has done much to imprison all other forms of friendly feeling, and to make men less generous, less kindly, more self-assertive and more cruel. Whatever sexual ethic may come to be ultimately accepted must be free from superstition and must have recognizable and demonstrable grounds in its favor."[3] Today few people realize the repressive state of the old ideas. This is probably the finest tribute one can give to Russell's success.

Of course, Russell's revolt did not overturn all the repressive ideas, and recently, with the tremendous resurgence of religious fundamentalism, there has been something of a counter-revolution, and a re-establishment of some of the old conventions. But the relations between men and women ought never again to suffer from some of the evils Russell attacked; and on many points his views on sexual morality still stand as ideals of tolerance and understanding.

NOTES

1. See "Marriage and Morals," this volume p. 270.
2. See "New Morals for Old," this volume p. 154.
3. "Marriage and Morals," p. 266.

14

Education Without Sex Taboos

*In 1927, owing to the needs of his two children, Russell became increasing-
ly interested in education and sexual morality. His controversial views
were closely linked with his observation of the joy people took in fighting
and killing during the First World War. Russell believed these characteristics to be largely the outcome of experiences and teachings people were
exposed to early in life. A peaceful and happy world could not be achieved
without drastic changes in education. In sexual matters, although not only
in these, irrational prohibitions and dishonesty are exceedingly harmful.*

*"Education Without Sex Taboos" is one of Russell's earliest essays on
the topic of sexual morality. Here, he frankly admits that his own problems
with sexuality were due in large part to his own puritanical upbringing.
Russell states his belief that the conventional moral instruction of his day,
which taught that "everything to do with sex is wicked," ill-prepared both
men and women for marriage and any sexual relationship they might
enter into. In addition, conventional moralists, who endeavored to be
"proper," stirred up morbid curiosity in children about sex.*

*According to Russell, one could only cure the Victorian attitude toward
sex by embarking upon a frank and honest education respecting sexual
matters. Only through honest education could sexual morality take its
proper place as one of the greatest treasures of mankind.*

This subject is part of the larger question: How can we bring up our
children without the usual vices and yet without making them feel
odd? By the "usual" vices, I mean those which are considered to be
virtues and carefully inculcated in a conventional moral training;
namely, cruelty, cowardice and jealousy. Before discussing the spe-

From *The New Republic* 52 (November 16, 1927): 346-348. Reprinted by permission of
the publisher.

cial problem of sex education, I should like to say a few words on the more general topic.

Take, first, cruelty. Already, because I think it a mistake to give a training in cruelty, I have been obliged to offend all my neighbors beyond hope of forgiveness. This has arisen as follows: Beacon Hill School, which opened on September 21, [1927] has two hundred and forty acres of ground, almost all wild woodland. The hunt has hitherto been allowed to pursue the fox over this ground and has asked me to give the same permission, which I have refused. Those who know English county society will realize that in so doing I have committed a worse offense than the advocacy of atheism, pacifism or free love. Yet I could not give the children at the school a right outlook if I deliberately permitted the torture of animals for human amusement.

Pacifism, though less heinous than dislike of fox-hunting, is yet a very difficult matter in education. I do not desire to check the bloodthirsty play-impulses of children, but I do desire not to teach them that their most important duty is to kill each other when they grow up. This means that most history textbooks have to be avoided, and that the children have to be brought up without certain nationalist sentiments which are part of the equipment of most normal citizens.

Religion was, until lately, a very difficult matter, but now the number of adults who do not adhere to any Church is sufficiently large to prevent a free-thinker from feeling odd. It is still held, even by many who have no religious beliefs themselves, that the young ought to have them, since otherwise they cannot be taught "virtue." I am myself at a loss to understand how anything which is really virtue can depend upon falsehood. Certainly, for my part, I am not prepared to tell children anything I do not believe. And from what I have seen of the children (now grown up) of other free-thinkers, I should say that they compare very favorably, from a moral point of view, with the children of parsons. I do not think that, on this head, there is any real difficulty.

But sex taboos are a far more serious matter, because they enter into and poison the life of instinct, and because very few adults are really free from them. I believe them to be totally irrational and very harmful. I need not go over the ground covered in psychoanalytic literature, since competent people now recognize that the artificial ignorance of children on sex matters and the severity of the prohibitions imposed upon them are responsible for a great deal of nervous disorder in later life. There is, however, another aspect of the question, which is, in a way, more important, since it concerns normal people and not only those who suffer from nervous disorders. The teaching that everything to do with sex is wicked—which is what a child learns from conventional moral instruction—unfits many people for marriage, some in one way and some in another. Girls who have been strictly brought up become incapable of unrestrained love; though they may believe that marriage is a sacrament, the part of it that seems to them sacred is the prohibition of adultery. Thus jealousy becomes surrounded with all the attributes of virtue, and love is kept like a tiger in the zoo, as something interesting but too dangerous to be at large. Among well-to-do young women this attitude as given place to another, which is its antithesis, but has the defects of a revolt. Having rejected, superficially but not fundamentally, the view that all sex is sin, they have taken up with the view that sex is a trivial amusement. The poetry, the sense of mystic union, the blossoming and unfolding of all that is best in our nature, which belong to a deep love, are not for them: love, like alcohol, is snatched in an atmosphere of prohibition, trivial, crude and poisonous. The puritan succeeds much more easily in destroying the poetry of what he considers sin than in preventing the acts which he deplores. It was not in an atmosphere of prohibition that Keats wrote:

> O for a draught of vintage! that hath been
> Cooled a long age in the deep-delvéd earth,
> Tasting of Flora and the country-green
> Dance, and Provençal song, and sunburnt mirth!

Such drinking as I have seen in America in recent years would not have lent itself to treatment in verse. And the same thing is true of love, when those who practice it believe in their instincts that they would be better if they did not. I have known men who could not have sexual relations with women whom they respected, who lived platonically with their wives, whom they deeply loved, and had trivial affairs with women whom they despised. All this is a result of bad education in matters of sex.

Coming now to the concrete problem of the education of children, it is, of course, evident that if the right result is to be produced, they must not, at any age, be left in charge of people whose outlook is wrong. The most highly trained nurses have been taught to deal with masturbation in a manner calculated to produce insanity. And the foundations of deceitfulness in later life are laid when a child is taught, in the name of decency, to be furtive about evacuation. Moreover, the usual motive to which ignorant women appeal in trying to produce what they consider right conduct is terror; thus the child comes to think that acts inspired by fear are better than those inspired by adventurousness. This produces a timorous adult, incapable of independent thought or feeling, and anxious only to escape the censure of neighbors. I think it quite likely that the inferiority of women to men, hitherto, in intellectual and artistic achievement, has been very largely due to the timidity which they acquired from sexual taboos. It is not to be supposed that this timidity is necessarily eliminated from the unconscious when conduct ceases to be be such as convention dictates. A very strong instinctive drive, such as that of sex, can break through imposed prohibitions, when weaker impulses, such as that of artistic creation, remain crushed.

Children should not at any age be taught that certain parts of the body are peculiar. In a civilized community, there would be no such thing as "decency," which is merely an externalization of indecency in thought and feeling. When we were equipping our school, we were looking one day for diagrams suitable for the teaching of physiology. We found some which were admirably made, one showing muscles, one nerves, one veins and arteries and so on. But, unfortunately, in all of them the sexual parts were omitted. To show such things to children is to give them a feeling that there is some mystery about these parts, which causes them to think about sexual matters, and to think in just the wrong way. We all, however virtuous and prudish, think a great deal more about sex than we should do if we had been brought up freely. Some mothers I have known, having learned that they ought to allow their little boys to be with them while they dress, nevertheless ask them to look away while they are washing, thus doing more harm than if they kept the children away altogether. Children should see each other and their parents naked whenever it so happens, and they should observe that their parents do not mind being naked before each other. But they should not see too much affection between their parents, as this gives rise to feelings of jealousy. I fear that in many homes this caution would be unnecessary.

Questions about sexual matters must be answered in the same tone of voice, and with the same manner, as any other questions. It will then be found that the interest in the subject is vastly less than the interest in trains and airplanes. I have found in both my own children great interest in the fact that children grow inside their mothers, because they feel that this is a fact about their own early lives. My boy (five and a half) knows that a seed comes from the father into the mother, but the fact does not interest him, and he has not yet asked how it is planted. When he asks, he will be told, but so far he has shown no signs of wanting to know.

I do not believe in teaching children about the "sacredness" of sex or motherhood or anything else. The right attitude seems to me to be purely scientific: the facts are so and so. Like all other facts, they should not be forced on children, but should be told them when they want to know them. The emotions that we may wish them to feel later on cannot, in any case, be felt before puberty, and should arise spontaneously, not as a result of teaching, since taught emotions are not genuine. I do not deny that emotions can be taught by Dr. Watson's methods; what I am thinking of is the method of moral exhortation.

I have not attempted to deal with the problems which arise after puberty and before the boy or girl is fully adult. These are difficult problems, as to which I have as yet not much experience of modern methods. I know the appalling misery that I went through myself in those years, owing to an old-fashioned education, and I know that the evil effects have pursued me down to the present day. I find that large numbers of men and women say the same thing. There is, therefore, every reason for condemning the methods of the past. But as to the exact method of handling the problems of adolescence, I cannot say that I have as yet any very decided opinion, for lack of sufficient intimate experience.

Whatever restrictions may be necessary in later life as regards sexual behavior, I am sure that the method of the taboo is not the right one for securing them. There should be freedom in thought and speech and feeling; so far as the police permit, there should be freedom to discard clothing, for instance, in bathing. The belief that sex is sinful, which must otherwise exist in the unconscious if not in conscious thought, is a potent source of unhappiness, leading to intolerance, cruelty and mental cowardice. I read in a letter to the newspaper from a religious person that we ought not to expose the body, because God made it. I could not follow the argument, nor understand why it should not involve hiding our noses, which, presumably, God also made. The whole conception that certain things are shameful, and must not be mentioned above a whisper, seems to me a mere relic of barbarism. So far from contributing to human happiness, it causes untold misery. And it produces that very pre-occupation with sex which it is supposed to prevent. Men and women brought up without this taboo will think about sex freely and fearlessly, but far less frequently and broodingly than the old-fashioned puritan, who is led by unconscious envy to see sin everywhere.

15

Why a Sexual Ethic Is Necessary

In this essay, which is the introduction to his famous volume on Marriage
and Morals, *Russell points out that the problem of determining which sexual morality is best, from the point of view of general happiness and well-
being, is extremely complicated; answers will differ as circumstances vary.
Russell believes that no sexual ethic can be either justified or condemned
on solid ground until it has been examined from all points of view.*

*In criticizing morality, Russell believes that one must eliminate all
elements of superstition, which are often subconscious, and take account of
any new discoveries of science that may make the wisdom of past ages no
longer rational.*

In characterizing a society, whether ancient or modern, there are
two elements, rather closely interconnected, which are of prime importance: one is the economic system, the other the family system.
There are at the present day two influential schools of thought, one
of which derives everything from an economic source, while the
other derives everything from a family or sexual source, the former
school that of Marx, the latter that of Freud. I do not myself adhere
to either school, since the interconnections of economics and sex do
not appear to me to show any clear primacy of the one over the other
from the point of view of causal efficacy. For example: no doubt the
industrial revolution has had and will have a profound influence
upon sexual morals, but conversely the sexual virtue of the Puritans
was psychologically necessary as a part cause of the industrial
revolution. I am not prepared myself to assign primacy to either the
economic or the sexual factor, nor in fact can they be separated with
any clearness. Economics is concerned essentially with obtaining

food, but food is seldom wanted among human beings solely for the benefit of the individual who obtains it; it is wanted for the sake of the family, and as the family system changes, economic motives also change. It must be obvious that not only life insurance but most forms of private saving would nearly cease if children were taken away from their parents and brought up by the State as in Plato's *Republic;* that is to say, if the State were to adopt the role of the father, the State would, *ipso facto,* become the sole capitalist. Thoroughgoing Communists have often maintained the converse, that if the State is to be the sole capitalist, the family, as we have known it, cannot survive; and even if this is thought to go too far, it is impossible to deny an intimate connection between private property and the family, a connection which is reciprocal, so that we cannot say that one is cause and the other is effect.

The sexual morals of the community will be found to consist of several layers. There are first the positive institutions embodied in law; such, for example, as monogamy in some countries and polygamy in others. Next there is a layer where law does not intervene but public opinion is emphatic. And lastly there is a layer which is left to individual discretion, in practice if not in theory. There is no country in the world and there has been no age in the world's history where sexual ethics and sexual institutions have been determined by rational considerations, with the exception of Soviet Russia. I do not mean to imply that the institutions of Soviet Russia are in this respect perfect; I mean only that they are not the outcome of superstition and tradition, as are, at least in part, the institutions of all other countries in all ages. The problem of determining what sexual morality would be best from the point of view of general happiness and well-being is an extremely complicated one, and the answer will vary according to a number of circumstances. It will be different in an industrially advanced community from what it would be in a primitive agricultural régime. It will be different where medical science and hygiene are effective in producing a low death rate from what it would be where plagues and pestilences carry away a large proportion of the population before it becomes adult. Perhaps when we know more, we shall be able to say that the best sexual ethic will be different in one climate from what it would be in another, and different again with one kind of diet from what it would be with another.

The effects of a sexual ethic are of the most diverse kinds—personal, conjugal, familial, national and international. It may well happen that the effects are good in some of these respects, where they are bad in others. All must be considered before we can decide what on the balance we are to think of a given system. To begin with the purely personal: these are the effects considered by psychoanalysis. We have here to take account not only of the adult behavor inculcated by a code, but also of the early education designed to produce obedience to the code, and in this region, as every one now knows, the effects of early taboos may be very curious and indirect. In this department of the subject we are at the level of personal well-being. The next stage of our problem arises when we consider the relations of men and women. It is clear that some sex relations have more value than others. Most people would agree that a sex relation is better when it has a large psychical element than when it is purely physical. Indeed the view which has passed from the poets into the common consciousness of civilized men and women is that love increases in value in proportion as more of the personalities of the people concerned enters into the relation. The poets also have taught many people to value love in proportion to its intensity; this, however, is a more debatable matter. Most moderns would agree that love should be an equal relation, and that on this ground, if on no other, polygamy, for example, cannot be regarded as an ideal system. Throughout this department of the subject it is necessary to consider both marriage and extra-marital relations, since whatever system of marriage prevails, extra-marital relations will vary correspondingly.

We come next to the question of the family. There have existed in various times and places many different kinds of family groups, but the patriarchal family has a very large preponderance, and, moreover, the monogamic patriarchal family has prevailed more and more over the polygamic. The primary motive of sexual ethics as they have existed in Western civilization since pre-Christian times has been to secure that degree of female virtue without which the patriarchal family becomes impossible, since paternity is uncertain. What has been added to this in the way of insistence on male virtue by Christianity had its psychological source in asceticism, although in quite recent times this motive has been reinforced by female jealousy, which became influential with the emancipation of women. This latter motive seems, however, to be temporary, since, if we may judge by appearances, women will tend to prefer a system allowing freedom to both sexes rather than one imposing upon men the restrictions which hitherto have been suffered only by women.

Within the mongamic family there are, however, many varieties. Marriages may be decided by the parties themselves or by their parents. In some countries the bride is purchased; in others, e.g., France, the bridegroom. Then there may be all kinds of differences as regards divorce, from the Catholic extreme, which permits no divorce, to the law of old China, which permitted a man to divorce his wife for being a chatterbox. Constancy or quasi-constancy in sex relations arises among animals, as well as among human beings, where, for the preservation of the species, the participation of the male is necessary for the rearing of the young. Birds, for example, have to sit upon their eggs continuously to keep them warm, and also have to spend a good many hours of the day getting food. To do both is, among many species, impossible for one bird, and therefore male cooperation is essential. The consequence is that most birds are models of virtue. Among human beings the cooperation of the father is a great biological advantage to the offspring, especially in unsettled times and among turbulent populations; but with the growth of modern civilization the role of the father is being increasingly taken over the by the State, and there is reason to think that a father may cease before long to be biologically advantageous, at any rate in the wage-earning class. If this should occur, we must expect a complete breakdown of traditional morality, since there will no longer be any reason why a mother should wish the paternity of her child to be indubitable. Plato would have us go a step further, and put the State not only in place of the father but in that of the mother also. I am not myself sufficiently an admirer of the State, or sufficiently impressed with the delights of orphan asylums, to be enthusiastic in favor of this scheme. At the same time it is not impossible that economic forces may cause it to be to some extent adopted.

The law is concerned with sex in two different ways, on the one hand to enforce whatever sexual ethic is adopted by the community in question, and on the other hand to protect the ordinary rights of individuals in the sphere of sex. The latter have two main departments: on the one hand the protection of females and non-adults from assault and from harmful exploitation, on the other hand the prevention of venereal disease. Neither of these is commonly treated purely on its merits, and for this reason neither is so effectively dealt with as it might be. In regard to the former, hysterical campaigns about the White Slave Traffic lead to the passage of laws easily evaded by professional malefactors, while affording opportunities of blackmail against harmless people. In regard to the latter, the view that venereal disease is a just punishment for sin prevents, the adoption of the measures which would be the most effective on purely medical grounds, while the general attitude that venereal disease is shameful causes it to be concealed, and therefore not promptly or adequately treated.

We come finally to the question of population. This is in itself a vast problem which must be considered from many points of view. There is the question of the health of mothers, the question of the health of children, the question of the psychological effects of large and small families respectively upon the character of children. These are what may be called the hygienic aspects of the problem. Then there are the economic aspects, both personal and public: the question of the wealth per head of a family or a community in relation to the size of the family or the birth rate of the community. Closely connected with this is the bearing of the population question upon international politics and the possibility of world peace. And, finally, there is the eugenic question as to the improvement or deterioration of the stock through the different birth and death rates of the different sections of the community. No sexual ethic can be either justified or condemned on solid grounds until it has been examined from all the points of view above enumerated. Reformers and reactionaries alike are in the habit of considering one or at most two of the aspects of the problem. It is especially rare to find any combination of the private and the political points of view, and yet it is quite impossible to say that either of these is more important than the other, and we can have no assurance *a priori* that a system which is good from a private point of view would also be good from a political point of view, or vice versa. My own belief is that in most ages and in most places obscure psychological forces have led men to adopt systems involving quite unnecessary cruelty, and that this is still the case among the most civilized races at the present day. I believe also that the advances in medicine and hygiene have made changes in sexual ethics desirable both from a private and from a public point of view, while the increasing role of the State in education is gradually rendering the father less important than he has been throughout historical times. We have, therefore, a twofold task in criticizing the current ethics: on the one hand we have to eliminate the elements of superstition, which are often subconscious; on the other hand we have to take account of those entirely new factors which make the wisdom of past ages the folly instead of the wisdom of the present.

16

The Place of Sex Among Human Values

Here Russell points out that while he is in agreement with the church in thinking that obsession with sexual topics is evil, he begs to differ with respect to the best methods of avoiding this evil. Russell elaborates his belief that the attitude of the church results in sex-obsessed moralists who are incapable of thinking cleanly and wholesomely on the topic of sexual morality. He points out that one of the most dangerous fallacies of these moralists has been to reduce intimate relations between couples to just the sexual act. This, Russell believes, is only done with one intention: to degrade sex.

The writer who deals with a sexual theme is always in danger of being accused, by those who think that such themes should not be mentioned, of an undue obsession with his subject. It is thought that he would not risk the censure of prudish and prurient persons unless his interest in the subject were out of all proportion to its importance. This view, however, is only taken in the case of those who advocate changes in the conventional ethic. Those who stimulate the appeals to harry prostitutes and those who secure legislation, nominally against the White Slave Traffic, but really against voluntary and decent extra-marital relations; those who denounce women for short skirts and lipsticks; and those who spy upon sea beaches in the hope of discovering inadequate bathing costumes, are none of them supposed to be the victims of a sexual obsession. Yet in fact they probably suffer much more in this way than do writers who advocate greater sexual freedom. Fierce morality is generally a reaction against lustful emotions, and the man who gives expression to it is generally filled with indecent thoughts—

From *Marriage and Morals* by Bertrand Russell, pp. 288-302. Copyright 1929 by George Allen and Unwin. Reprinted by permission of the publisher.

thoughts which are rendered indecent, not by the mere fact that they have a sexual content, but that morality has incapacitated the thinker from thinking cleanly and wholesomely on this topic. I am quite in agreement with the Church in thinking that obsession with sexual topics is an evil, but I am not in agreement with the Church as to the best methods of avoiding this evil. It is notorious that St. Anthony was more obsessed by sex than the most extreme voluptuary who ever lived; I will not adduce more recent examples for fear of giving offense. Sex is a natural need, like food and drink. We blame the gormandiser and the dipsomaniac because in the case of each an interest which has a certain legitimate place in life has usurped too large a share of his thoughts and emotions. But we do not blame a man for a normal and healthy enjoyment of a reasonable quantity of food. Ascetics, it is true, have done so, and have considered that a man should cut down his nutriment to the lowest point compatible with survival, but this view is not now common, and may be ignored. The Puritans, in their determination to avoid the pleasures of sex, became somewhat more conscious than people had been before of the pleasures of the table. As a seventeenth-century critic of Puritanism says:

> Would you enjoy gay nights and pleasant dinners?
> Then must you board with saints and bed with sinners.

It would seem, therefore, that the Puritans did not succeed in subduing the purely corporeal part of our human nature, since what they took away from sex they added to gluttony. Gluttony is regarded by the Catholic Church as one of the seven deadly sins, and those who practice it are placed by Dante in one of the deeper circles of hell, but it is a somewhat vague sin, since it is hard to say where a legitimate interest in food ceases, and guilt begins to be incurred. Is it wicked to eat anything that is not nourishing? If so, with every salted almond we risk damnation. Such views, however, are out of date. We all know a glutton when we see one, and although he may be somewhat despised, he is not severely reprobated. In spite of this fact, undue obsession with food is rare among those who have never suffered want. Most people eat their meals and then think about other things until the next meal. Those, on the other hand, who, having adopted an ascetic philosophy, have deprived themselves of all but the minimum of food, become obsessed by visions of banquets and dreams of demons bearing luscious fruits. And marooned

Antarctic explorers, reduced to a diet of whale's blubber, spend their days planning the dinner they will have at the Carlton when they get home.

Such facts suggest that, if sex is not to be an obsession, it should be regarded by the moralists as food has come to be regarded, and not as food was regarded by the hermits of the Thebaid. Sex is a natural human need like food and drink. It is true that men can survive without it, whereas they cannot survive without food and drink, but from a psychological standpoint the desire for sex is precisely analogous to the desire for food and drink. It is enormously enhanced by abstinence, and temporarily allayed by satisfaction. While it is urgent, it shuts out the rest of the world from the mental purview. All other interests fade for the moment, and actions may be performed which will subsequently appear insane to the man who has been guilty of them. Moreover, as in the case of food and drink, the desire is enormously stimulated by prohibition. I have known children refuse apples at breakfast and go straight out into the orchard and steal them, although the breakfast apples were ripe and the stolen apples unripe. I do not think it can be denied that the desire for alcohol among well-to-do Americans is much stronger than it was twenty years ago. In like manner, Christian teaching and Christian authority have immensely stimulated interest in sex. The generation which first ceases to believe in the conventional teaching is bound, therefore, to indulge in sexual freedom to a degree far beyond what is to be expected of those whose views on sex are unaffected by superstitious teaching, whether positively or negatively. Nothing but freedom will prevent undue obsession with sex, but even freedom will not have this effect unless it has become habitual and has been associated with a wise education as regards sexual matters. I wish to repeat, however, as emphatically as I can, that I regard an undue preoccupation with this topic as an evil, and that I think this evil widespread at the present day, especially in America, where I find it particularly pronounced among the sterner moralists, who display it markedly by their readiness to believe falsehoods concerning those whom they regard as their opponents. The glutton, the voluptuary, and the ascetic are all self-absorbed persons whose horizon is limited by their own desires, either by way of satisfaction or by way of renunciation. A man who is healthy in mind and body will not have his interests thus concentrated upon himself. He will look out upon the world and find it in objects that seem to him worthy of his attention. Absorption in self is not, as some have supposed, the natural condition of unregenerate man. It is a disease brought on, almost always, by some thwarting of natural impulses. The voluptuary who gloats over thoughts of sexual gratification is in general the result of some kind of deprivation, just as the man who hoards food is usually a man who has lived through a famine or a period of destitution. Healthy, outward-looking men and women are not to be produced by the thwarting of natural impulse, but by the equal and balanced development of all the impulses essential to a happy life.

I am not suggesting that there should be no morality and no self-restraint in regard to sex, any more than in regard to food. In regard to food we have restraints of three kinds, those of law, those of manners, and those of health. We regard it as wrong to steal food, to take more than our share at a common meal, and to eat in ways that are likely to make us ill. Restraints of a similar kind are essential where sex is concerned, but in this case they are much more complex and involve much more self-control. Moreover, since one human being ought not to have property in another, the analogy of stealing is not adultery but rape, which obviously must be forbidden by law. The questions that arise in regard to health are concerned almost entirely with venereal disease, a subject which we have already touched upon in connection with prostitution. Clearly, the diminution of professional prostitution is the best way, apart from medicine, of dealing with this evil, and diminution of professional prostitution can be best effected by that greater freedom among young people which has been growing up in recent years.

A comprehensive sexual ethic cannot regard sex merely as a natural hunger and a possible source of danger. Both these points of view are important, but it is even more important to remember that sex is connected with some of the greatest goods in human life. The three that seem paramount are lyric love, happiness in marriage, and art. Of lyric love and marriage we have already spoken. Art is thought by some to be independent of sex, but this view has fewer adherents now than it had in former times. It is fairly clear that the impulse to every kind of aesthetic creation is psychologically connected with courtship, not necessarily in any direct or obvious way, but none the less profoundly. In order that the sexual impulse may lead to artistic expression, a number of conditions are necessary. There must be artistic capacity; but artistic capacity, even within a given race, appears as though it were common at one time and uncommon at another, from which it is safe to conclude that environment, as opposed to native capacity, has an important part to play in the development of the artistic impulse. There must be a certain kind of freedom, not the sort that consists in rewarding the artist, but the sort that consists in not compelling him or inducing him to form habits which turn him into a philistine. When Julius II imprisoned Michelangelo, he did not in any way interfere with that kind of freedom which the artist needs. He imprisoned him because he considered him an important man, and would not tolerate the slightest offense to him from anybody whose rank was less than papal. When, however, an artist is compelled to kowtow to rich patrons or town councillors, and to adapt his work to their aesthetic canons, his artistic freedom is lost. And when he is compelled by fear of social and economic persecution to go on living in a marriage which has become intolerable, he is deprived of the energy which artistic creation requires. Societies that have been conventionally virtuous have not produced great art. Those which have, have been composed of men such as Idaho would sterilize. America at present imports most of its artistic talent from Europe, where, as yet, freedom lingers, but already the Americanization of Europe is making it necessary to turn to the negroes. The last home of art, it seems, is to be somewhere on the Upper Congo, if not in the uplands of Tibet. But its final extinction cannot be long delayed, since the rewards which America is prepared to lavish upon foreign artists are such as must inevitably bring about their artistic death. Art in the past has had a popular basis, and this has depended upon joy of life. Joy of life, in its turn, depends upon a certain spontaneity in regard to sex. Where sex is repressed, only work remains, and a gospel of work for work's sake never produced any work worth doing. Let me not be told that some one has collected statistics of the number of sexual acts *per diem* (or shall we say *per noctem?*) performed in the United States, and that it is at least as great per head as in any other country. I do not know whether this is the case or not, and I am not in any way concerned to deny it. One of the most dangerous fallacies of the conventional moralists is the reduction of sex to the sexual act, in order to be better able to belabor it. No civilized man, and no savage that I have ever heard of, is satisfied in his instinct by the bare sexual act. If the impulse which leads to the act is to be satisfied, there must be courtship, there must be love, there must be companionship. Without these, while the physical hunger may be appeased for the moment, the mental hunger remains unabated, and no profound satisfaction can be obtained. The sexual freedom that the artist needs is freedom to love, not the gross freedom to relieve the bodily need with some unknown woman; and freedom to love is what, above all, the conventional moralists will not concede. If art is to revive after the world has been Americanized, it will be necessary that America should change, that its moralists should become less moral and its immoralists less immoral, that both, in a word, should recognize the higher values involved in sex, and the possibility that joy may be of more value than a bank-account. Nothing in America is so painful to the traveller as the lack of joy. Pleasure is frantic and bacchanalian, a matter of momentary oblivion, not of delighted self-expression. Men whose grandfathers danced to the music of the pipe in Balkan or Polish villages sit throughout the day glued to their desks, amid typewriters and telephones, serious, important and worthless. Escaping in the evening to drink and a new kind of noise, they imagine that they are finding happiness, whereas they are finding only a frenzied and incomplete oblivion of the hopeless routine of money that breeds money, using for the purpose the bodies of human beings whose souls have been sold into slavery.

It is not my intention to suggest, what I by no means believe, that all that is best in human life is connected with sex. I do not myself regard science, either practical or theoretical, as connected with it, nor yet certain kinds of important social and political activities. The impulses that lead to the complex desires of adult life can be arranged under a few simple heads. Power, sex, and parenthood appear to me to be the source of most of the things that human beings do, apart from what is necessary for self-preservation. Of these three, power begins first and ends last. The child, since he has very little power, is dominated by the desire to have more. Indeed, a large proportion of his activities spring from this desire. His other dominant desire is vanity—the wish to be praised and the fear of being blamed or left out. It is vanity that makes him a social being and gives him the virtues necessary for life in a community. Vanity is a motive closely intertwined with sex, though in theory separable from it. But power has, so far as I can see, very little connection with sex, and it is love of power, at least as much as vanity, that makes a child work at his lessons and develop his muscles. Curiosity and the pursuit of knowledge should, I think, be regarded as a branch of the love of power. If knowledge is power, then the love of knowledge is the love of power. Science, therefore, except for certain branches of biology and physiology, must be regarded as lying outside the province of sexual emotions. As the Emperor Frederick II is no longer alive, this opinion must remain more or less hypothetical. If he were still alive, he would no doubt decide it by castrating an eminent mathematician and an eminent composer and observing the effects upon their respective labors. I should expect the former to be nil and the latter to be considerable. Seeing that the pursuit of knowledge is one of the most valuable elements in human nature, a very important sphere of activity is, if we are right, exempted from the domination of sex.

Power is also the motive to most political activity, understanding this word in its widest sense. I do not mean to suggest that a great statesman is indifferent to the public welfare; on the contrary, I believe him to be a man in whom parental feeling has become widely diffused. But unless he has also a considerable love of power he will fail to sustain the labors necessary for success in a political enterprise. I have known many highminded men in public affairs, but unless they had a considerable dose of personal ambition they seldom had the energy to accomplish the good at which they aimed. On a certain crucial occasion, Abraham Lincoln made a speech to two recalcitrant senators, beginning and ending with the words: "I am the President of the United States, clothed with great power." It can hardly be questioned that he found some pleasure in asserting this fact. Throughout all politics, both for good and for evil, the two chief forces are the economic motive and the love of power; an attempt to interpret politics on Freudian lines is, to my mind, a mistake.

If we are right in what we have been saying, most of the greatest men, other than artists, have been actuated in their important activities by motives unconnected with sex. If such activities are to persist and are, in their humbler forms, to become common, it is necessary that sex should not overshadow the remainder of a man's emotional and passionate nature. The desire to understand the world and the desire to reform it are the two great engines of progress, without which human society would stand still or retrogress. It may be that too complete a happiness would cause the impulses to knowledge and reform to fade. When Cobden wished to enlist John Bright in the free trade campaign, he based a personal appeal upon the sorrow that Bright was experiencing owing to his wife's recent death. It may be that without this sorrow Bright would have had less sympathy with the sorrows of others. And many a man has been driven to abstract pursuits by despair of the actual world.

To a man of sufficient energy, pain may be a valuable stimulus, and I do not deny that if we were all perfectly happy we should not exert ourselves to become happier. But I cannot admit that it is any part of the duty of human beings to provide others with pain on the off chance that it may prove fruitful. In ninety-nine cases out of a hundred pain proves merely crushing. In the hundredth case it is better to trust to the natural shocks that flesh is heir to. So long as there is death there will be sorrow, and so long as there is sorrow it can be no part of the duty of human beings to increase its amount, in spite of the fact that a few rare spirits know how to transmute it.

17

Our Sexual Ethics

Written seven years after the publication of Marriage and Morals *and four years before Russell encountered the hostile reaction to his appointment at the City College of New York, this essay contains one of Russell's last published elaborations of sexual morality, sex education, and relationships both within and outside marriage.*

I

Sex, more than any other element in human life, is still viewed by many, perhaps by most, in an irrational way. Homicide, pestilence, insanity, gold and precious stones—all the things, in fact, that are the objects of passionate hopes or fears—have been seen, in the past, through a mist of magic or mythology; but the sun of reason has now dispelled the mist, except here and there. The densest cloud that remains is in the territory of sex, as is perhaps natural since sex is concerned in the most passionate part of most people's lives.

It is becoming apparent, however, that conditions in the modern world are working to effect a change in the public attitude toward sex. As to what change, or changes, this will bring about, no one can speak with any certainty; but it is possible to note some of the forces now at work, and to discuss what their results are likely to be upon the structure of society.

In so far as human nature is concerned, it cannot be said to be *impossible* to produce a society in which there is very little sexual intercourse outside of marriage. The conditions necessary for this result, however, are such as are made almost unattainable by modern

Originally published in *The American Mercury* 38 (May 1936).

life. Let us, then, consider what they are.

The greatest influence toward effecting monogamy is immobility in a region containing few inhabitants. If a man hardly ever has occasion to leave home and seldom sees any woman but his wife, it is easy for him to be faithful; but if he travels without her or lives in a crowded urban community, the problem is proportionately more difficult. The next greatest assistance to monogamy is superstition: those who genuinely believe that "sin" leads to eternal punishment might be expected to avoid it, and to some extent they do so, although not to so great an extent as might be expected. The third support of virtue is public opinion. Where, as in agricultural societies, all that a man does is known to his neighbors, he has powerful motives for avoiding whatever convention condemns. But all these causes of correct behavior are much less potent than they used to be. Fewer people live in isolation; the belief in hell-fire is dying out; and in large towns no one knows what his neighbor does. It is, therefore, not surprising that both men and women are less monogamous than they were before the rise of modern industrialism.

Of course, it may be said that, while an increasing number of people fail to observe the moral law, that is no reason for altering our standards. Those who sin, we are sometimes told, should know and recognize that they sin, and an ethical code is none the worse for being difficult to live up to. But I should reply that the question whether a code is good or bad is the same as the question whether or not it promotes human happiness. Many adults, in their hearts, still believe all that they were taught in childhood and feel wicked when their lives do not conform to the maxims of the Sunday school. The harm done is not merely to introduce a division between the conscious reasonable personality and the unconscious infantile personality; the harm lies also in the fact that the valid parts of conventional morality become discredited along with the invalid parts, and it comes to be thought that, if adultery is excusable, so are laziness, dishonesty, and unkindness. This danger is inseparable from a system which teaches the young, *en bloc,* a number of beliefs that they are almost sure to discard when they become mature. In the process of social and economic revolt, they are likely to throw over the good along with the bad.

The difficulty of arriving at a workable sexual ethic arises from the conflict between the impulse to jealousy and the impulse to polygamy. There is no doubt that jealousy, while in part instinctive, is to a very large degree conventional. In societies in which a man is considered a fit object for ridicule if his wife is unfaithful, he will be jealous where she is concerned, even if he no longer has any affection for her. Thus jealousy is intimately connected with the sense of property and is much less where this sense is absent. If faithfulness is no part of what is conventionally expected, jealousy is much diminished. But although there is more possibility of lessening jealousy than many people suppose, there are very definite limits so long as fathers have rights and duties. So long as this is the case, it is inevitable that men should desire some assurance that they are the fathers of their wives' children. If women are to have sexual freedom, fathers must fade out, and wives must no longer expect to be supported by their husbands. This may come about in time, but it will be a profound social change, and its effects, for good or ill, are incalculable.

In the meantime, if marriage and paternity are to survive as social institutions, some compromise is necessary between complete promiscuity and lifelong monogamy. To decide on the best compromise at any given moment is not easy; and the decision should vary from time to time, according to the habits of the population and the reliability of birth-control methods. Some things, however, can be said with some definiteness.

In the first place, it is undesirable, both physiologically and educationally, that women should have children before the age of twenty. Our ethics should, therefore, be such as to make this a rare occurrence.

In the second place, it is unlikely that a person without previous sexual experience, whether man or woman, will be able to distinguish between mere physical attraction and the sort of congeniality that is necessary in order to make marriage a success. Moreover, economic causes compel men, as a rule, to postpone marriage, and it is neither likely that they will remain chaste in the years from twenty to thirty nor desirable psychologically that they should do so; but it is much better that, if they have temporary relations, that they should not be with professionals but with girls of their own class, whose motive is affection rather than money. For both these reasons, young unmarried people should have considerable freedom as long as children are avoided.

In the third place, divorce should be possible without blame to either party and should not be regarded as in any way disgraceful. A childless marriage should be terminable at the wish of one of the partners, and any marriage should be terminable by mutual consent—a year's notice being necessary in either case. Divorce should, of course, be possible on a number of other grounds—insanity, desertion, cruelty, and so on; but mutual consent should be the most usual ground.

In the fourth place, everything possible should be done to free sexual relations from the economic taint. At present, wives, just as much as prostitutes, live by the sale of their sexual charms; and even in temporary free relations the man is usually expected to bear all the joint expenses. The result is that there is a sordid entanglement of money with sex, and that women's motives not infrequently have a mercenary element. Sex, even when blessed by the church, ought not to be a profession. It is right that a woman should be paid for housekeeping or cooking or the care of children, but not merely for having sexual relations with a man. Nor should a woman who has once loved and been loved by a man be able to live ever after on alimony when his love and hers have ceased. A woman, like a man, should work for her living, and an idle wife is no more intrinsically worthy of respect than a gigolo.

II

Two very primitive impulses have contributed, though in very different degrees, to the rise of the currently accepted code of sexual behavior. One of these is modesty and the other, as mentioned above, is jealousy. Modesty, in some form and to some degree, is almost universal in the human race and constitutes a taboo which must only be broken through in accordance with certain forms and ceremonies, or, at the least, in conformity with some recognized etiquette. Not everything may be seen, and not all facts may be mentioned. This is not, as some moderns suppose, an invention of the Victorian age; on the contrary, anthropologists have found the most elaborate forms of prudery among primitive savages. The conception of the obscene has its roots deep in human nature. We may go against it from a love of rebellion, or from loyalty to the scientific spirit, or from a wish to feel wicked, such as existed in Byron; but we do not thereby eradicate it from among our natural impulses. No doubt convention determines, in a given community, exactly what is to be considered indecent, but the universal existence of *some* convention of the kind is conclusive evidence of a source which is not merely conventional. In almost every human society, pornography and exhibitionism are reckoned as offenses, except when, as not infrequently occurs, they form part of religious ceremonies.

Asceticism—which may or may not have a psychological connection with modesty—is an impulse which seems to arise only where a certain level of civilization has been reached, but may then become powerful. It is not to be found in the earlier books of the Old Testament, but it appears in the later books, in the Apocrypha and in the New Testament. Similarly, among the Greeks there is little of it in early times, but more and more as time goes on. In India, it arose at a very early date and acquired great intensity. I will not attempt to give a psychological analysis of its origin, but I cannot doubt that it is a spontaneous sentiment, existing, to some slight extent, in almost all civilized human beings. Its faintest form is reluctance to imagine a revered individual—especially a person possessed of religious sanctity—engaged in love-making, which is felt to be scarcely compatible with the highest degree of dignity. The wish to free the spirit from bondage to the flesh has inspired many of the great religions of the world and is still powerful even among modern intellectuals.

But jealousy, I believe, has been the most potent single factor in the genesis of sexual morality. Jealousy instinctively rouses anger; and anger, rationalized, becomes moral disapproval. The purely instinctive motive must have been reinforced, at an early stage in the development of civilization, by the desire of males to be certain of paternity. Without security in this respect the patriarchal family would have been impossible, and fatherhood, with all its economic implications, could not have become the basis of social institutions. It was, accordingly, wicked to have relations with another man's wife but not even mildly reprehensible to have relations with an unmarried woman. There were excellent practical reasons for condemning the adulterer, since he caused confusion and very likely bloodshed. The siege of Troy was an extreme example of the upheavals due to disrespect for the rights of husbands, but something of the sort, though on a smaller scale, was to be expected even when the parties concerned were less exalted. There were, of course, in those days, no corresponding rights of wives; a husband had no duty to his wife, though he had the duty of respecting the property of other husbands. The old system of the patriarchal family, with an ethic based on the feelings that we have been considering, was, in a sense, successful: men, who dominated, had considerable liberty, and women, who suffered, were in such complete subjection that their unhappiness seemed not important. It is the claim of women to equality with men that has done most to make a new system necessary in the world today. Equality can be secured in two ways: either by exacting from men the same strict monogamy as was, in the past, exacted from women; or by allowing women, equally with men, a certain relaxation of the traditional code. The first of these ways was preferred by most of the pioneers of women's rights and is still preferred by the churches; but the second has many more adherents in practice, although most of them are in doubt as to the theoretical justifiability of their own behavior. And those who recognize that *some* new ethic is required find it difficult to know just what its precepts should be.

There is another source of novelty, and that is the effect of the scientific outlook in weakening the taboo on sexual knowledge. It has come to be understood that various evils—for example, venereal disease—cannot be effectively combated unless they are spoken of much more openly than was formerly thought permissible; and it has also been found that reticence and ignorance are apt to have injurious effects upon the psychology of the individual. Both sociology and psychoanalysis have led serious students to deprecate the policy of silence in regard to sexual matters, and many practical educators, from experience with children, have adopted the same position. Those who have a scientific outlook on human behavior, moreover, find it impossible to label any action as "sin"; they realize that what we do has its origin in our heredity, our education, and our environment, and that is by control of these causes, rather than by denunciation, that conduct injurious to society is to be prevented.

In seeking a new ethic of sexual behavior, therefore, we must not ourselves be dominated by the ancient irrational passions which gave rise to the old ethic, though we should recognize that they may, by accident, have led to some sound maxims, and that, since they still exist, though perhaps in a weakened form, they are still among the data of our problem. What we have to do positively is to ask ourselves what moral rules are most likely to promote human happiness, remembering always that, whatever the rules may be, they are not likely to be universally observed. That is to say, we have to consider the effect which the rules will in fact have, not that which they would have if they were completely effective.

III

Let us look at the next question of knowledge on sexual subjects, which arises at the earliest age and is the least difficult and doubtful of the various problems with which we are concerned. There is no sound reason, of any sort or kind, for concealing facts when talking to children. Their questions should be answered and their curiosity satisfied in exactly the same way in regard to sex as in regard to the habits of fishes, or any other subject that interests them. There should be no sentiment, because children cannot feel as adults do and see no occasion for high-flown talk. It is a mistake to begin with the loves of the bees and the flowers; there is no point in leading up to the facts of life by devious routes. The child who is told what he wants to know and allowed to see his parents naked will have no pruriency and no obsession of a sexual kind. Boys who are brought up in official ignorance think and talk much more about sex than boys who have always heard this topic treated on a level with any other. Official ignorance and actual knowledge teach them to be deceitful and hypocritical with their elders. On the other hand, real ignorance, when it is achieved, is likely to be a source of shock and anxiety, and to make adaptation to real life difficult. All ignorance is regrettable, but ignorance on so important a matter as sex is a serious danger.

When I say that children should be told about sex, I do not mean that they should be told only the bare physiological facts; they should be told whatever they wish to know. There should be no attempt to represent adults as more virtuous than they are, or sex as occurring only in marriage. There is no excuse for deceiving children. And when, as must happen in conventional families, they find that their parents have lied, they lose confidence in them and feel justified in lying to them. There are facts which I should not obtrude upon a child, but I would tell him anything sooner than say what is not true. Virtue which is based upon a false view of the facts is not real virtue. Speaking not only from theory but from practical experience, I am convinced that complete openness on sexual subjects is the best way to prevent children from thinking about them excessively, nastily, or unwholesomely, and also the almost indispensable preliminary to an enlightened sexual morality.

Where adult sexual behavior is concerned, it is by no means easy to arrive at a rational compromise between the antagonistic considerations that have each their own validity. The fundamental difficulty is, of course, the conflict between the impulse to jealousy and the impulse to sexual variety. Neither impulse, it is true, is universal: there are those (though they are few) who are never jealous, and there are those (among men as well as among women) whose affections never wander from the chosen partner. If either of these types could be made universal, it would be easy to devise a satisfactory code. It must be admitted, however, that either type can be made more common by conventions designed to that end.

Much ground remains to be covered by a complete sexual ethic, but I do not think we can say anything very positive until we have more experience, both of the effects of various systems and of the changes resulting from a rational education in matters of sex. It is clear that marriage, as an institution, should only interest the state because of children and should be viewed as a purely private matter so long as it is childless. It is clear, also, that, even where there are children, the state is only interested through the duties of fathers, which are chiefly financial. Where divorce is easy, as in Scandinavia, the children usually go with the mother, so that the patriarchal family tends to disappear. If, as is increasingly happening where wage earners are concerned, the state takes over the duties that have hitherto fallen upon fathers, marriage will cease to have any *raison d'être* and will probably be no longer customary except among the rich and the religious.

In the meantime, it would be well if men and women could remember, in sexual relations, in marriage, and in divorce, to practice the ordinary virtues of tolerance, kindness, truthfulness, and justice. Those who, by conventional standards, are sexually virtuous too often consider themselves thereby absolved from behaving like decent human beings. Most moralists have been so obsessed by sex that they have laid much too little emphasis on other more socially useful kinds of ethically commendable conduct.

Part Four

Marriage and Divorce

Introduction

In 1929 Russell wrote: "Very few men or women who have had a conventional upbringing have learned to feel decently about sex and marriage. Their education has taught them that deceitfulness and lying are considered virtues by parents and teachers; that sexual relations, even within marriage, are more or less disgusting, and that in propagating the species men are yielding to their animal nature while women are submitting to a painful duty. This attitude has made marriage unsatisfying both to men and women, and the lack of instinctive satisfaction has turned to cruelty masquerading as morality."[1]

In spite of erroneous opinion to the contrary, Russell had often proselytized in favor of the institution of marriage. "The essence of a good marriage," he wrote, "is respect for each other's personality, combined with that deep intimacy, physical, mental and spiritual, which makes a serious love between man and woman the most fructifying of all human experiences."[2] Russell also believed in the need for marriage, especially for the well-being of any children that could possibly be involved. However, he offered some unconventional qualifications to the then-current view of matrimony. He felt that trial marriages were in some cases desirable, that both the husband and the wife should have premarital sexual experiences, and that an occasional affair by either the husband or the wife should not necessarily be grounds for divorce.

Although Russell's views on marriage, sexual morality, and divorce would seem quite ordinary, if not benign, by today's standards, in Russell's day such suggestions aroused fierce controversy.

Russell's best-selling book *Marriage and Morals,* first published

231

in 1929, created such a storm of protest that Dr. William T. Manning, the Episcopal Bishop of New York, condemned the invitation extended to Russell to lecture at nine American schools and colleges. Manning saw these invitations as evidence of a world-wide anti-Christian conspiracy and persuaded, among others, Nicholas Murray Butler, the president of Columbia University, to withdraw that institution's invitation to Russell. In agreeing to this action, Butler appeared to have forgotten that, in 1915, he had awarded Russell the Nicholas Murray Butler gold medal, in recognition of his outstanding contributions to philosophy.

By 1931 Russell had achieved in America much the same notoriety that Sigmund Freud had reached in Vienna. In 1940 he was offered a professorship at the City College of New York to teach a graduate course in logic and mathematics; once again the ire of Bishop Manning was aroused. In that now-famous controversy, Russell's appointment was legally revoked on the grounds that he was morally unfit to teach. Similar reactions occurred elsewhere, and for a time Russell was subject to an almost complete boycott throughout the United States. This attitude was in marked contrast to the enthusiastic reception accorded *Marriage and Morals* by the majority of New York reviewers. Typical of the latter view was a description of the book as "the most humane and persuasive volume in the recent books on marriage."[3]

Late in life, Russell admitted to mixed feelings about his writings on marriage. He wrote: "I do not know what I think now about the subject of marriage. There seems to be insuperable objections to every general theory about it. Perhaps easy divorce causes less unhappiness than any other system, but I am no longer capable of being dogmatic on the subject of marriage."[4]

NOTES

1. Bertrand Russell. *Marriage and Morals* (London: George Allen & Unwin, 1929), pp. 80-81.

2. "Marriage and Morals," this volume p. 271

3. Barry Feinberg and Ronald Kasrils (ed.). *Bertrand Russell's America: His Transatlantic Travels and Writings*. Volume One. (London: George Allen & Unwin, 1973), p. 113.

4. Bertrand Russell. *The Autobiography of Bertrand Russell: 1914-1944* (Boston: Little, Brown & Company, 1968), p. 228.

18

Marriage and the Population Question

This essay on marriage, written during the height of the First World War when Russell became actively concerned about social reform, contains his earliest published call for the reform of the institution of marriage, which at that time was heavily dominated by the teaching of the church and a Victorian outlook. Here, Russell speaks out against a state of affairs that allowed a widespread but very flimsy hypocrisy, involving many infractions of the code.

Russell begins by addressing two questions: First, how does marriage affect the development and character of those who become married? and second, what is the influence of marriage on the propagation and education of children?

In addition, he discusses the oppression of married women at the time—a situation in which the husband reigned supreme and the wife was relegated to the status of being little more than a willing slave unable to pursue any fulfilling interests outside of her marital obligations.

The influence of the Christian religion on daily life has decayed very rapidly throughout Europe during the last hundred years. Not only has the proportion of nominal believers declined, but even among those who believe the intensity and dogmatism of belief is enormously diminished. But there is one social institution which is still profoundly affected by the Christian tradition—I mean the institution of marriage. The law and public opinion as regards marriage are dominated even now to a very great extent by the teachings of the Church, which continue to influence in this way the lives of men, women, and children in their most intimate concerns.

It is marriage as a political institution that I wish to consider, not marriage as a matter for the private morality of each individual.

Originally published in *The International Journal of Ethics* 26 (July 1916): 443-61.

Marriage is regulated by law, and is regarded as a matter in which the community has a right to interfere. It is only the action of the community in regard to marriage that I am concerned to discuss: whether the present action furthers the life of the community, and if not, in what ways it ought to be changed.

There are two questions to be asked in regard to any marriage system: first, how it affects the development and character of the men and women concerned; secondly, what is its influence on the propagation and education of children. These two questions are entirely distinct, and a system may well be desirable from one of these two points of view when it is very undesirable from the other. I propose first to describe the present English law and public opinion and practice in regard to the relations of the sexes, then to consider their effects as regards children, and finally to consider how these effects, which are bad, could be obviated by a system which would also have a better influence on the character and development of men and women.

The law in England is based upon the expectation that the great majority of marriages will be lifelong. A marriage can only be dissolved if either the wife or the husband, but not both, can be proved to have committed adultery. In case the husband is the "guilty party," he must also be guilty of cruelty or desertion. Even when these conditions are fulfilled, in practice only the well-to-do can be divorced, because the expense is very great.[1] A marriage cannot be dissolved for insanity or crime, or for cruelty, however abominable, or for desertion, or for adultery by both parties; and it cannot be dissolved for any cause whatever if both husband and wife have agreed that they wish it dissolved. In all the cases the law regards the man and woman as bound together for life. A special official, the King's Proctor, is employed to prevent divorce when there is collusion and when both parties have committed adultery.[2]

This interesting system embodies the opinions held by the Church of England some fifty years ago, and by most Nonconformists then and now. It rests upon the assumption that adultery is sin, and that when this sin has been committed by one party to the marriage, the other is entitled to revenge if he is rich. But when both have committed the same sin, or when the one who has not committed it feels no righteous anger, the right to revenge does not exist. As soon as this point of view is understood, the law, which at first seems somewhat strange, is seen to be perfectly consistent. It rests, broadly speaking, upon four propositions: (1) that sexual intercourse outside marriage is sin; (2) that resentment of adultery by the "innocent" party is a righteous horror of wrong-doing; (3) that this resentment, but nothing else, may be rightly regarded as making a common life impossible; (4) that the poor have no right to fine feelings. The Church of England, under the influence of the High Church, has ceased to believe the third of these propositions, but it still believes the first and second, and does nothing actively to show that it disbelieves the fourth.

The penalty for infringing the marriage law is partly financial, but depends mainly upon public opinion. A rather small section of the public genuinely believes that sexual relations outside marriage are wicked; those who believe this are naturally kept in ignorance of the conduct of friends who feel otherwise, and are able to go through life not knowing how others live or what others think. This small section of the public regards as depraved not only actions, but opinions, which are contrary to its principles. It is able to control the professions of politicians through its influence on elections, and the votes of the House of Lords through the presence of the Bishops. By these means it governs legislation, and makes any change in the marriage law almost impossible. It is able, also, to secure in most cases that a man who openly infringes the marriage law shall be dismissed from his employment or ruined by the defection of his customers or clients. A doctor or lawyer, or a tradesman in a country town, cannot make a living, nor can a politician be in Parliament, if he is publicly known to be "immoral." Whatever a man's own conduct may be, he is not likely to defend publicly those who have been branded, lest some of the odium should fall on him. Yet so long as a man has not been branded, few men will object to him, whatever they may know privately of his behavior in these respects.

Owing to the nature of the penalty, it falls very unequally upon different professions. An actor or journalist usually escapes all punishment. An urban working man can almost always do as he likes. A man of private means, unless he wishes to take part in public life, need not suffer at all if he has chosen his friends suitably. Women, who formerly suffered more than men, now suffer less, since there are large circles in which no social penalty is inflicted, and a very rapidly increasing number of women who do not believe the conventional code. But for the majority of men outside the working classes the penalty is still sufficiently severe to be prohibitive.

The result of this state of things is a widespread but very flimsy hypocrisy, which allows many infractions of the code, and forbids

only those which must become public. A man may not live openly
with a woman who is not his wife, an unmarried woman may not
have a child, and neither man nor woman may get into the divorce
court. Subject to these restrictions, there is in practice a very great
freedom. It is this practical freedom which makes the state of the
law seem tolerable to those who do not accept the principles upon
which it is based. What has to be sacrificed to propitiate the holders
of strict views is not pleasure, but only children and a common life
and truth and honesty. It cannot be supposed that this is the result
desired by those who maintain the code, but equally it cannot be
denied that this is the result which they do in fact achieve. Extramatrimonial relations which do not lead to children and are accompanied by a certain amount of deceit remain unpunished, but severe
penalties fall on those which are honest or lead to children.

Within marriage, the expense of children leads to continually
greater limitation of families. The limitation is greatest among those
who have the most sense of parental responsibility and most wish
to educate their children well, since it is to them that the expense of
children is most severe. But although the economic motive for limiting families has hitherto probably been the strongest, it is being
continually reinforced by another. Women are acquiring freedom—
not merely outward and formal freedom, but inward freedom, enabling them to think and feel genuinely, not according to received
maxims. To the men who have prated confidently of women's natural instincts, the result would be very surprising if they were aware
of it. Very large numbers of women, when they are sufficiently free
to think for themselves, do not desire to have children, or at most
desire one child in order not to miss the experience which a child
brings. There are women who are intelligent and active-minded who
resent the slavery to the body which is involved in having children.
There are ambitious women, who desire a career which leaves no
time for children. There are women who love pleasure and gaiety,
and women who love the admiration of men; such women will at
least postpone childbearing until their youth is past. All these
classes of women are rapidly becoming more numerous, and it may
be safely assumed that their numbers will continue to increase for
many years to come.

It is too soon to judge with any confidence as to the effects of
women's freedom upon private life and upon the life of the nation.
But I think it is not too soon to see that it will be profoundly different from the effect expected by the pioneers of the women's

movement. Men have invented, and women in the past have often accepted, a theory that women are the guardians of the race, that their life centers in motherhood, that all their instincts and desires are directed, consciously or unconsciously, to this end. Tolstoy's Natacha illustrates this theory: she is charming, gay, liable to passion, until she is married; then she becomes merely a virtuous mother, without any mental life. This result has Tolstoy's entire approval. It must be admitted that it is very desirable from the point of view of the nation, whatever we may think of it in relation to private life. It must also be admitted that it is probably common among women who are physically vigorous and not highly civilized. But in countries like France and England it is becoming increasingly rare. More and more women find motherhood unsatisfying, not what their needs demand. And more and more, there comes to be a conflict between their personal development and the future of the community. It is difficult to know what ought to be done to mitigate this conflict, but I think it is worthwhile to see what are likely to be its effects if it is not mitigated.

Owing to the combination of economic prudence with the increasing freedom of women, there is at present a selective birth rate of a very singular kind.[3] In France the population is practically stationary, and in England it is rapidly becoming so; this means that some sections are dwindling while others are increasing. Unless some change occurs, the sections that are dwindling will practically become extinct, and the population will be almost wholly replenished from the sections that are now increasing.[4] The sections that are dwindling include the whole middle-class and the skilled artisans. The sections that are increasing are the very poor, the shiftless and drunken, the feeble-minded—feeble-minded women, especially, are apt to be very prolific. There is an increase in those sections of the population which still actively believe the Catholic religion, such as the Irish and the Bretons, because the Catholic religion forbids limitation of families. Within the classes that are dwindling, it is the best elements that are dwindling most rapidly. Working-class boys of exceptional ability rise, by means of scholarships, into the professional class; they naturally desire to marry into the class to which they belong by education, not into the class from which they spring; but as they have no money beyond what they earn, they cannot marry young, or afford a large family. The result is that in each generation the best elements are extracted from the working classes and artificially sterilized, at least in comparison with those who are left. In the professional classes the young women who have initiative, energy, or intelligence are as a rule not inclined to marry young, or to have more than one or two children when they do marry. Marriage has been in the past the only obvious means of livelihood for women; pressure from parents and fear of becoming an old maid combined to force many women to marry in spite of a complete absence of inclination for the duties of a wife. But now a young woman of ordinary intelligence can easily earn her own living, and can acquire freedom and experience without the permanent ties of a husband and a family of children. The result is that if she marries she marries late.

For these reasons, if an average sample of children were taken out of the population of England, and their parents were examined, it would be found that prudence, energy, intellect, and enlightenment were less common among the parents than in the population in general; while shiftlessness, feeble-mindedness, stupidity, and superstition were more common than in the population in general. It would be found that those who are prudent or energetic or intelligent or enlightened actually fail to reproduce their own numbers; that is to say, they do not on the average have as many as two children each who survive infancy. On the other hand, those who have the opposite qualities have, on the average, more than two children each, and more than reproduce their own numbers.

It is impossible to estimate the effect which this will have upon the character of the population without a much greater knowledge of heredity than exists at present. But so long as children continue to live with their parents, parental example and early education must have a great influence in developing their character, even if we leave heredity entirely out of account. Whatever may be thought of genius, there can be no doubt that intelligence, whether through heredity or through education, tends to run in families, and that the decay of the families in which it is common must lower the mental standard of the population. It seems unquestionable that if our economic system and our moral standards remain unchanged, there will be, in the next two or three generations, a rapid change for the worse in the character of the population in all civilized countries, and an actual diminution of numbers in the most civilized.

The diminution of numbers, in all likelihood, will rectify itself in time through the elimination of those characteristics which at present lead to a small birth-rate. Men and women who can still believe the Catholic faith will have a biological advantage; gradually a race will grow up which will be impervious to all the assaults of reason, and will believe imperturbably that limitation of families leads to hell-fire. Women who have mental interests, who care about art or literature or politics, who desire a career or who value their liberty, will gradually grow rarer, and be more and more replaced by a placid maternal type which has no interests outside the home and no dislike of the burden of motherhood. This result, which ages of masculine domination have vainly striven to achieve, is likely to be the final outcome of women's emancipation and of their attempt to enter upon a wider sphere than that to which the jealousy of men confined them in the past.

Perhaps, if the facts could be ascertained, it would be found that something of the same kind occurred in the Roman Empire. The decay of energy and intelligence during the second, third, and fourth centuries of our era has always remained more or less mysterious. But there is reason to think that then, as now, the best elements of the population in each generation failed to reproduce themselves, and that the least vigorous were, as a rule, those to whom the continuance of the race was due. One might be tempted to suppose that civilization, when it has reached a certain height, becomes unstable, and tends to decay through some inherent weakness, some failure to adapt the life of instinct to the intense mental life of a period of high culture. But such vague theories have always something glib and superstitious which makes them worthless as scientific explanations or as guides to action. It is not by a literary formula, but by detailed and complex thought, that a true solution is to be found.

Let us first be clear as to what we desire. There is no importance in an increasing population; on the contrary, if the population of Europe were stationary, it would be much easier to promote economic reform and to avoid war. What is regrettable *at present* is not the decline of the birth-rate in itself, but the fact that the decline is greatest in the best elements of the population. There is reason, however, to fear in the future three bad results: first, an absolute decline in the numbers of English, French, and Germans; secondly, as a consequence of this decline, their subjugation by less civilized races and the extinction of their tradition; thirdly, a revival of their numbers on a much lower plane of civilization, after generations of selection of those who have neither intelligence nor foresight. If this result is to be avoided, the present unfortunate selectiveness of the birth-rate must be somehow stopped.

The problem is one which applies to the whole of Western civilization. There is no difficulty in discovering a theoretical solution, but there is great difficulty in persuading men to adopt a solution in practice, because the effects to be feared are not immediate and the subject is one upon which people are not in the habit of using their reason. If a rational solution is ever adopted, the cause will probably be international rivalry. It is obvious that if one State—say Germany—adopted a rational means of dealing with the matter, it would acquire an enormous advantage over other States unless they did likewise. After the war, it is possible that population questions will attract more attention than they did before, and it is likely that they will be studied from the point of view of international rivalry. This motive, unlike reason and humanity, is perhaps strong enough to overcome men's objections to a scientific treatment of the birth-rate.

In the past, at most periods and in most societies, the instincts of men and women led of themselves to a more than sufficient birth-rate; Malthus's statement of the population question had been true enough up to the time when he wrote. It is still true of barbarous and semi-civilized races, and of the worst elements among civilized races. But it has become false as regards the more civilized half of the population in Western Europe and America. Among them, instinct no longer suffices to keep numbers even stationary.

We may sum up the reasons for this in order of importance, as follows:

1. The expense of children is very great if parents are conscientious.

2. An increasing number of women desire to have no children, or only one or two, in order not to be hampered in their own careers.

3. Owing to the excess of women, a large number of women remain unmarried. These women, though not debarred in practice from relations with men, are debarred by the code from having children. In this class are to be found an enormous and increasing number of women who earn their own living as typists, in shops, or otherwise. The war has opened many employments to women from which they were formerly excluded, and this change is probably only in part temporary.

If the sterilizing of the best parts of the population is to be arrested, the first and most pressing necessity is the removal of the economic motives for limiting families. The expense of children ought to be borne wholly by the community. Their food and clothing and education ought to be provided, not only to the very poor as a matter of charity, but to all classes as a matter of public interest. In addition to this, a woman who is capable of earning money, and who abandons wage-earning for motherhood, ought to receive from the State as nearly as possible what she would have received if she had not had children. The only condition attached to State maintenance of the mother and the children should be that both parents are physically and mentally sound in all ways likely to affect the children. Those who are not sound should not be debarred from having children, but should continue, as at present, to bear the expense of children themselves.

It ought to be recognized that the law is only concerned with marriage through the question of children, and should be indifferent to what is called "morality," which is based upon custom and texts of the Bible, not upon any real consideration of the needs of the community. The excess women, who at present are in every way discouraged from having children, ought no longer to be discouraged. If the State is to undertake the expense of children, it has the right, on eugenic grounds, to know who the father is, and to demand a certain stability in a union. But there is no reason to demand or expect a lifelong stability, or to exact any ground for divorce beyond mutual consent. This would make it possible for the women who must at present remain unmarried to have children if they wished it. In this way an enormous and unnecessary waste would be prevented, and a great deal of needless unhappiness would be avoided.

There is no necessity to begin such a system all at once. It might be begun tentatively with certain exceptionally desirable sections of the community. It might then be extended gradually, with the experience of its working which had been derived from the first experiment. If the birth-rate were very much increased, the eugenic conditions exacted might be made more strict.

There are of course various practical difficulties in the way of such a scheme: the opposition of the Church and the upholders of traditional morality, the fear of weakening parental responsibility, and the expense. All these, however, might be overcome. But there remains one difficulty which it seems impossible to overcome completely in England, and that is, that the whole conception is antidemocratic, since it regards some men as better than others, and would demand that the State should bestow a better education upon the children of some men than upon the children of others. This is contrary to all the principles of progressive politics in England. For this reason it can hardly be expected that any such method of dealing with the population question will ever be adopted in its entirety of this country. Something of the sort may well be done in Germany, and if so, it will assure German hegemony as no merely military victory could do. But among ourselves we can only hope to see it adopted in some partial, piecemeal fashion, and probably only after a change in the economic structure of society which will remove most of the artificial inequalities that progressive parties are rightly trying to diminish.

So far we have been considering the question of the reproduction of the race, rather than the effect of sex relations in fostering or hindering the development of men and women. From the point of view of the race, what seems needed is a complete removal of the economic burdens due to children from all parents who are not physically or mentally unfit, and as much freedom in the law as is compatible with public knowledge of paternity. Exactly the same changes seemed called for when the question is considered from the point of view of the men and women concerned.

In regard to marriage, as with all the other traditional bonds between human beings, a very extraordinary change is taking place, wholly inevitable, wholly necessary as a stage in the development of a new life, but by no means wholly satisfied until it is completed. All the traditional bonds were based on *authority*—of the king, the feudal baron, the priest, the father, the husband. All these bonds, just because they were based on authority, are dissolved, and the creation of other bonds to take their place is as yet very incomplete. For this reason human relations have at present an unusual triviality, and do less than they did formerly to break down the hard walls of the Ego.

The ideal of marriage in the past depended upon the authority of the husband, which was admitted as a right by the wife. The husband was free, the wife was a willing slave. In all matters which concerned husband and wife jointly, it was taken for granted that the husband's fiat should be final. The wife was expected to be faithful, while the husband, except in very religious societies, was only expected to throw a decent veil over his infidelities. Families could not be limited except by continence, and a wife had no recognized right to demand continence, however she might suffer from frequent children.

So long as the husband's right to authority was unquestioningly believed by both men and women, this system was fairly satisfactory, and afforded to both a certain instinctive fulfillment which is rarely achieved among educated people now. Only one will, the husband's, had to be taken into account, and there was no need of the difficult adjustments required when common decisions have to be reached by two equal wills. The wife's desires were not treated seriously enough to enable them to thwart the husband's needs, and the wife, unless she was exceptionally selfish, did not seek self-development, or see in marriage anything but an opportunity for duties. Since she did not seek or expect much happiness, she suffered less, when happiness was not attained, than a woman does now: her suffering contained no element of indignation or surprise, and did not readily turn into bitterness and sense of injury.

The saintly, self-sacrificing woman whom our ancestors praised had her place in a certain organic conception of society, the conception of the ordered hierarchy of authorities which dominated the Middle Ages. She belongs to the same order of ideas as the faithful servant, the loyal subject, and the orthodox son of the Church. This whole order of ideas has vanished from the civilized world, and it is to be hoped that it has vanished for ever, in spite of the fact that the society which it produced was vital and in some ways full of nobility. The old order has been destroyed by the new ideals of justice and liberty, beginning with religion, passing on to politics, and reaching at last the private relations of marriage and the family. When once the question has been asked, "Why should a woman submit to a man?" when once the answers derived from tradition and the Bible have ceased to satisfy, there is no longer any possibility of maintaining the old subordination. To every man who has the power of thinking impersonally and freely, it is obvious, as soon as the question is asked, that the rights of women are precisely the same as the rights of men. Whatever dangers and difficulties, whatever temporary chaos, may be incurred in the transition to equality, the claims of reason are so insistent and so clear that no opposition to them can hope to be long successful.

Mutual liberty, which is now demanded, is making the old form of marriage impossible. But a new form, which shall be an equally good vehicle for instinct, and an equal help to spiritual growth, has not yet been developed. For the present, women who are conscious of liberty as something to be preserved are also conscious of the difficulty of preserving it. The wish for mastery is an ingredient in most men's sexual passions, especially in those which are strong and serious. It survives in many men whose theories are entirely opposed to despotism. The result is a fight for liberty on the one side and for life on the other. Women feel that they must protect their individuality; men feel, often very dumbly, that the repression of instinct which is demanded of them is incompatible with vigor and initiative. The clash of these opposing moods makes all real mingling of personalities impossible; the man and woman remain hard, separate units, continually asking themselves whether anything of value to themselves is resulting from the union. The effect is that relations tend to become trivial and temporary, a pleasure rather than the satisfaction of a profound need, an excitement, not an attainment. The fundamental loneliness into which we are born remains untouched, and the hunger for inner companionship remains unappeased.

No cheap and easy solution of this trouble is possible. It is a trouble which affects most the most civilized men and women, and is an outcome of the increasing sense of individuality which springs inevitably from mental progress. I doubt if there is any radical cure except in some form of religion, so firmly and sincerely believed as to dominate even the life of instinct. The individual is not the end and aim of his own being: outside the individual, there is the community, the future of mankind, the immensity of the universe in which all our hopes and fears are a mere pin-point. A man and woman with reverence for the spirit of life in each other, with an equal sense of their own unimportance beside the whole life of man, may become comrades without interference with liberty, and may achieve the union of instinct without doing violence to the life of mind and spirit. As religion dominated the old form of marriage, so religion must dominate the new. But it must be a new religion based upon liberty, justice, and love, not upon authority and law and hell-fire.

A bad effect upon the relations of men and women has been produced by the romantic movement, through directing attention to what ought to be an incidental good, not the purpose for which relations exist. Love is what gives intrinsic value to a marriage, and, like art and thought, it is one of the supreme things which make human life worth preserving. But though there is no good marriage without love, the best marriages have a purpose which goes beyond love. The love of two people for each other is too circumscribed, too separate from the community, to be by itself the main purpose of a good life. It is not in itself a sufficient source of activities, it is not sufficiently prospective, to make an existence in which ultimate satisfaction can be found. It brings its great moments, and then its times which are less great, which are unsatisfying because they are less great. It becomes, sooner or later, retrospective, a tomb of dead joys, not a well-spring of new life. This evil is inseparable from any purpose which is to be achieved in a single supreme emotion. The only adequate purposes are those which stretch out into the future, which can never be fully achieved, but are always growing, and infinite with the infinity of human endeavor. And it is only when love is linked to some infinite purpose of this kind that it can have the seriousness and depth of which it is capable.

For the great majority of men and women seriousness in sex relations is most likely to be achieved through children. Children are to most people rather a need than a desire: instinct is as a rule only consciously directed towards what used to lead to children. The desire for children is apt to develop in middle life, when the adventure of one's own experience is past, when the friendships of youth seem less important than they once did, when the prospect of a lonely old age begins to terrify, and the feeling of having no share in the future becomes oppressive. Then those who, while they were young, have had no sense that children would be a fulfillment of their needs, begin to regret their former contempt for the normal, and to envy acquaintances whom before they had thought humdrum. But owing to economic causes it is often impossible for the young, and especially for the best of the young, to have children without sacrificing things of vital importance to their own lives. And so youth passes, and the need is felt too late.

Needs without corresponding desires have grown increasingly common as life has grown more different from that primitive existence from which our instincts are derived, and to which, rather than to that of the present day, they are still very largely adapted. An unsatisfied need produces, in the end, as much pain and as much distortion of character as if it had been associated with a conscious desire. For this reason, as well as for the sake of the race, it is important to remove the present economic inducements to childlessness. There is no necessity whatever to urge parenthood upon those who feel disinclined to it, but there is necessity not to place obstacles in the way of those who have no such disinclination.

In speaking of the importance of preserving seriousness in the relations of men and women, I do not mean to suggest that relations which are not serious are always harmful. Traditional morality has erred by laying stress on what ought not to happen, rather than on what ought to happen. What is important is that men and women should find, sooner or later, the best relation of which their natures

are capable. It is not always possible to know in advance what will
be the best, or to be sure of not missing the best if everything that
can be doubted is rejected. Among primitive races, a man wants a
female, a woman wants a male, and there is no such differentiation
as makes one a much more suitable companion than another. But
with the increasing complexity of disposition that civilized life
brings, it becomes more and more difficult to find the man or woman
who will bring happiness, and more and more necessary to make it
not too difficult to acknowledge a mistake.

The present marriage law is an inheritance from a simpler age,
and is supported, in the main, by unreasoning fears and by contempt for all that is delicate and difficult in the life of the mind.
Owing to the law, large numbers of men and women are condemned,
so far as their ostensible relations are concerned, to the society of an
utterly uncongenial companion, with all the embittering consciousness that escape is practically impossible. In these circumstances,
happier relations with others are often sought, but they have to be
clandestine, without a common life, and without children. Apart
from the great evil of being clandestine, such relations have some
almost inevitable drawbacks. They are liable to emphasize sex unduly, to be exciting and disturbing; and it is hardly possible that
they should bring a real satisfaction of instinct. It is the combination of love, children, and a common life that makes the best
relation between a man and a woman. The law at present confines
children and a common life within the bounds of monogamy, but it
cannot confine love. By forcing many to separate love from children
and a common life, the law cramps their lives, prevents them from
reaching the full measure of their possible development, and inflicts
a wholly unnecessary torture upon those who are not content to
become frivolous.

To sum up: The present state of the law, of public opinion, and
of our economic system is tending to degrade the quality of the race
by making the worst half of the population the parents of more
than half of the next generation. At the same time, women's claim
to liberty is making the old form of marriage a hindrance to the
development of both men and women. A new system is required, if
the European nations are not to degenerate, and if the relations of
men and women are to have the strong happiness and organic
seriousness which belonged to the best marriages in the past. The
new system must be based upon the fact that to produce children is
a service to the community, and ought not to expose parents to

heavy pecuniary penalties. It will have to recognize that neither the law nor public opinion should concern itself with the private relations of men and women, except where children are concerned. It ought to remove the inducements to make relations clandestine and childless. It ought to admit that, although lifelong monogamy is best when it is successful, the increasing complexity of our needs makes it increasingly often a failure for which divorce is the best preventive. Here, as elsewhere, liberty is the basis of political wisdom. And when liberty has been won, what remains to be desired must be left to the conscience and religion of individual men and women.

NOTES

1. There was a provision for suits *in forma pauperis*, but for various reasons this provision was nearly useless; a new and somewhat better provision has recently been made, but is still very far from satisfactory.

2. The following letter (*New Statesman*, December 4, 1915) illustrates the nature of his activities:

DIVORCE AND WAR

To the Editor of the "New Statesman."

Sir,—The following episodes may be of interest to your readers. Under the new facilities for divorce offered to the London poor, a poor woman recently obtained a decree *nisi* for divorce against her husband, who had often covered her body with bruises, infected her with a dangerous disease, and committed bigamy. By this bigamous marriage the husband had ten illegitimate children. In order to prevent this decree being made absolute, the Treasury spent at least £200 of the taxes in briefing a leading counsel and an eminent junior counsel and in bringing about ten witnesses from a city a hundred miles away to prove that this woman had committed causal acts of adultery in 1895 and 1898. The net result is that this woman will probably be forced by destitution into further adultery, and that the husband will be able to treat his mistress exactly as he treated his wife, with impunity, so far as disease is concerned. In nearly every other civilized country the marriage would have been dissolved, the children could have been legitimated by subsequent marriage, and the lawyers employed by the Treasury would not have earned the large fees they did from the community for an achievement which seems to most other lawyers thoroughly anti-social in its effects. If any lawyers really feel that society is benefited by this sort of litigation, why cannot they give their services for nothing, like the lawyers who assisted the wife? If we are to practice economy in war-time, why cannot the King's Proctor be satisfied with a junior counsel only? The fact remains that many persons situated like the husband and wife in question prefer to avoid having illegitimate children, and the birth-rate accordingly suffers.

The other episode is this: A divorce was obtained by Mr. A. against Mrs. A. and Mr. B. Mr. B. was married and Mrs. B., on hearing of the divorce proceedings, obtained a decree *nisi* against Mr. B. Mr. B. is at any moment liable to be called to the Front, but Mrs. B. has for some months declined to make the decree *nisi* absolute, and this prevents him marrying Mrs. A., as he feels in honor bound to do. Yet the law allows any petitioner, male or female, to obtain a decree *nisi* and to refrain from making it abso-lute for motives which are probably discreditable. The Divorce Law Com-missioners strongly condemned this state of things, and the hardship in question is immensely aggravated in war-time, just as the war has given rise to many cases of bigamy owing to the chivalrous desire of our soldiers to obtain for the *de facto* wife and family the separation allowance of the State. The legal wife is often united by similar ties to another man. I com-mend these facts to consideration in your columns, having regard to your frequent complaints of a falling birth-rate. The iniquity of our marriage laws is an important contributory cause to the fall in question.

Yours, etc.,
E. S. P. HAYNES

November 29th.

3. Some interesting facts were given by Mr. Sidney Webb in two letters to *The Times,* October 11 and 16, 1906; there is also a Fabian tract on the subject: "The Decline in the Birth-Rate," by Sidney Webb (No. 131). Some further information may be found in "The Declining Birth-Rate: Its Na-tional and International Significance," by A. Newsholme, M.D., M.R.C.S. (Cassell, 1911).

4. The fall in the death-rate, and especially in the infant mortality, which has occurred concurrently with the fall in the birth-rate, has hitherto been sufficiently great to allow the population of Great Britain to go on increasing. But there are obvious limits to the fall of the death rate, whereas the birth-rate might easily fall to a point which would make an actual diminution of numbers unavoidable.

19

The Ostrich Code of Morals:
Is Companionate Marriage Moral?

"The Ostrich Code of Morals" centered around a debate given to the American Public Forum on 3 December 1927 pitting Bertrand Russell against Professor William McDougall on this question: Is trial-marriage moral or immoral? The answer, according to both Russell and McDougall, depends very largely upon what one thinks about conventional marriage. If marriage is nothing more than a simple relationship between a man and a woman, then the morality of trial-marriage rests solely with the consciences of the individuals involved. If, on the other hand, marriage is also a bond with society, then the latter not only can but should condemn as immoral any form of wedlock that disregards the social consequences of marriage. Here, at the very beginning, is where Russell and his opponent part company.

The moral outlook Russell projects in this debate is both rational and humane; he advocates divorce by mutual consent, as well as trial-marriage for young people who are not yet ready to assume the responsibilities of parenthood. He concludes his debate with the hope that with the perpetuation of greater sexual freedom a society of more rational and caring people will emerge. These important remarks on trial-marriage were later elaborated upon to form the core of his book Marriage and Morals *published two years later.*

Even though Russell discussed the subjects of trial-marriage, enlightened sexual ethics, and divorce by mutual consent in a carefully thought-out and socially responsible manner, the ideas expressed in "The Ostrich Code of Morals" started a vast public campaign in the United States against his views.

Originally published as part of a debate titled "Is Companionate Marriage Moral?" in *Forum* vol. 80, no. 1 (July, 1928): 7-10.

Russell, however, was not the only one to encounter fierce opposition for harboring progressive ideas on sexuality and marriage. In the late Twenties, trial-marriages for young people had already been popularly advocated by Denver judge Ben B. Lindsey. Lindsey's writings immediately came under savage attack by fundamentalist clergy and the Ku Klux Klan both of whose efforts succeeded in ousting him from office. In this essay, Russell, who had corresponded with Lindsey over the previous year, began with a tribute to Lindsey "whose courage and humanity I cannot sufficiently admire." Russell continued to communicate with Lindsey and on one occasion wrote: "I am much disgusted by the injustice and persecution to which you have been subjected . . . . I continue to be surprised by the fact that America persecutes Americans for the opinions which it hires foreigners at great expense to express."*

I wish to begin with a tribute to Judge Ben B. Lindsey, whose courage and humanity I cannot sufficently admire. Having long used his office for the unprecedented purpose of promoting human happiness, he has, not unnaturally, been ousted by a combination of sadists of all parties. But what Denver has lost the world has gained. If I understand aright his advocacy of "companionate marriage," his purpose is, in the highest and best sense, conservative, not subversive.

Companionate marriage has two aspects, one legal, the other social. The legal aspect is threefold. First, there is to be recognition of marriages not intended (at first, at any rate) to lead to children, and in such marriages the parties are to be encouraged to obtain the best available information on birth control. Secondly, so long as the marriage remains childless, divorce by mutual consent is to be permitted. Thirdly, the wife is, in general, to have no claim to alimony if the marriage is dissolved. But as soon as there are children the marriage is to become, *ipso facto,* an ordinary marriage.

The social aspect of companionate marriage is a matter of custom and public opinion. At present when a man marries, he expects to support his wife, and she often expects it of him. Whether there are children or not, it is expected that both will behave, from an economic point of view, as if there were. Moreover, they are expected, unless for some serious reason, to live together continuously, so that it is impossible for the wife to have work in a different place

---

*Barry Feinberg and Ronald Kasrils (eds.). *Bertrand Russell's America: His Transatlantic Travels and Writings.* Volume One. (London: George Allen & Unwin, Ltd., 1973), p. 107.

from that in which her husband lives. In companionate marriage these conventional expectations are to be absent. The husband and wife will be together as much as they choose, but no more. Since children are not expected, there is no reason why the wife should not earn her living, and every reason why she should. There will be no interference with each other's work, none of the fuss and flummery which at present make marriage disgusting to young people of spirit, none of the foolish pretense of protection by the male and dependence on the part of the female.

What are the advantages to be expected from the legal and social recognition of such an institution?

The root fact is that few men can afford the usual type of marriage while they are very young. Outside of the wage-earning class, most men wait till they are nearly thirty before undertaking the financial responsibilities involved. But their sexual instinct does not wait. In the old days they found an outlet with prostitutes. Because this was easily concealed, it never troubled the moralists much. Nowadays, young women, for the most part, no longer feel bound to abstain from extramarital intercourse, with the result that unmarried men can have decent relations with women with whom they have much in common mentally—relations not founded upon a cash nexus, but upon mutual affection. It is this that so pains our moralists. For my part, I think it immeasurably better than prostitution. Nevertheless, as it exists at present it still has grave defects—defects due chiefly to the influence of elderly morality upon law and custom.

The great evil in the present system is that the sexual relations of the young have to be surreptitious. This tends to make them frivolous, promiscuous, and unduly exciting, because a quasipermanent relation with one person is harder to conceal than a series of casual and more or less accidental affairs. And the mere fact of concealment, combined with the terror of pregnancy, is very bad morally and nervously. Young people in co-educational colleges are led by this state of affairs to spend far too much time and thought on sex, to the great detriment of their work. It is just as if we could only obtain food by hunting. In the old days when that was true, the pursuit of food took up almost the whole of a man's energy, leaving little over for anything more valuable.

The same thing seems to be happening with regard to sex, owing to the fact that there is no conventionally recognized way in which the young can satisfy their instincts. The pursuit of the female by the male, and the male by the female, occupies far too much time and thought, and in a manner which precludes the higher satisfaction to be derived from sex. It would be far better if young people could live together openly, without interfering with each other's work, without economic ties, without children until they deliberately chose to have children. I have no doubt that the improvement in health, in morals, and in intelligence would be quite enormous if this were rendered possible.

What are the arguments against Judge Lindsey's plan? They are two: objections to birth control, and objections to divorce by mutual consent. Let us take them in turn.

(1) Objections to birth control are, to begin with, hypocritical. Nine-tenths of the married people who publicly object to it do, in fact, practice it. This is evident when we compare the size of families at the present day with the size of families sixty years ago.

(2) Objections to birth control are futile. The young will employ contraceptives whatever the old may say. The only effect of legal obstacles is to cause the employment of bad and unscientific methods, leading to a percentage of failures, generally followed by the highly undesirable practice of abortion. There is also a tendency to cause stupid people to breed faster than intelligent people, so long as some intelligence is required to find out about contraceptives. This leads to a progressive mental deterioration of the race.

(3) It is positively desirable that young people should have experience of sex without at first having children. Abstinence is nervously and mentally undesirable. Children, when the parents are very young, are a financial burden, a barrier to the most useful career, and not likely to be wisely and adequately cared for.

(4) Without birth control, we cannot dispense with the old checks on the increase of population—war, pestilence, and famine. This has been obvious since the time of Malthus. Every opponent of birth control, unless he is incapable of arithmetic, must be assumed to be a supporter of war, pestilence, and famine. In fact, most of them are supporters of war—or at least were so during the Great War.

(5) Thus the practice of birth control should be regarded, not merely as permissible, but as a public duty; and every citizen should be helped to perform this duty.

I come now to divorce by mutual consent. I confess that the objections to this, where there are no children, seem to me to be based wholly on instinctive, unconscious cruelty. The elderly people who make our laws are often no longer capable of sexual pleasure, and are frequently conscious of having missed its best forms when they were young. This leads to a species of envy, and they try to impose a morality which shall prevent the young from being happier than they were. What more admirable method than to say that when two young people have made a mistake of which both are conscious, they shall nevertheless remain tied to each other, and be prevented from escaping except by some act at which moralists can point the finger of scorn?

As Judge Lindsey points out, most divorces are in fact collusive, and are obtained by means of perjury. Is it not ridiculous to inflict all this upon people who wish to part? Was ever anything so absurd as the law which says that a marriage may be dissolved if only one of the parties desires it, but not when both do? What would be thought of such a provision in any other sphere? Suppose, when a man rents a house, the lease could only be terminated when one party desired it and the other did not. Everyone would see the absurdity at once, and would say that of course the lease should be terminable when both parties so desired. It must be understood that in this whole discussion of companionate marriage we are only concerned with childless unions, in which there is no one to be considered except the husband and wife.

The fact is, of course, that the crew of traditional moralists on this whole matter are not rational. Their explicit basis is texts of Scripture and theological dogma; their real basis is envy, cruelty, and love of interference. I hope and believe that the greater sexual freedom now prevailing among the young is bringing into existence a generation less cruel than that which is now old, and that a rational ethic in sex matters will, therefore, during the next twenty years, more and more prevail over the doctrines of taboo and human sacrifice which pass traditionally as "virtue."

20

My Own View of Marriage

In this essay, written in the year preceding the publication of Marriage and Morals, *Russell elaborates on his belief that the conventional view of marriage lacks a rational basis; that the newer absence of morality tends to sweep away all that had real value in the relations of men and women; and that what is needed is a new morality, no less serious than the old, but based upon a truer psychology and a just appreciation of human needs.*

The subject of marriage is a much more complicated one than seems to be generally thought by those who write about it. There are, broadly speaking, two views, both of which are widely held but neither of which appears to me to have any validity. There is the romantic view, embodied in fairy tales, according to which the prince and princess marry and live happy ever after; this is the view which has led to the frequency of divorce, for as soon as the couple are not living happy ever after he comes to the conclusion that it was not the princess and she that it was not really the prince; then each makes another experiment, probably equally unsuccessful. And the reason of the repeated failures is that both have had an entirely impossible conception of what the relation between two people can be.

Then there is the view, expressed with brutal frankness by St. Paul, that "it is better to marry than to burn;" in this view, sexual pleasure is wholly regrettable, but human nature is so weak that few will forego it wholly; marriage, however, can be relied upon to reduce the pleasure to a minimum and to turn husband and wife

Originally published in *The Outlook* 48 (March 7, 1929): 376-77.

into mutual policemen. This view describes itself as the belief that marriage is a sacrament.

Each of these opposing views is too extreme, the one in that it regards pleasure as the end of life, the other since it thinks the same of the prevention of pleasure. Pleasure in itself is a good, but not a very important good, and it cannot satisfactorily be made the end of life because it does not entail progressive activity. To achieve happiness it is necessary to have some end never completely realized, but always in process of realization. Ambition, parental affection, scientific curiosity, artistic creativeness, supply such activities; a man or woman who is absorbed in one of these and is not wholly unsuccessful can achieve a measure of happiness, but a man or woman who lives for pleasurable moments is certain, ultimately, to be the prey of unendurable boredom.

It is in this respect that marriage is distinguished from temporary extramatrimonial relations. Marriage is complicated, owing to the fact that it involves two very diverse elements—the relation of the man and woman to each other, and the relation to their children. (Where there are no children the essence of marriage is absent.) In a happy marriage the husband and wife love each other and their children, and their love for each other is fulfilled, not merely in sex, but in co-operation for their children; this is a motive which in decent people survives at moments when mere pleasure has lost its vividness, or when perhaps some psychological strain has introduced difficulties into the merely personal aspects of the relation. But when marriage is wholly successful, the satisfaction which it affords is extraordinarily complete, since the sexual and parental instincts co-operate to reinforce each other.

It is at the production of such marriages that laws and morals ought to aim. This end is certainly not achieved by the conventional ethics which maintain that two wholly inexperienced people should enter upon an indissoluble relation; to find a person with whom one can live harmoniously through life is not easy, and is all but impossible to the totally inexperienced, who cannot distinguish sex hunger from the deeper affection which will survive satisfaction and be intensified by it. There should, therefore, be experience before marriage, both for men and women; there must also be the possibility of dissolving marriage for grave cause. The conventional view, however, as to what constitutes grave cause is, to my mind, wholly mistaken. Occasional adultery on either side is quite compatible with deep and lasting affection, and if this were generally realized jealousy would not nearly so often wreck the happiness of married people, as it does at present. Jealousy is, of course, rooted in instinct, but the occasions which bring it into play depend very largely upon beliefs and social conventions. What is expected does not cause the same jealousy as what is unexpected, and jealousy becomes far more terrible when it is reinforced by the belief that a sin has been committed. I do not say that the control of jealousy is altogether easy, but it is certainly not more difficult than lifelong faithfulness to one person. It would be absurd to pretend that a happy or decent life is possible without self-control, but I maintain that a large part of the necessary self-control should go into the curbing of jealousy, whereas conventional morality regards jealousy as wholly admirable. I am not, however, advocating unfaithfulness; I am merely advocating a tolerant attitude to it when it occurs.

There are, however, other causes sufficiently grave to call for the dissolution of a marriage in spite of the harm that may be done to children; among the more obvious of these I should mention insanity, crime, and habitual drunkenness. Where such things exist in one partner to a marriage, it is better for the children that that partner should not have access to them. There are other situations in which divorce might be desirable, but they are very difficult to define with legal precision. When the parents hate each other, they are apt to institute a competition for the children's affections; this produces an atmosphere which is almost bound to create grave nervous disorders in the children, for whom, therefore, divorce is as desirable as it is for their parents. I do not quite know how such cases can be brought within the purview of the law except through the vague idea of incompatibility, which amounts, in effect, to divorce by mutual consent. Probably in fact divorce by mutual consent, given a right public opinion, would do less harm than the continuance of a marriage which has become nothing but a legal bondage. It should, however, be recognized that wherever there are children it shows a failure of self-control and a lack of parental responsibility in one, if not both partners, when they cannot so adjust their differences as to co-operate in regard to the welfare of their children.

What is of real importance in a successful marriage is the merging of the ego in a wider unit. That man and wife are one flesh should be something more than a mere phrase; there should be an instinctive physical sympathy as the substructure upon which mental companionship is built. Modern men and women are much too much inclined to a certain hardness and completeness of the ego. In a great many marriages, even when they are not unhappy, there is no profound interpenetration, no merging of the individual life into a wider, more satisfying common existence. It is in this merging that the real excellence of marriage consists, and where it is absent no profound happiness can exist. Although many people resist this breaking down of the walls of self, it is nevertheless a profound human need, and where it is not corrected there will be a sense of dissatisfaction, of which the causes will very likely remain unknown. But where this complete union has been achieved it extends also to the children, towards whom parental love will be free and spontaneous and not tainted with jealousy. This result is not to be achieved without generosity, fearlessness, and passion, three things at which the traditional moralist looks askance. There must be no attempt to fetter one's partner, no fear of the possible pain to which one exposes one's self by a complete abandonment to love, no inhibition of passion as the result of a niggardly morality.

One of the difficulties in all modern civilization is the association of well-regulated and orderly conduct with personal prudence. Personal prudence carried beyond a point is death to all the finer qualities and all the spiritual joys that life has to offer. It is for this reason that all the great mystics have inveighed against it; "cast thy bread upon the waters;" "take no thought for the morrow;" "he that loseth his life shall find it"—all these are condemnations of prudence. Yet it would be impossible to carry through marriage and the care of young children without prudence. I think there is, however, a distinction to be made between the prudence which is personal and concerned with avoiding hurt to one's self, and that other prudence which springs from love and is concerned with avoiding hurt to the object of affection. Personal prudence in marriage means the certainty of missing all that gives importance to marriage as an enrichment of the individual life; but prudence in regard to the welfare of one's children is clearly one of the most imperative duties, though even this may be overridden by some great public need.

The psychological difference between the two kinds of prudence is clear, since one has its root in fear, the other in love; unfortunately, the prudence which is rooted in fear has been much reinforced by conventional morality. We think better of a man who grows rich than of a man who grows poor, of a woman incapable of love than of a woman seduced. In all this our outlook is lacking in courage and magnamimity, and this is at the basis of a very large number of matrimonial troubles. Not infrequently husband and wife begin their married life with a determination on each side to preserve as much privacy as possible, the wife aiming at privacy chiefly in physical matters, the husband in matters concerned with his business; in this way an attitude of mutual antagonism grows up and there is never that complete surrender to a common life out of which alone a true marriage can grow. People have some strange notion that there is something sacred about their individuality, and so they tend to make the sex relation trivial and purely physical instead of being a profound and fructifying union of two whole persons. This may be connected with the individualism that has grown up from the Christian doctrine of personal salvation as opposed to the more primitive belief in the family.

Man is a complex creature, but his life should be built upon a basis of instinct, using this word not in its technical sense, but in the broader sense common in popular usage. Sex, parenthood, and power are the chief instinctive passions, and much harm has come through confused mixtures of the three as well as from an intellectual simplification of each. Each has its penumbra in the emotional life, and, as a source of profound satisfaction, none brings its full possible contribution to human happiness unless it comes with the right surroundings. The impulse to power is obviously the source of political activity, also of the business activities of men who are already rich. It is the source also of the intellectual life; the impulse to knowledge comes primarily from the feeling that knowledge is power.

Parenthood is an impulse quite distinct from sex, as any one may see who will take the trouble to read the Old Testament. It is mainly a desire to escape from death, to leave some portion of one's ego functioning in the world after the death of the rest of the body; but in order for it to be developed to its full extent in women it requires the physical care of the child, and in order to exist in men in any satisfying form it requires certainty as to paternity. This is, of course, the crux in all theories which would relax the rigidity of the marriage bond on the side of women; this also is the justification for male jealousy; but in the practical working out of this problem men have found in their marriage relations an outlet for their impulses to power rather than for their feelings of affection. The psychological problem to be faced, and I do not pretend that it is an easy one, is this: can a man retain any certainty of paternity if marriage is an equal partnership instead of a slavery involving in fact if not in form a more or less Oriental seclusion; or, if this is impossible, will women's demands for freedom lead to a return to the matriarchal system?

I do not think the psychology of modern marriage has as yet been at all worked out, and I foresee a considerable period of difficulty before civilized mankind arrives again at an institution as solid and lasting as the old patriarchal family. Perhaps this stage will never be reached until the state assumes the economic role of the father and the family, as we know it, ceases to exist. I sincerely hope not, for marriage and the family supply elements in life which are very valuable and which nothing else in the modern world can give. Life in its biological aspect is a continuous stream in which the division into different individuals is incidental and unimportant; to realize this aspect of life is to leave the prison of self by one of the many gates into a larger world, and for ninety-nine men and women out of one hundred it is the easiest of these gates.

Sex alone does not have this merit, but only sex in connection with parenthood, for then it becomes something transcending the emotion of the moment and forming part of the stream of life from the beginning to the unknown end. The true education in sexual morality would consist of giving to young people a sense of the importance and dignity of marriage so conceived. The old-fashioned morality had a basis which was not rational, while the newer absence of morality tends to sweep away all that has real value in the relations of men and women; to preserve this we need a new morality, not less serious than the old, but based upon a truer psychology and a just appreciation of human needs.

21

Marriage and Morals

This essay, published as the concluding chapter of Marriage and Morals, *contains Russell's vivid and forceful summation of the most salient points covered in this controversial book. It is largely due to the eloquence of his final remarks that this essay contains some of the most widely quoted passages of Russell's work on marriage and morality.*

In the course of our discussion we have been led to certain conclusions, some historical, some ethical. Historically, we found that sexual morality, as it exists in civilized societies, has been derived from two quite different sources, on the one hand desire for certainty as to fatherhood, on the other an ascetic belief that sex is wicked, except in so far as it is necessary for propagation. Morality in pre-Christian times, and in the Far East down to the present day, had only the former source, except in India and Persia, which are the centers from which asceticism appears to have spread. The desire to make sure of paternity does not, of course, exist in those backward races which are ignorant of the fact that the male has any part in generation. Among them, although masculine jealousy places certain limitations upon female license, women are on the whole much freer than in early patriarchal societies. It is clear that in the transition there must have been considerable friction, and the restraints upon women's freedom were doubtless considered necessary by men who took an interest in being the fathers of their own children. At this stage, sexual morality existed only for women. A man might not commit adultery with a married woman, but otherwise he was free.

From *Marriage and Morals* by Bertrand Russell, pp. 303-320. Copyright © 1929 by George Allen and Unwin. Reprinted by permission of the publisher.

With Christianity, the new motive of avoidance of sin enters in, and the moral standard becomes in theory the same for men as for women, though in practice the difficulty of enforcing it upon men has always led to a greater toleration of their failings than those of women. Early sexual morality had a plain biological purpose, namely to ensure that the young should have the protection of two parents during their early years and not only of one. The purpose was lost sight of in Christian theory, though not in Christian practice.

In quite modern times there have been signs that both the Christian and the pre-Christian parts of sexual morality are undergoing modification. The Christian part has not the hold that it formerly had, because of the decay of religious orthodoxy and the diminishing intensity of belief even among those who still believe. Men and women born during the present century, although their unconscious is apt to retain the old attitudes, do not, for the most part, consciously believe that fornication as such is sin. As for the pre-Christian elements in sexual ethics, these have been modified by one factor, and are in process of being modified by yet another. The first of these factors is the use of contraceptives, which are making it increasingly possible to prevent sexual intercourse from leading to pregnancy, and are therefore enabling women, if unmarried, to avoid children altogether, and if married, to have children only by their husbands, without in either case finding it necessary to be chaste. This process is not yet complete, because contraceptives are not yet wholly reliable, but one may, I think, assume that before very long they will become so. In that case, assurance of paternity will become possible without the insistence that women shall have no sexual intercourse outside marriage. It may be said that women could deceive their husbands on the point, but after all it has been possible from the earliest times for women to deceive their husbands, and the motive for deception is much less strong when the question is merely who shall be the father than when it is whether there shall be intercourse with a person who may be passionately loved. One may, therefore, assume that deceit as to paternity, though it may occasionally occur, will be less frequent than deceit as to adultery has been in the past. It is also by no means impossible that the jealousy of husbands should, by a new convention, adapt itself to the new situation, and arise only when wives propose to choose some other man as the father of their children. In the East, men have always tolerated liberties on the part of eunuchs which most European husbands would resent. They have tolerated them because they introduce no doubt as to paternity. The same kind of toleration might easily be extended to liberties accompanied by the use of contraceptives.

The bi-parental family may, therefore, survive in the future without making such great demands upon the continence of women as it had to make in the past. A second factor, however, in the change which is coming over sexual morals, is liable to have more far-reaching effects. This is the increasing participation of the State in the maintenance and education of children. This factor, so far, operates in Europe more than in America, and affects mainly the wage-earning classes, but they, after all, are a majority of the population, and it is quite likely that the substitution of the State for the father, which is gradually taking place where they are concerned, will ultimately extend to the whole population. The part of the father, in animal families as with the human family, has been to provide protection and maintenance, but in civilized communities protection is provided by the police, and maintenance may come to be provided wholly by the State, so far, at any rate, as the poorer sections of the population are concerned. If that were so, the father would cease to serve any obvious purpose. With regard to the mother, there are two possibilities. She may continue her ordinary work and have her children cared for in institutions, or she may, if the law so decides, be paid by the State to care for her children while they are young. If the latter course is adopted, it may be used for a while to bolster up traditional morality, since a woman who is not virtuous may be deprived of payment. But if she is deprived of payment she will be unable to support her children unless she goes to work, and it will, therefore, be necessary to put her children in some institution. It would seem probable, therefore, that the operation of economic forces may lead to the elimination of the father, and even to a great extent of the mother, in the care of children whose parents are not rich. If so, all the traditional reasons for traditional morality will have disappeared, and new reasons will have to be found for a new morality.

The break-up of the family, if it comes about, will not be, to my mind, a matter for rejoicing. The affection of parents is important to children, and institutions, if they exist on a large scale, are sure to become very official and rather harsh. There will be a terrible degree of uniformity when the differentiating influence of different home environments is removed. And unless an international government is previously established, the children of different countries will be taught a virulent form of patriotism which will make it nearly certain that they will exterminate each other when grown up. The necessity for an international government arises also in regard to population, since in its absence nationalists have a motive for encouraging a greater increase of numbers than is desirable, and, with the progress of medicine and hygiene, the only remaining method of disposing of excessive numbers will be war.

While the sociological questions are often difficult and complicated, the personal questions are, to my mind, quite simple. The doctrine that there is something sinful about sex is one which has done untold harm to individual character—a harm beginning in early childhood and continuing throughout life. By keeping sex love in a prison, conventional morality has done much to imprison all other forms of friendly feeling, and to make men less generous, less kindly, more self-assertive and more cruel. Whatever sexual ethic may come to be ultimately accepted must be free from superstition and must have recognizable and demonstrable grounds in its favor. Sex cannot dispense with an ethic, any more than business or sport or scientific research or any other branch of human activity. But it can dispense with an ethic based solely upon ancient prohibitions propounded by uneducated people in a society wholly unlike our own. In sex, as in economics and in politics, our ethic is still dominated by fears which modern discoveries have made irrational, and the benefit to be derived from those discoveries is largely lost through failure of psychological adaptation to them.

It is true that the transition from the old system to the new has its own difficulties, as all transitions have. Those who advocate any ethical innovation are invariably accused, like Socrates, of being corrupters of youth; nor is this accusation always wholly unfounded, even when in fact the new ethic which they preach would, if accepted in its entirety, lead to a better life than the old ethic which they seek to amend. Every one who knows the Mahometan East asserts that those who have ceased to think it necessary to pray five times a day have also ceased to respect other moral rules which we consider more important. The man who proposes any change in sexual morality is especially liable to be misinterpreted in this way, and I am conscious myself of having said things which some readers may have misinterpreted.

The general principle upon which the newer morality differs from the traditional morality of puritanism is this: we believe that instinct should be trained rather than thwarted. Put in these general terms, the view is one which would win very wide acceptance among modern men and women, but it is one which is fully valid only when accepted with its full implications and applied from the earliest years. If in childhood instinct is thwarted rather than trained, the result may be that it has to be to some extent thwarted throughout later life, because it will have taken on highly undesirable forms as a result of thwarting in early years. The morality which I should advocate does not consist simply of saying to grown-up people or to adolescents: "Follow your impulses and do as you like." There has to be consistency in life; there has to be continuous effort directed to ends that are not immediately beneficial and not at every moment attractive; there has to be consideration for others; and there should be certain standards of rectitude. I should not, however, regard self-control as an end in itself, and I should wish our institutions and our moral conventions to be such as to make the need for self-control a minimum rather than a maximum. The use of self-control is like the use of brakes on a train. It is useful when you find yourself going in the wrong direction, but merely harmful when the direction is right. No one would maintain that a train ought always to be run with the brakes on, yet the habit of difficult self-control has a very similar injurious effect upon the energies available for useful activity. Self-control causes these energies to be largely wasted on internal friction instead of external activity; and on this account it is always regrettable, though sometimes necessary.

The degree to which self-control is necessary in life depends upon the early treatment of instinct. Instincts, as they exist in children, may lead to useful activities or harmful ones, just as the steam in a locomotive may take it toward its destination or into a siding where it is smashed by an accident. The function of education is to guide instinct into the directions in which it will develop useful rather than harmful activities. If this task has been adequately performed in early years, a man or woman will, as a rule, be able to live a useful life without the need of severe self-control, except, perhaps, at a few rare crises. If on the other hand early education has consisted in a mere thwarting of instinct, the acts to which instinct prompts in later life will be partly harmful, and will therefore have to be continually restrained by self-control.

These general considerations apply with peculiar force to sexual impulses, both because of their great strength and because of the fact that traditional morality has made them its peculiar concern. Most traditional moralists appear to think that, if our sexual impulses were not severely checked, they would become trivial, anarchic and gross. I believe this view to be derived from observation of those who have acquired the usual inhibitions from their early years and have subsequently attempted to ignore them. But in such men the early prohibitions are still operative even when they do not succeed in prohibiting. What is called conscience, that is to say the unreasoning and more or less unconscious acceptance of precepts learnt in early youth, causes men still to feel that whatever the conventions prohibit is wrong, and this feeling may persist in spite of intellectual convictions to the contrary. It thus produces a personality divided against itself, one in which instinct and reason no longer go hand in hand, but instinct has become trivial and reason has become anemic. One finds in the modern world various different degrees of revolt against conventional teaching. The commonest of all is the revolt of the man who intellectually acknowledges the ethical truth of the morality he was taught in youth, but confesses, with a more or less unreal regret, that he is not sufficiently heroic to live up to it. For such a man there is little to be said. It would be better that he should alter either his practice or his beliefs in such a way as to bring harmony between them. Next comes the man whose conscious reason has rejected much that he learnt in the nursery, but whose unconscious still accepts it in its entirety. Such a man will suddenly change his line of conduct under the stress of any strong emotion, especially fear. A serious illness or an earthquake may cause him to repent and to abandon his intellectual convictions as the result of an upbrush of infantile beliefs. Even at ordinary times his behavior will be inhibited, and the inhibitions may take an undesirable form. They will not prevent him from acting in ways that are condemned by traditional morals, but they will prevent him from doing so in a whole-hearted way, and will thus eliminate from his actions some of the elements that would have given them value. The substitution of a new moral code for the old one can never be completely satisfactory unless the new one is accepted with the whole personality, not only with that top layer which constitutes our conscious thought. To most people this is very difficult if throughout their early years they have been exposed to the old morality. It is therefore impossible to judge a new morality fairly until it has been applied in early education.

Sex morality has to be derived from certain general principles, as to which there is perhaps a fairly wide measure of agreement, in spite of the wide disagreement as to the consequences to be drawn from them. The first thing to be secured is that there should be as much as possible of that deep, serious love between man and woman which embraces the whole personality of both and leads to a fusion by which each is enriched and enhanced. The second thing of importance is that there should be adequate care of children, physical and psychological. Neither of these principles in itself can be considered in any way shocking, yet it is as a consequence of these two principles that I should advocate certain modifications of the conventional code. Most men and women, as things stand, are incapable of being as whole-hearted and as generous in the love that they bring to marriage as they would be if their early years had been less hedged about with taboos. They either lack the necessary experience, or they have gained it in furtive and undesirable ways. Moreover, since jealousy has the sanction of moralists, they feel justified in keeping each other in a mutual prison. It is, of course, a very good thing when a husband and wife love each other so completely that neither is ever tempted to unfaithfulness; it is not, however, a good thing that unfaithfulness, if it does occur, should be treated as something terrible, nor is it desirable to go so far as to make all friendship with persons of the other sex impossible. A good life cannot be founded upon fear, prohibition, and mutual interference with freedom. Where faithfulness is achieved without these, it is good, but where all this is necessary it may well be that too high a price has been paid, and that a little mutual toleration of occasional lapses would be better. There can be no doubt that mutual jealousy, even where there is physical faithfulness, often causes more unhappiness in a marriage than would be caused if there were more confidence in the ultimate strength of a deep and permanent affection.

The obligations of parents toward children are treated far more lightly than seems to me right by many persons who consider themselves virtuous. Given the present system of the biparental family, as soon as there are children it is the duty of both parties to a marriage to do everything that they can to preserve harmonious relations, even if this requires considerable self-control. But the control required is not merely, as conventional moralists pretend, that involved in restraining every impulse to unfaithfulness; it is just as important to control impulses to jealousy, ill-temper, masterfulness, and so on. There can be no doubt that serious quarrels between parents are a very frequent cause of nervous disorders in children; therefore whatever can be done to prevent such quarrels should be done. At the same time, where one or both parties have not sufficient self-control to prevent disagreements from coming to the knowledge of the children, it may well be better that the marriage should be dissolved. It is by no means the case that the dissolution of a marriage is invariably the worst thing possible from the point of view of the children; indeed it is not nearly so bad as the spectacle of raised voices, furious accusations, perhaps even violence, to which many children are exposed in bad homes.

It must not be supposed that the sort of thing which a sane advocate of greater freedom desires is to be achieved at once by leaving adults, or even adolescents, who have been brought up under the old severe restrictive maxims, to the unaided promptings of the damaged impulses which are all the moralists have left to them. This is a necessary stage, since otherwise they will bring up their children as badly as they were brought up; but it is no more than a stage. Sane freedom must be learnt from the earliest years, since otherwise the only freedom possible will be a frivolous, superficial freedom, not freedom of the whole personality. Trivial impulses will lead to physical excesses, while the spirit remains in fetters. Instinct rightly trained from the first can produce something much better than what results from an education inspired by a Calvinistic belief in original sin, but when such an education has been allowed to do its evil work, it is exceedingly difficult to undo the effect in later years. One of the most important benefits which psycho-analysis has conferred upon the world is its discovery of the bad effects of prohibitions and threats in early childhood; to undo this effect may require all the time and technique of a psycho-analytic treatment. This is true not only of those obvious neurotics who have suffered damage visible to every one; it is true also of most apparently normal people. I believe that nine out of ten of those who have had a conventional upbringing in their early years have become in some degree incapable of a decent and sane attitude toward marriage and sex generally. The kind of attitude and behavior that I should regard as the best has been rendered impossible for such people; the best that can be done is to make them aware of the damage that they have sustained and to persuade them to abstain from maiming their children in the same way in which they have been maimed.

The doctrine that I wish to preach is not one of license; it involves exactly as much self-control as is involved in the conventional doctrine. But self-control will be applied more to abstaining from interference with the freedom of others than to restraining one's own freedom. It may, I think, be hoped that with the right education from the start this respect for the personality and freedom of others may become comparatively easy; but for those of us who have been brought up to believe that we have a right to place a veto upon the actions of others in the name of virtue, it is undoubtedly difficult to forgo the exercise of this agreeable form of persecution. It may even be impossible. But it is not to be inferred that it would be impossible to those who had been taught from the first a less restrictive morality. The essence of a good marriage is respect for each other's personality combined with that deep intimacy, physical, mental, and spiritual, which makes a serious love between man and woman the most fructifying of all human experiences. Such love, like everything that is great and precious, demands its own morality, and frequently entails a sacrifice of the less to the greater; but such sacrifice must be voluntary, for, where it is not, it will destroy the very basis of the love for the sake of which it is made.

22

Is Modern Marriage a Failure?

In 1930, one year after the publication of his best-selling book, Marriage and Morals, *Russell was invited to debate John Cowper Powys on the topic "Is Modern Marriage a Failure?" This speech, in which Russell asserted that the institution of marriage was declining and that "complete fidelity was not to be expected in most marriages" (which is not to say that Russell advocated infidelity), was to provide the grounds for the vicious campaign brought against his appointment to the City College of New York in 1940.*

BERTRAND RUSSELL

Ladies and Gentlemen: The proposition which I have to maintain is that modern marriage is a failure. Now I know that that is a much more difficult proposition to secure your assent to than the proposition that Mr. Powys is going to maintain. For after all either you are not married or you are. Those of you who are not married no doubt look forward to a marriage which is going to be not a failure, and those of you who are married are not going to let on. So quite clearly he seems to me to have the more popular side of this argument.

You understand that we are going to debate whether *modern* marriage is a failure. We are not going to debate marriage in general or marriage among the Fiji Islanders or among various interesting peoples of whom the anthropologists like to write, because although those peoples live in the present day it is agreed that they are not to be counted as modern. It is modern marriage that we have to consider; marriage as we know it among each other, not, of course,

Originally published by the Discussion Guild (New York, 1930).

among ourselves, among each other. That is what we have to consider. Not either marriage as it has existed in the past when, as we all know, it was invariably idyllic, nor yet marriage as it will exist in the future when perhaps it will have so nearly dissolved that there will be nothing to be said against it. It is not either of those sorts of marriage that we are to discuss but just marriage here and now as we all know it.

And I might say that marriage as we know it among our friends is very far from being that success which it is cracked up to be. I am comparing marriage with what it might be, marriage as it might exist, as perhaps in certain cases it does exist, comparing that with marriage as we actually know it. And as we actually know marriage in the majority of cases it falls very far short indeed of what we can easily imagine marriage to be if it were amended to a certain extent in certain directions.

Marriage, as everybody knows, is the legal and social regulation of the procreative impulse. It is not the procreative impulse itself. The procreative impulse itself is a thing which we inherit from the animals, but marriage as a legal and social institution with moral sanctions attached to it is a definitely human institution. And it is this legal and social arrangement that we have to consider.

There is, of course, among many types of animals a permanent or quasi-permanent union which has many of the characteristics of marriage as we know it. Among the great majority of birds, for example, there is union either for a season, or perhaps for life. It is quite the common thing among birds and they live most exemplary lives. I believe cases of sin among birds are practically unknown. You may say broadly speaking that those animals have a permanent union of the sexes among which the support and protection of the male is necessary to the female and to the young during the infancy of the young. That is so, for example, with most birds because the female has to sit upon the eggs and hasn't time to go and get herself any food, and after the young are hatched out she still does not have time to get them all the juicy worms they want. And therefore, without a husband, the economic support of the household would fail, and the husband among birds serves as he does among ourselves the economic function of providing the necessary food. You will find that there is this institution as one may call it (though it is not of course among animals a *legal* institution) wherever either protection or support from the male is necessary during the infancy of the young. And that, of course, is the primary reason why there is such an institution as marriage among human beings.

But among animals there is a curious difference from what there is among human beings, and that is that wherever any permanent union exists among animals, instinct takes care of it. When once two animals have mated then the male ceases to be attracted to any other female and the female ceases to be attractive to any other male. That is very convenient, and it enables these animals, as I say, to live blameless lives. Unfortunately among human beings instinct is not so nicely adjusted to our legal institutions, and that is the source of all the trouble. If only we could have our instincts arranged as neatly as those of the animals in question we shouldn't be here debating this problem tonight. But unfortunately we don't feel all our impulses all day long exactly in accord with what the law expects us to do. The result is that marriage very often produces various undesigned bad results.

I should subject marriage to three tests:

First, does it minister to the happiness of the husband and wife?

Second, how does it answer in regard to the bearing of children?

And third, how does it answer in regard to the rearing of children?

For after all those are the three main things that you may look for in a good system. That is, it should make the husband and wife happy; it should lead to the bearing of a suitable number of healthy children; and it should lead to those children being reared in the proper way. Those seem to me to be the three tests to which you may expose any marriage system.

Now how does modern marriage come out when you test it by these three tests? Take first of all the happiness of the couple themselves. Very often they are extremely happy for a while, but it doesn't often happen, as far as I have observed, that that happiness persists throughout a long life. It does happen sometimes, but the statistical proportion of cases, as far as I have been able to observe, is not a very large one.

I have been traveling around your country lately a very great deal. I have been North, South, East and West, everywhere, and staying mainly in hotels. In most of the hotels that I stay in I find that there is a dinner going on of either the Elks or the Mooses or the Rotary Club or what not, and that at this dinner only males are assembled without their wives, and I have not observed any great degree of melancholy at the lack of the women being present. They may of course be concealing the ache in their hearts. I can only say, if so, they do it very successfully indeed. And I think if you were to observe quite frankly and honestly men who have been married for ten years or more, you would find that the great majority of them are very glad when they can get an evening off. And I think probably the same thing applies to the wives.

The problem with which every wife and every husband is faced is the problem of securing an evening off himself or herself without the other one having an evening off, too. And that problem has so far proved insoluble, so that in general they sit together bored to death but each consoled in his or her boredom by the thought that the other is equally bored.

You no doubt are all aware of the great principle in economics which is called the principle of marginal utility. That is a very fine long word, but what it means is this, that supposing you eat one chocolate cream, you may think it is very nice; you eat a second one and you think, "Well, yes, that is rather nice"; and you eat a third and you think, "Well, that is quite enough," and if you are compelled to eat a fourth, you think it is quite disgusting. That is called the principle of marginal utility.

Now supposing you apply this principle to marriage and you will see how it works out. The first year is quite all right; the second year is so so; the third perhaps is passable and after that you begin to think, "Well, really a little variation of this monotony might be quite pleasant." It is very easy to understand how the thing is by analogy. I, for my part, am very fond of eating bacon and eggs for my breakfast, but if there had been a law passed to say that if I had once tasted bacon and eggs for breakfast, I must never taste any other breakfast dish as long as I live, I think I should hate bacon and eggs. And that is precisely what the law does, and it has the natural effect that prohibitions have, of making people think that what is prohibited must be much nicer than what they have got. Very often it isn't, but they think it must be, and that inevitably produces all kinds of friction and all kinds of awkward situations. It produces a result in which the husband and wife—I am talking now of people who are virtuous; I am not talking of those that fail in any degree in obedience to the moral law; I am talking of those who are perfectly and absolutely virtuous—where the husband and the wife are each other's policeman, where each, that is to say, takes care that the other one doesn't in any way break the law, and so they don't. That does not mean that they have on the whole a very delightful or charming relation; sometimes they might be quite glad if there were such stag parties as I was speaking of to break up the monotony of invariable domesticity. There comes in this way to be acknowledged and admitted as a perfectly proper thing an extraordinary amount of mutual interference, of each having a right to say "no" to the other, and that is endured by each party because of its being mutual, but it doesn't on that account become a good thing. Interference of one person with another is not a desirable thing at all, and it does not lead to good results.

For one thing, it closes people's perceptiveness and their powers of sympathy. They learn, if they are very anxious not to err in any way, they learn not to see anybody else, because if they do see them they may be led astray, and so the world gradually gets closed in and they grow less and less perceptive as time goes on.

Of course people are not all such complete patterns of virtue as I have been speaking of and when they are not you find that they are led to divorce. I think divorce is generally recognized to be a failure in a marriage, but I have been talking of the failures that are not embodied in divorce. I am not quite sure that divorce always is such a failure as the continuance of the sort of thing that I have been speaking of, because after all they do try again and perhaps succeed better as a result of experience. But in a great many cases which are viewed conventionally as a complete and perfect success, you have this trouble of people's sympathies becoming unperceptive, people learning to interfere with each other with the sense that they have a perfect right to do so and losing all the power of adventurousness in life, of freshness and new ideas and all the rest, and going on saying what they said thirty years ago because it would be so awfully dangerous to let themselves think anything new.

All that is part of the result of modern marriage where you have surviving a certain kind of system that did extremely well when you had a pleasant community rather sparse, all knowing each other, but which is far less adaptable to the densely populated urban areas in which most highly civilized people live at the present day.

Now I come onto the second point in regard to marriage, and that is the bearing of children. Marriage clearly is an institution concerned primarily and first of all, or it should be so concerned, with the bearing of children. That is its primary purpose. It should not be its primary purpose to provide sexual satisfaction for the parties, because that can be provided without marriage, but the primary purpose of it is the bearing of children. That is why there has to be an institution. That is why it has to be a thing that the state takes cognizance of. Otherwise, it might just as well let people go their own way.

Now, as a matter of fact, law and public opinion and public morals do not recognize at all clearly or at all explicitly that children are the main purpose of marriage. For example, to take a clear case, you can get a marriage annulled for impotence, but you cannot get a marriage annulled for childlessness. If you recognized that children are the purpose of marriage, then childlessness clearly, if it were established as unavoidable, would be a ground for the annulling of marriage. That shows you that children are not recognized by the law or by the church as the main fundamental purpose of marriage in spite of a certain amount of language that might lead you to suppose that it is so.

In modern marriage procreation, which should be its main purpose, is to an increasing degree sacrificed to swank, sacrificed to the desire to make a display among your neighbors, to seem to be rich and grand, to have a great many superfluities and a great many useless luxuries. That is really the thing to which in the main the bearing of children has been to an increasing degree sacrificed in the modern world, and is still being increasingly sacrificed, because the birth rate continues to go down and down.

Consider among the people that you know how many there are among young married couples who think that they would rather have a grand piano or a new car or a larger apartment or whatever it may be than have another child just now, and, consequently, they set to work to have all this swank, and the main purpose of the swank is to impress the neighbors. The neighbors are not impressed with your having another child but they are impressed with your having a new car. I don't quite know why; I never quite understand neighbors; but I have noticed that that is the way they feel.

And so you have a situation where the birth rate goes down and down and where for economic reasons the people who have the most money have the smallest number of children. All the people who have a lot of money can tell you that they have small families because they can't afford large ones. It is a very curious situation, but what they mean is that they can't afford to have a large family and also to be grander than their neighbors at the same time, and that it is obviously absolutely necessary to be grander than your neighbors. Therefore, you can't have these children.

I am not urging that people should have large families in the old sense. I believe that the ideal and perfect citizen has 2.4 children.

That is a very, very difficult ideal that we can't hope to achieve. But although that is what the ideal citizen would do, the actual well-to-do citizens of practically every civilized country in our day has, on the average, fewer children than that, and he is not in fact reproducing his own numbers. The well-to-do classes in civilized States are, to an increasing extent, being replaced from either below in the same community or from outside by people who have not yet acquired the taste for grand pianos, and that shows that there is something unstable about the civilization that we have developed. It is not a self-perpetuating civilization. It is one which inevitably must change, because those who are of it do not reproduce their numbers. If that sort of civilization were in each generation acquired by the new people who enter it from below or the outside, then they also would die out. If that is not to happen, then we must develop a new type of civilization which will reproduce its own numbers. Our present civilization is not self-perpetuating. It lives upon the vital capital of the world, and that shows that there is something about it that is not quite right—I don't know what—but something that is not quite right.

I should be inclined myself to say that the whole of our effective standards of values are far too economic and far too little biological. When you read the Old Testament, for example—I don't know whether any of you have, but it is quite worth reading, I assure you—when you read the Old Testament, you will find that a man considers it a blessing to have a large family, and he is very much concerned with his seed, with his descendants, with the thought that this or that advantageous thing will happen to his descendants, and the greatest misfortune that can happen to a man is to leave no descendants. We don't feel that sort of thing nowadays at all. We don't care about that kind of family tree, that kind of continuity of the race. A man thinks about what he can do himself, what he personally can achieve in the way of a good income, or a good career, or fame, or whatever it may be, or, it may be, merely the notoriety of some famous crime, or anything that will put him on some kind of a pinnacle personally. The old conception of something where he is merely the transmitter of an earlier thing, that whole conception we no longer entertain, because we have grown too entirely individualistic, so wrapped up in the individual as opposed to the race; that is why we have this spurious economic standard of values instead of the biologic standards of values you will find in the old literature.

I think the individual in the modern world overshadows the race to a quite extraordinary extent. A very great many people prefer amusement, even of the most casual and frivolous sort, to the more permanent, and it seems to me, solid happiness that you can derive from the existence of children of your own. That sort of rather solid and rather serious happiness seems somehow not to appeal to people in the present day because their lives are so rooted in themselves, because the individual is the important thing. And that applies not only to the frivolous, but also to a great many of the serious-minded people. The serious-minded people are occupied with their own virtue. They want themselves to be virtuous, and that, to my mind, is a rather poor and ambiguous aim, because you will never succeed in it by aiming at it. You have to aim at something else before you can be any good. And the result of all this is that modern marriage, considered from the point of view of the bearing of children, is a preposterous failure. There are not nearly so many children born as would need to be born in order to keep the more civilized sections of the more civilized nations at the same level of numbers.

And now I come to the third purpose which marriage should serve, and that is the rearing of children. In the old days, of course, the family played a tremendously important part in education. It still does, I believe, in Iceland, but it does not do so in the parts of the world that are familiar to most of those who are here. In the parts of the world that we know of, the serious part of education is done in school. The thing that is left to parents in the way of education is to provide the children with the spectacle of domestic bliss, and that part of the work it seems to me they do not perform quite adequately. It seems to me that a school teacher whose work was as inadequately performed would be very likely to get the sack.

There are, of course, marriages that appear models of happiness. We in this room exemplify that, but when we consider the people who are not here present, we must all recognize that among our neighbors other types of marriage exist. I can think of four such types: There are those where the husband bullies the wife; there are those where the wife bullies the husband; there are those where they are equally-matched and bickering goes on all the time; and finally, there are those where the whole process is put an end to by divorce.

Now, I won't say what percentage of modern marriages falls into one or the other of those four types, but I am afraid it is quite a large percentage, and all those four types are undoubtedly very bad for children. The fact that divorce is bad for children, I think is generally recognized. The moralists, who seem to me to take some sort of malicious pleasure in the thought of how unhappy married people can be when they are held together by the law and who therefore support the law that holds them together, these men have made a great deal of the harm that children suffer from divorce, and I think they are quite right. Children do suffer a great deal from divorce. Children get nervous disorders. They get various kinds of upsets of one sort or another, ranging from sleepwalking to kleptomania, because of troubles between their parents, which upset the children's sense of security and make them feel that they live in a dangerous world, because it does make a young child feel that he lives in a dangerous world when he finds his parents separated. But, and I think this is the point that the conventional moralists are very often overlooking, the same kind of nervous damage, and, perhaps, an even greater nervous damage, is done to children when they are forced perpetually to see bickering between their parents—still more if they are compelled to see actual brutality on the part of the man toward the woman. Anything of that sort has an extremely bad effect on children. It fills them probably first with horror, then with a kind of indifference, and later on with an impulse to imitation. In any event, the effect is very undesirable. So I am not at all sure that divorce isn't a better thing in an immense number of cases than the spectacle of domestic discord that the child otherwise has to see.

I think that for many children, in fact almost all children of marriages in which the husband and wife are not really close friends and cooperators in regard to the children and aware of the importance of the task that they have undertaken in having children, I think in a great many of such marriages the spectacle of home life that the child gets is positively bad for him and he might be better off if he saw no home life at all. We have an idyllic picture of home life, and sometimes it is verified, but very often it is not, and very often when it is not, the fact that the idyllic picture has been put forward as the normal thing makes the failure to realize that all the worse from the point of view of the child. If children were brought up to think all parents quarrelled, they wouldn't so much mind. But they are brought up to feel almost all of them get on and they are just unfortunate that their own parents don't. So they get not only the effect of seeing their own parents quarrel, but also that a peculiar misfortune has happened to them. That is the sort of thing that results from the kind of idyllic optimism always thought to be so very good for the young.

It is always thought that the young should be told everybody is virtuous, everybody is charming, there are no evils in the world whatsoever. And then when the child does come across any of the evils in the world the shock is appalling. I think the only rule with children as with grownups is to bring them up to the truth. That, however, is beside the point.

The causes, as it seems to me, of what is wrong with modern marriage are two-fold. On the one hand what I touched on a moment ago, that our life is too economic and too little biological, with the consequence that sex life has seemed to us the important thing in marriage rather than the cooperation in the rearing of children. That is one thing that is wrong. The other thing that is wrong is the very ancient passion of jealousy. Now jealousy is a very strong passion indeed if you don't learn to control it, and it has been so strong in the past that it led men to shut up women and to cause the lives of women to be most appallingly restricted and painful. That was a very great evil from which women have been partially emancipated. But unfortunately, the passion of jealousy not having been recognized for the evil that it is, as women have become emancipated they seem to have thought that it was their right to pass on to men some of the oppression which had formerly been meted out to them, and that does not seem to be at all a desirable thing. If there is going to be emancipation I don't see why we men shouldn't share in it. It is a somewhat one-sided business it seems to me to emancipate the women and give them a right to become tyrants in their turn. There is not much point in that, and all this business of jealousy should be recognized for what it is. It should be recognized as an evil passion which it is possible to control. People will tell you it is impossible to control it, and those very men will tell you that it is perfectly possible to control the passion of illicit love. The passion of illicit love is quite as instinctive as jealousy, and if you can control the one, you can control the other. And I maintain that if you are to control one or the other it is better to control a restrictive passion which aims at depriving somebody of a joy rather than an expansive passion which aims at giving joy. All expansive passions are better than restrictive ones. And marriage being based as it is mainly on jealousy, being rooted in jealousy as the reason for its existence—not the only reason but the reason for marriage as we have it here and now, the reason that distinguishes marriage as it is from marriage as it might be in so far as it is rooted in jealousy, to that extent it is a restrictive institution and a bad institution and to that extent it is the cause of unhappiness, and not only of unhappiness but of limitation of sympathy, lack of receptiveness, lack of new thought, lack of intelligence, lack of initiative, all kinds of spiritual and mental death that comes from the fact that a man's life and a woman's life are dominated by fear, by the fear that at any moment if you let yourself go you may do something you shouldn't do. That attitude of fear is not the sort of attitude with which a man or a woman should go through life. We want something more adventurous, more fearless, more bold. I think that is the root cause of what I should regard as the failure of modern marriage.

Now my time is finished, and I suppose you are to hear what a fine, admirable institution modern marriage is.

JOHN COWPER POWYS

Ladies and Gentlemen: Mr. Russell has very persuasively and logically indicated the evils of modern life in regard to the prevalence of the economic view over the biological, and incidentally over other aspects of noble human life which are being sacrificed, as my opponent said, to this contemptible desire to show off in the eyes of your neighbor. He divided the matter of marriage into three; first of all, their coming together for purely sex enjoyment; secondly, their coming together for the procreation of children; and thirdly, their coming together for the rearing of children, and he indicated that in all three cases modern marriage was a failure.

But how is modern marriage a failure when in each of the three cases indicated by Mr. Russell what is a failure is the condition, mechanical, economical, industrial, commercial and megalopolitan of modern life, but this does not touch marriage except on my side, for I contend that among the few remaining strongholds against the evils of our commercial, industrial, mechanized and over-economic life, marriage remains the most formidable. Naturally, the invasion has begun and as I follow Mr. Russell's arguments, I hope to be able to show you that in each of his three aspects of modern marriage, the particular evil upon which he animadverts so logically is not the existence of the fortress against modern life, but of those invading powers from modern life that have by reason of a certain weakness in the defenders of the fortress obtained a lodgment there.

First then with regard to the two persons coming together for mutual happiness and enjoyment. Now when you contemplate marriage as it exists today, you are struck at the very start by a striking and curious phenomenon, namely, that a large percentage of unhappy people in marriage, not the majority but I admit a large percentage, are the ones who make the noise, whereas that larger percentage, in my opinion the majority, who are happy, are for obvious reasons silent about their happiness and they are silent about their happiness because as I said at the beginning, the institution of marriage is one of the few fortresses left against modern life, and one of the most irritating aspects of modern life is publicity, therefore, you may be perfectly certain that those who are secretively, furtively and proudly happy will be the last people in the world to take the world into their confidence, whereas, the others who are miserable, having given up the whole thing, are continually clamoring and squealing, and since they make the noise and it is their clamor that has approached our philosophical visitor in this country, it is natural enough that he has taken the view he has of modern marriage in America.

Now Mr. Russell drew a withering picture of these two unfortunate persons sitting opposite one another, the man escaping on certain occasions to his happy associates, the Rotarians or the Eks or the Moose or the Lions or the Eagles or even the Pythian portion of Freemasonry. I have traveled at least as much as my antagonist in various portions of this country. I too have attended these peculiar meetings, functions and dinners, and I dispute the gusto and the zest and Rabelaisian enjoyment of life which these occasions display. On the contrary, Mr. Russell, the existence of a certain personage on these occasions, and again and again have I been confronted by this personage, disproves the release and enjoyment and liberation and gusto and complacency of these fortunate men free from their domestic prison.

I am referring to that particular individual who leads these worthy Rotarians in their music. I have noted an individual from another order of society altogether, a choirmaster or a Y.M.C.A. organizer, and this young man with a peculiar cast of countenance as in a vaudeville performance, will put his foot on some high chair, will jest with the unfortunate elderly grocers and candlestick makers who happen to be sitting near him, calling them "Charlie" and

"Dick" and "Bob" and "Will," and calling upon them to perform, and these uncomfortable, shy, embarrassed people are swept into a chorus, the chorus being, (Mr. Russell has referred to ham and eggs) a peculiar song of which the burden seems to be some particular occult repetition in which those words—I will not repeat them—continue to occur and I have never seen a look of more miserable, more embarrassed, shyer discomfort than on the faces of these unfortunate men enjoying themselves.

But, to return to the poor prisoners in their domestic box, and my proof to you that their marriage is not a failure—and mark you this extends all over this country, but abounds and reaches undoubtedly its climacteric in what is called the Middle West—I deny that marriage is a failure in the Middle West and for this reason: The typical American husband and wife in Indiana, in Arkansas, in Ohio, are partners in a great game. Their coming together has been sexual but it has speedily become much more than this. I question Mr. Russell's imagery of that particular piece of candy which turned out so nasty after having been tasted three times. As a matter of fact, my travels in the Middle West and my visits to what are called homes in the Middle West have led me to regard the domestic happiness of Middle Western husbands and wives as a very living and a very growing thing. It is indeed in its way—I do not say in the profoundest, sophisticated way, but still in a natural healthy and human way—a legitimate, dignified, quiet, human experience and the pleasure of it does not diminish but rather grows. It grows with the appearance of children, but it also grows with the greater understanding of the humor of the two people. They confront one another but not in boredom. There is at any rate in the Middle West, at any rate in Indiana, a growing wonder in such a menage that the man should be a man, that he should wear trousers instead of petticoats, that he should shave with a Gillette razor, that he should have a penchant for hot cakes at a certain hour in the morning and perhaps a penchant for more than two percent alcoholic beer on other occasions; that he should dig in his garden; that he should like to see a certain number of flower beds in the front and a certain number of vegetables growing in the back; that he should have, first of all, a Ford car and then a more expensive car; that he should build rather a more comfortable—I won't say a very luxurious but a more comfortable house for himself, his wife and his growing family; or, put the family out for a time, for himself and his wife; and here is also an equal wonder, constantly amazing to this man, that his mate should be as she is. Between the two of them at any rate the wife in the Middle West plays the role of housekeeper, of cook, of waitress, of general supervisor and of confidante in the husband's business, and also of his mistress. This situation may not exist in the East but it certainly exists all over the Middle West. The husband shares his business interests with the wife and these two are partners in the struggle against the world and they enjoy their partnership. They enter the great arena, they contend against their neighbors but not merely for swank or show. In the great legitimate struggle for existence they want to have larger rows of potatoes and peas and beans. Well, Mr. Russell, that is harmless and innocent competition. They want to have the feeling that their business is going well; that they are playing some kind of a role in civic affairs and together by degrees they grow more and more intimate.

Finally, in addition to being a cook and a housekeeper and being occupied all the time and sharing her husband's business activities, the typical Middle Western wife is, allow me to say so, though this sounds perhaps scandalous, a very passable courtesan.

Now I touch here upon a very delicate matter but I must not shrink from it for it is necessary to my refutation of the boredom referred to by Mr. Russell. In the Middle West the women (though I do not say they are all as beautiful as Helen of Troy) devote a good deal of attention to feminine adornment, not of a very recondite kind and I dare say not of the kind that would pass on Fifth Avenue, still less in the Champs Elysees, but still provocative enough for the situation, and if Mr. Russell had listened more closely to the conversation of his Elks and Moose and Rotarians he would have found that a large part of it consisted in a very masculine and world-old jesting, of I dare say a crude character but still deeply felt, about what? Not about their escape from their domestic prison but about the charming, winning, attractive and very human peculiarities of their ladies as ladies, little masculine jests about women's tastes, women's frippery, women's vanity, women's irony, women's weakness, etc., indicating that secretly in the background of these men's happiness is the fact that they have this quaint—I do not say Cleopatra-like and very often a homely enough—object of worship; but still not dressed in trousers. That is the whole point.

In modern marriage as in all marriage the thrill comes from the fact that they are of opposite sexes and if, according to Mr. Russell, boredom comes like a withering blight upon this difference, it only means that something is fundamentally wrong. And I contend that in America this is rare; this is not the rule; you cannot judge America by New York; you cannot judge America even by Boston; you must take the great swing of the country and I contend that the magic, the glamor, above all the mystery of sex in a very definite way remains five years, ten years, fifteen years. They have this gift; Providence has given it to them; five, ten, fifteen years, twenty years after marriage they are conscious of the piquant, the provocative, the mysterious difference spiritually, mentally, esthetically, morally and above all nervously, between the man and the woman. This, I contend, is the great, the grand purpose of marriage, whose end both at first and now is to intensify our interest in life and to offer us an escape from life. Marriage above everything else intensifies, (Mr. Russell is wrong) intensifies the interest in life. The quarreling may come. Try to interfere with these quarreling husbands and wives and you will see the deep link that exists underneath these disturbances. No, no, the difference between a man and a woman is not realized to its full potentialities until they are married.

Mr. Russell would say a love affair would do as well. Not at all. Anyone who knows anything about love affairs knows this, that they do not take the place of that perpetual intercourse, intimate and sometimes I admit, quarrelsome but always *interesting,* that binds two people together. Indeed, you may go so far as to say that until you have been married for ten, for fifteen, for twenty years to one person, the greatest experience possible to human beings is outside your knowledge and your intellectual grasp.

Human beings do not realize the implicit mystery of men being men and women being women until they have struggled together in this condition of tragic tension.

Passing on then to the next point of my opponent, the matter of the procreation of children. Mr. Russell said that modern marriage is a failure because the birth rate goes down and down, but he forgot the growing mass of immigrants in this country. I am aware that the pure American Nordic stock—I might say Anglo-Saxon stock, for some of the Germans and Scandinavians in the Northern States are still prolific—is rapidly sinking. But Mr. Russell must be aware that this going down of the population is confined to certain old American families and does not extend to the recent comers to this land.

Now then, in the struggle for existence in America, the poor people, the proletarians who work with their hands and who have more children, continually encroach upon the privileges of the brain

workers who are no longer manual workers, the commercial workers, the industrial leaders and so on, in the higher or at any rate in
the more white collar levels of society, and as they come up, these
foreigners, from being manual workers, they bring up their prolific
tendencies. Only by degrees—and we have not reached this yet—
only by degrees will the foreign-born proletariat of America begin to
acquire this Anglo-Saxon tendency in America by means of birth
control and by this competition with their neighbors, to have very
small families, but this is in the future and Mr. Russell especially
limited our debate to the immediate present, and in the immediate
present we have only to go to the East Side in New York and see the
bonfires tonight lit by those crowds of swarming children in the
Jewish, Italian and other foreign quarters to understand that even
in a great metropolis young blood is not going to fail, and procreation of children as an element of American marriage has not been
destroyed by the economic conditions of modern life.

Now, thirdly, the rearing of children. Mr. Russell said that in
the rearing of children the education was largely taken out of the
parents' hands by the school system. That is true in so far as actual
scholastic information is concerned. Education in the narrow, technical sense of the word, but education in the more human, in the
more psychological sense of the word still remains, and Mr. Russell
allowed that it still remains in indicating so eloquently the bad
effect upon children of the quarrels of their parents. I noticed that
he laid more stress upon the bad effect upon children of separation
and divorce. This, apparently, is worse for children than the little
bickerings and even the more dangerous quarrels that occur in the
best regulated homes.

As a matter of fact, here again I would like to propose against
Mr. Russell's failure of modern marriage, my own definition of exactly where and how modern marriage is a success. I would say
modern marriage is a success in that it is one of the surviving
fortresses against the mechanization, industrialization, commerciali-
zation of human life; that modern marriage is a success in so far as
it intensifies our awareness, our dramatic awareness of the mystery
of life, and in the second place that it offers, and this is what I am
coming to with regard to the rearing of children, it offers an escape,
and the only escape, from life.

I take the words of my distinguished opponent, who pointed out
that children come up against a shock when their parents are divorced. For the first time they realize the insecure foundations upon

which human life is built. Mr. Russell allows that a certain protection from life is what children need, and I would go so far as to enlarge that opinion and maintain that a certain protection from life is what we all need, and can only find in marriage, even in an imperfect marriage, even in a marriage disturbed by quarrels.

Now, if you consider the condition of children who are tossed to and from one parent to another, or because of the quarrels of parents, end up in an institution, Mr. Russell, in one of his recent books, has expressed horror of orphanages and other institutions, and I hold the view that marriage is a success in modern times, in so far as that, even with imperfect parents, it protects a child from certain ghastly lonelinesses and shocks that it would get in an institution. Children looking back upon their childhood, for children are much wiser than many of us philosophers, children looking back upon their childhood, forget the absurd quarrels of their parents, and even when they remember them, they remember them with a kind of humorous enjoyment. Their quarrels endear their parents to them; their quarrels prove that their parents are weak and human and fallible like themselves, and in a family there is a great deal left to the instinct of nature.

My opponent is a great philosopher and above all a mathematician. It is therefore only too natural for him to lay stress upon the legal, biological, scientific and scholastic aspects of this problem. There are, however, in nature, in life, as Shakespeare points out at least once in his work, there are occasions when certain mysterious instincts have play and in regard to marriage these instincts are given a freedom that they are not given under any other condition. In a love affair, in a passing love affair, the atmosphere is so electric, the emotional disturbance so acute, the abandonment so extreme, that the instincts to which I am now referring, such as have to do with the invisible balance, the occult play, between that phenomenon known as a male animal and that other phenomenon known as a female animal, do not arrive at their most interesting point. They are disturbed and agitated. Whereas in marriage the mere fact that custom—I will not now speak of law—custom, tradition, the opinion of the neighbors, the general atmosphere in the community make it difficult for these people to separate helps these instincts to create a new unity in the world. Thus your man and your woman may be very often quarrelsome, but even the quarrels of such married people have a peculiar connotation of pleasure to those engaged.

With regard to this matter of the rearing of children, it is, I
think, clear that children prefer the security of a home where the
husband is very male and the mother is very female and where
these two by their little instinctive by-play and back-chat and hu-
mors and quarrels, and various forms of human intimacy—I say
the children prefer the recognized and familiar atmosphere of such
a home to the great unknown world symbolized by life in a hotel or
life in an orphanage, or life first with one parent by himself and
then with the other parent by herself. In other words, I am defending modern marriage on what I would like to call both sensuous and
mystical grounds.

Mr. Russell in his brilliant book, from which he has taken a few
of the arguments in this debate, in his brilliant book upon morals
and marriage, indicates that in his opinion the mystical element of
marriage, the mystical element of this coming together of the man
and the woman may be completely disregarded. I do not share this
view. It seems to me that we do not know enough at present about
the constitution of the universe to be absolutely sure that mysterious
forces, magical powers, may not come from outside or from beyond,
I do not know whither or whence, and fall upon a particular des-
ignated couple of human beings who have by some element of
mysticism in themselves, religion in themselves, idealism in themselves, come to have faith that such a spiritual force is a possible
contingency.

Now it seems to me that it is unphilosophical in our distinguished philosopher, it seems to me that it is not true skepticism to
omit altogether what Rabelais who certainly has spoken of marriage
in those famous Panurge scenes—shall I marry, shall I not marry?
If I marry I shall be a cuckold, if I marry my wife will beat me
up—indicates as the other alternative.

Now Rabelais ends his philosophizing on this very point, surrounding life with a suggestion of mystery. His phrase—"I go to see
the great perhaps"—indicates my attitude to modern marriage.

"With this ring I thee wed. With my body I thee worship, and
with all my worldly goods I thee endow." It is, I admit, rather
singular that in the American version of our English prayer book
with which Mr. Russell and I are so familiar, the expression, "with
my body I thee worship" has been left out, for it is precisely upon
this point that my present argument turns. But as Mr. Russell says,
we are not confining our discussion of modern marriage to America
alone. So I am allowed to use a passage expurgated for moral rea-

sons from my own marriage ceremony. I am allowed to use this on my side as an evidence of a certain reliance between these two people bound by this convenant upon what I will not call the supernatural, but upon the unknown.

Now it seems to me if the purpose of marriage is the heightening of life and the escape from life, this element of mystery is very important and may it not be that the extreme boredom of Mr. Russell's domestic victim comes from the fact that the passage I quoted is left out from the American marriage service?

One word and I have done. In order to intensify life in the bringing together of the man and the woman, a certain amount of self control is necessary. Mr. Russell said that jealousy is a bad motive, but going out to new loves may be a good motive. Now we have all seen in New York and elsewhere quite as much misery caused by the going out to new loves as caused by jealousy and I would ask Mr. Russell why is it that divorced people as soon as they escape from the first prison rush to enter the prison again?

Does this not prove that modern marriage so far from being a failure, satisfies some deep instinct in human nature? In his book Mr. Russell has indicated that the instinct of—well, to put it plainly, of consummating marriage is not universal. I am prepared to accept that, but there is a universal instinct in connection with rushing into marriage and this is the lovers instinct to swear before man and the Gods eternal fidelity. That is a deep, irrevocable human instinct.

Now then, if custom, if tradition support our married people in keeping up this mystical covenant that with their eyes they have willingly, exultantly sworn to, then it seems to me a mistake to consider this boredom as a result of the original vow. Boredom does not come from a difficult thing. Boredom does not come from a heroic thing. Boredom does not come from a day by day struggle to retain a loyalty that is not easy in the face of a corrosive world. Anything but boredom springs from this, and this and nothing less than this is the essence of modern marriage. They respect one another. They are tender to one another and the more they know of one another, the more they realize the essential pathos, mystery and beauty even in the dullest, stupidest, most tedious cases of a man and a woman.

BERTRAND RUSSELL

Ladies and Gentlemen, I think I have seldom heard an abler ad-

of a bad cause than I listened to this evening. I was rather
.ering what anybody could say on such a side of such a topic,
. I know now what can be said.

Mr. Powys told us that marriage is a mystery, that no one knows
why anybody marries. And he represented that this is a matter
which is altogether beyond human reason. Now, from that point we
can go on. Another very elegant device in his speech was dependent
upon the generally recognized fact that New Yorkers never go further west than Buffalo. I don't know whether that is true or not, but
I can't help thinking Mr. Powys believes it, because, so far as I have
seen the Middle West, it is not so very unlike the rest of the habit-
able globe, but as represented in Mr. Powys' remarks, it was a kind
of marvelous Paradise, where everybody's heroic dreams come true,
where wives find extraordinary pleasure in being both cooks and
housekeepers and in the evening when they are tired, helping their
husbands out with the accounts. Well, I don't know, perhaps, as Mr.
Broun already said, there are different parts of the Middle West. I
cannot but subscribe to that sentiment. Then there was one thing
very painful to me in Powys's address, and that was where he took
away from me one of my illusions, namely, that men at these dinners of Elks, etc., really enjoyed themselves. It seems that like the
Prisoner of Chillon, they leave their prison with a sigh. I have not
myself observed that; so far as I have seen them, they seemed to be
having quite a reasonably good time, but evidently on a further
study, you penetrate this region of mystery he spoke of and in this
region of mystery, they are really very unhappy. There certainly
does seem to be something curiously mysterious about these things.
Mr. Powys quoted the marriage service in which the man says,
"With all my worldly goods I thee endow." He did not mention that
for something like 300 years after that marriage service was created,
the law was that the man endowed the wife with nothing, but the
wife did endow him with all her worldly goods. That is another
example of mystery.

Well, I am afraid it is hopeless for me to follow into those regions. I am a poor, humdrum fellow, who can but follow evidence,
and moreover, as Mr. Powys rather unkindly pointed out, I am a
mathematician, and so I am quite unable to pursue him into those
regions.

I should like nevertheless to say a few words about some of the
things he mentioned. He said repeatedly that marriage offers an
escape from life. Now he doesn't seem to have concluded from that

that marriage is a form of death. He said again that no one knows the best that life has to offer until you have been married twenty years in tragic tension. There again I am dealing with a mystery; whether he meant that at the end of that time you might get a divorce, I don't know. Perhaps he will tell us when he speaks again wherein the joy of twenty years of tragic tension consists.

He made some rather curious observations, I thought, on the subject of the bearing of children. I was pointing out that in what one calls typically modern marriage there is a deficiency of children. That is to say, there are not enough to keep up the population. He replied by saying that there are certain sections of the population who still do keep it up. Quite true. But those are the sections which are not what you call modern, and in proportion as they become modern they cease to have these large families. Everybody knows that that is so. If you read the statistics you will find that it is not a fact confined to America. At one stage of Mr. Powys's remarks he said that he was not confining his purview to America, but at that stage he most certainly was doing so, because you will find that this fall in the birth rate is an old phenomenon in France, a very marked phenomenon in England, Germany, in practically every known country with the exception of Ecuador. There is reason to think if the world goes on as it is now that in another 300 years the whole population of the world will be Ecuadorians. I don't know whether that is a thing which Mr. Powys views with joy, but for my part I think it would be rather a pity if we did not ourselves leave descendants to inherit that remarkable intelligence which I see before me.

He spoke a great deal about the human elements which people derive from education in the home. Now I agree entirely with him as to the possibility of that sort of thing, as to the fact that it sometimes occurs, as to the fact that it used to occur often, but I do not agree that it is a particular typical modern phenomenon. A typically modern wage earning family are much too busy to do very much with their children, and what is done for them is done in the school, and the school has to do the moral education as well as the actual technical instruction. The moral education more and more is taken over by the school in the modern working class family, and I think everybody knows that that is so and that it is an inevitable result in industrialism.

I noticed a curious vacillation in Mr. Powys. I thought sometimes he said "Industrialism is bad. Marriage which exists in an industrial community must share some of the evils of industrialism, but marriage is less industrialized than any other institution and is therefore the best institution of our time." That as far as I could follow him was his argument. At other times he would turn round and argue in quite a different kind of way, and I never could quite make out whether he was really talking about modern marriage as it is in the present day or about marriage as it used to exist among the ancient Romans or the ancient Spartans or in some entirely pre-industrial community where there were no schools and no inherited wealth and none of the sort of things that make trouble in our day. I don't think he himself has quite made up his mind whether he is talking about modern marriage or about marriage in an ideal past or in an ideal region such as the Middle West.

He made a somewhat curious assertion, that married people like quarreling, and I suppose that is based upon the fact that they do quarrel. He must have been, I think, under the impression that what people do they like doing, but I don't know whether that is true. Perhaps it is true of some people. They say it takes two to make a quarrel, but I don't think that is true in marriage. And so far as I have observed marriage a great many people are compelled to quarrel who don't in the least enjoy it, because some perfectly practical and definite issue comes up in which you have got to take one side or the other. A committee of two with no chairman is a very awkward form of government.

He states, as I said a moment ago, that protection from life is only to be found in marriage. Now I don't feel that I quite understand that statement. I don't know what he means by life and I don't know exactly how marriage protects you from it. I suppose it protects you from a breach of promise action. I can see that in that sense marriage does protect you from life, but I think it must be a rather gloomy experience which would lead you to identify a circumstance of that sort with life, and I am sure I hope that that is not the view that I am intended to take of life.

Marriage, we are told, is something which depends upon the thrill that belongs to beings of opposite sexes. Now I had had that idea myself, I confess. But I am not quite sure that that is in itself a complete proof that marriage is altogether and always a success, for, great as that thrill may be at certain stages of one's existence, it becomes considerably less after about thirty years. You cease really to be surprised that your wife is a woman after you have been married that long. And so I really feel that as an argument to prove that marriage remains delightful after ten or twenty years of tragic tension, well I can't feel that that is really a complete and absolute answer.

Mr. Powys made a great point of the fact that when married people quarrel they nevertheless resent outside interference. That I know is quite true. I know of a case of a husband and wife who did not speak to each other for twenty-six years. At the end of twenty-six years the landlord raised the rent and then they spoke to each other. That, I quite admit. I did not maintain and I do not maintain that husband and wife hate each other more than they hate some people, like the landlord or whoever it may be. But that is not a complete proof that they love each other, and I don't think it proves that you are completely happy together if you resent someone coming in and spoiling both your games at the same time. So that that really is no conclusive answer.

He argued also that it is better to leave jealousy its former place in life since new loves cause misery. Now there I think he was assuming that new loves were to be combined with the present amount of jealousy, and also that they were to be allowed to break up the home. I think the necessity that arises there is more a certain restraint, a certain degree of permanence in the matter of institutions, and a certain control on both sides in order to make such an adjustment of rival claims that each side may get its due, and I at any rate should not wish to see each passing fancy break up a marriage.

That is the situation to a great extent in the present day in this country in certain sections. You find that people imagine when they marry that they are going to get all this romantic satisfaction that Mr. Powys talks of and when it fails at any point they divorce and try again, and again fail, and that, it seems to me, comes of viewing marriage as a mystery, because when you find that it is by no means mysterious you think you must try another marriage. It is much better, it seems to me, to view all human institutions in a more or less realistic spirit as just what they are, and then you will be less disappointed when you find that they are not what they are not.

So that for my part I don't apologize for not being romantic. I don't apologize for the lack of mystery. I know always that every person who speaks of mystery appears to be seeing deeper into things and perhaps they are. But it is not the way that I see the world. I observe the world and I see all sorts of things that don't seem to be at all mysterious, and if they seem mysterious to others, well they have a wisdom that is hidden from me. But I don't feel that there is any mystery about people marrying, and it is curious to to me that Mr. Powys, who considers marriage such a great success, nevertheless considers it an absolute mystery why people enter into it. I don't know that he offered me anything very definite to answer. It seemed to me we did not meet. He was talking about one sort of thing and I was talking about another. I was talking about the world as one can observe it with the ordinary outward eye; he was talking of the world as the poet views it when he is in a fine frenzy rolling. I haven't got the poet's eye and I fear I am deficient in the fine frenzy. I can only see the world as it appears to me, and I can only say that a great many of the people that I met in the Middle West certainly did not have rows of beans and I knew even several who kept cooks. And it seems to me therefore that in all this there is a certain idealism, if I may say so. And I suppose I may define idealism as the habit of seeing things as embodiments of an ideal rather than as the actual facts which they are.

I am sure I wish I could believe that twenty years of tragic tension are thoroughly enjoyable to those who go through them. I should think more highly of the happiness of human life if I could believe that. But I for my part cannot. I think that suffering is suffering and happiness is happiness. And I don't think that you alter those facts by giving them grand names.

The matter of worldly goods exactly illustrates the sort of thing I mean. The prayerbook uses these lovely phrases about "with all my worldly goods I thee endow" and it doesn't mean a thing, a single word of it. It is just a nice way to talk and it makes you feel happy, but if you are going to take that as representing what life really is, well, then, I am afraid I cannot agree to that sort of method. To understand what life really is I think one must take it quite simply and quite stark, just as you see it, and take away all the beautiful phrases and all the lovely poetry, etc., and try to see it as novelists see it, rather than as the poet sees it. You know the poet always thinks that it is spring. Nevertheless the calendar is against him on that subject. I feel that just as the calendar is a somewhat mundane institution, very deficient in imagination, so one's view of the world should be equally deficient in imagination, equally direct, equally simple and equally devoid of all the trappings of poetry and all the delights of imagination with which Mr. Powys so beautifully and so very charmingly invested this world that we live in. The world that he portrays is a very lovely world. Would that I could live in it. But I should not advise any of you to go away from here and settle in the Middle West in the hopes that you will find it.

JOHN COWPER POWYS

I can only express my regret that my own years prevent me from
offering myself as a youthful candidate for Mr. Russell's school for
in that fortunate academia or Stoic Porch I am conscious that a
good life is taught of such a balanced fulfillment of human nature
that in addition to knowing what is happening in this real world of
ours, observed so naturally and directly and modestly and simply, I
have a shrewd idea that a good deal of imagination and not a little
of those rare and fine esthetic susceptibilities that Mr. Russell's
culture draws from the ancient nations to which he has referred,
would incidentally sweeten the cup of stark reality given to his
fortunate pupils. But since I am compelled by the present stringency
of our debate to confine myself to Mr. Russell's own self-denying
ordinance which I know he breaks at home, it is necessary for me to
take up his definite challenge and indicate to you and to you, Mr.
Chairman—it is something to have a Chairman who has the mysterious power of transportation—that when I speak of a thing being
mysterious, I do not mean to imply that it is anything ideal or even
religious, but simply that it cannot at present be explained by any
of our scientific processes, not even by those mysterious mathematical processes of our great philosopher.

I merely imply that the coming together of a man and a woman
in what has now, in the modern world, come to be regarded as the
old-fashioned institution of marriage, is worthy of more careful consideration than its opponent gives it.

Mr. Russell indicated that my stress upon the tragic tension of
these two implied that they were suffering. Not necessarily. Mr.
Russell's classical knowledge and study in fable will inform him
that the word "tragic" does not imply, by any means, sordid or even
continuous misery. It implies a heightening of awareness of a certain, inherent clash. Now, I contend that this tragic awareness of
the essential difference between these partners whose intimacy gives
them a kind of escape from the chaos of the outer world is itself a
fulfillment, as no other can ever be, of that good life of which Mr.
Russell is so well known an exponent. For the custom of marriage,
even as it is held in our modern industrial world, does still hold
these people together after that poetic springtime has passed away.
I contend that there is a poetry in autumn and even in winter, and
that the deepening of life in one place between two people, even
allowing for many tragic misunderstandings, reaches a depth of

awareness not ideal at all, of an awareness of these secrets of reality, this very reality, to which Mr. Russell has drawn our attention.

It appears to me that you get more of the reality of life in the contact between these two people, prolonged past the time of their amorous spring time than you get in the repeated love affairs, for in these love affairs, the superficial excitement is so lively, and the natural human stir of animal passion is so absorbing that the deeper aspects of reality are drugged. A man and a woman are enduring a kind of inebriation. I turn the tables on Mr. Russell. It is in the light love affairs on the side which are to be tolerated by my married man and married woman that the spring tide illusions are to be found, with each new amorous encounter, towards which my unfortunate partner must be so indulgent and must overcome his jealousy, her jealousy. I say in each one of these passing love affairs, there is so much excitement and disturbance of the senses that the longer, deeper, more permanent, more subtle and calmer secrets of life are muddied up, discolored, disturbed, and it seems to me since both Mr. Russell in his larger field, and myself in my own peripatetic existence are struggling after what he has so nobly called the good life, it seems to me that the attainment of the good life above everything else, demands a certain degree of peace, of calm, from these agitations. I have talked hitherto of these two together becoming partners in the struggle of life, becoming indeed a unit, in which the masculine and the feminine join together against life and are able to outwit it at many points, join together in fact against the strange and the dark and the horrible and the terrible, and are able to escape from those things in many ways.

Now turn to a further point. Every reality that has beauty and truth in it is double-edged and contains a contradiction reconciled in a deeper unit; and it is true that just as modern marriage can be an escape from the horrors of life and a kind of sanctuary, it also can be a most vivid, daring and deep experience; and in this sense you get this tension that I took the liberty of calling tragic. I hold the view that the essence of marriage lies in the coming together of the man and the woman independently of children. I hold the view that it would be a mistake to regard the marriage as lacking in its consummation until the woman is pregnant with her first child; I hold the view that the mystery is in life itself and that when two people held together by custom, grow into a certain rhythmic swing, not always comfortable, not always pleasant, but fruitful of a deeper insight, fruitful of a stronger self-control, fruitful of a tenderer sympathy. Their union is evocative of that mood of mutual forgiveness which is the essence of a human noble character. In this way, each forgiving the other, jealousy enters as a heightening of life and not as an evil.

Mr. Russell's attack upon jealousy is, I think, misplaced. I think it is unfair to jealousy. Jealousy, though it sounds a horrid thing, is in reality—Mr. Russell must allow this—a profound compliment to the person about whom it is exercised. If you are really indifferent, why, you do not care; and with the kind of married couple that would suffer and suffer acutely if one or the other had a passing amour with somebody else, that suffering, that jealousy is not a sign that their marriage is miserable, but on the contrary, it is a sign that the possession of the other is so precious a thing that they cannot bear the idea of sharing it with anyone else.

I must not go back to earlier epochs in the history of the world, but it seems to me that the issue between us can be brought to a clear focus in this point alone. Mr. Russell contends that human beings get more of the good life, more fulfillment in adventures that go out, in meeting new people, in falling in love with new people, whereas I contend that there is more fulfillment of life and a deeper knowledge, not ideal, not necessarily poetical, but real, a deeper knowledge of reality of life to be derived from the psychological, intellectual and esthetic difference between two people when held together by custom than in the other way. Moreover when you consider these amours by the way that are to make marriage more tolerable for the two concerned, this assumes that the original covenant between them was ill advised. I would say wait until you have found your real mate. I would grant to Mr. Russell the first failure and the recovery from that, the first failure possibly before the pregnancy of the woman, before the birth of the child or even afterwards, though I would regret such an occurrence, but sooner or later it falls to most human beings to meet their real mate. Sooner or later—and when they have found their mate, then jealousy on both sides is legitimate; and it is legitimate in spite of what Mr. Russell has so wittily and amusingly for purposes of debate observed and well we know that term, it is as when Mark Antony said, "A plain blunt man that loves his friend." We know only too well the Socratic irony of our distinguished visitor upon those lines! No, no sir, that will not avail. You not least of all men, being the philosopher you are, but most of all men, know well that element, call it what you will, the unknown, the unknowable, that underlies all human experience. It is not a poetic idealism or a flight of rhetoric when I say that protected by custom and overshadowed by some kind of ritual; for human beings, as you yourself have allowed, are very childish; marriage is necessary in order to give dignity, awareness and beauty to life. Why do we wear clothes? Not only for the weather.

Why do men take off their hats to women? Not merely as a snobbish matter of convention. These things are symbols; and it is not a mere poetic flight, it is a secret of our experience of life, that when two human beings have lived together for a certain length of time, each separate identity becomes in a strange way sacred and dear. They may have their disputes; they may have their tragic misunderstandings; but if you are going to mitigate marriage by love affairs on the side, the result will be the destruction of the very essence of marriage, which is a certain real experience, growing deeper and deeper as life goes on, buttressed and fortified by the original spontaneous vow between them, and assisted (I will not say consecrated; I leave the religious problem out) by custom, tradition, aura, atmosphere, obtaining at the present moment with regard to this matter. No, it isn't true to say that members of this great house are on my side because those who are married, though inwardly it is distasteful to them, want to have their condition justified, and those who are not married, look at marriage very much in the humorous way Mr. Russell has described it. The real truth is that we all feel, the moment we approach this symbol, this ritual, this situation—I will not call it a sacrament, though the word sacrament meant the oath taken by a Roman soldier to his cause; that it has a stoic, stark, austere, rather than a springtime, ideal, sentimental, shadowy connotation. But I put that aside; let it be no sacrament; let it be no convention; let it be no religious mystery at all; let it merely be the coming together of a man and a woman, and, I contend, quite apart from children, that as years go by, this thing is the most fulfilling of the nobler nature, the subtler nature, the more imaginative nature; yes, Mr. Russell, and the more *rational* nature of human beings, than any other great institution of modern times! Together they dig in; together they experience; together they feel; together there is this tragic tension. But, after all, in the final issue, something emerges, a tenderness toward the other, a pathos in regard to the other, a strange feeling that only comes in marriage; that this other human skeleton, clothed in flesh like your own and yet not like your own, did not ask to be born into this bitter world any more than you asked, and the same curse of being born into the world at all lies upon her, lies upon him; and out of a real marriage emerges not mere poetical, springtime idealism, but that human virtue, the greatest and the last of all, that used to be called pity.

23

Do I Preach Adultery?

In 1940 Russell found himself embroiled in a fierce controversy surround-
ing his views on sexual morality and marriage. This controversy found its
apotheosis when Anglican Bishop Manning started a public campaign
against Russell's appointment to teach two graduate courses in logic and
mathematics at the City College of New York. Bishop Manning declared
that Russell's position should be revoked on the grounds that "Russell was
a recognized propagandist against both religion and morality and who
specifically defends adultery."*

Although in the United States there was a strong movement developing
to censor anything written by Russell, this essay was especially commis-
sioned so that Russell could clarify his sexual ethic, which, while serving
as the focal point of his attackers, had been so crudely distorted.

No, I do not preach adultery. I am aware that, by careful selection
and omission of context, I can be made to seem to do so in the eyes
of people already prejudiced against me. But what I really think is
something different, which I will try to make clear.

I believe, in common with the great majority, that a lifelong
affection for one partner, where it exists, is what is best. I believe
that where there is any possibility of the realization of this ideal, it
is wise and right to restrain such wandering desires as might im-
peril harmony. I believe that when people marry, it should be in the
hope that love will last, and with the intention of doing everything

Originally published in *Liberty* (May 1940).

*John Dewey. *The Bertrand Russell Case* (New York: Viking Press, 1941), p. 19.

in their power to cause it to last. Times of friction may occur without destroying the underlying bond; if so, they should be endured with self-control and mutual forbearance. In all this, my views are the same as my critics'.

The difficult questions arise when marriages are unhappy. The traditional view, that marriage is a sacrament which can be terminated only by death, is not that now taken by the law in the great majority of civilized countries, including the United States (with the exception of South Carolina). The sacramental view rests upon theological grounds, which this is not my place to argue. My views, in agreement with those of the legislatures that allow divorce, are based upon the belief that human institutions should minister to human happiness, and that that form of law and custom is best which does the most to promote the welfare of the parties concerned. It should, however, be noted that those who believe marriage to be sacramentally indissoluble are compelled to regard remarried divorced persons as adulterous. When, therefore, they say (as they do) that I preach adultery, they may mean merely that I hold the marriage of divorced persons to be legitimate. If so, their words convey a very false impression.

When a marriage is unhappy, there are various possibilities. Both parties, or one, or neither, may desire a divorce; both, or one, or neither, may remain physically faithful. I think that when either strongly and for a considerable period desires a divorce, there is little hope of the marriage again becoming happy. In some cases this is obviously impossible; for instance, where one party suffers from incurable insanity. The law ought to grant divorce for this cause, but if it does not, humane people do not blame the person who takes, seriously and with a sense of responsibility, the liberty which the law ought to allow to him or her.

Such cases, however, are exceptional. The really difficult cases are those in which husband and wife, in spite of a greater or less degree of unhappiness, still, for the sake of the children or for some other reason, think the marriage worth preserving. Such cases occupied my thoughts perhaps too much, at the time when I wrote *Marriage and Morals*. This book was written with a view to conditions in England, where divorce (at that time) was only possible for adultery. Subsequent experience in other countries, expecially America, has made me think the avoidance of divorce less often desirable than I then thought it. The chief argument against divorce is the effect on children, but a home life with parents who are on bad terms with each other is apt to be even more harmful to them than divorce.

Nevertheless, there are marriages which, though no longer very happy, may be considered worth preserving, and it is they that raise the question of adultery in its most difficult form. Different considerations are called for in regard to the two parties. We will suppose, for the sake of argument, that the husband, but not the wife, has been unfaithful. He is torn in one direction by love, she in the opposite direction by jealousy. Each, under the influence of passion, is likely to behave in an undesirable way. But traditional morality takes the view that, while his passion is wholly to be condemned, hers, provided it stops short of crime, is to be regarded as righteous. Such a judgment seems to me too simple. I should say to both: If you wish your marriage to be preserved, it will be necessary for at least one of you to practice self-restraint; if neither can do so, the marriage had better be dissolved.

The dissolution of a marriage is, however, to be avoided if possible, not only on account of the children but also for other reasons. As I said in *Marriage and Morals,* "A companionship which has lasted for many years and through many deeply felt events has a richness of content which cannot belong to the first days of love, however delightful these may be. And any person who appreciates what time can do to enhance values will not lightly throw away such companionship for the sake of new love."

This consideration has two sides. On the one hand, it should operate to restrain both parties from infidelity; on the other hand, if infidelity has occurred, it should lead the other party to be willing to cope with jealousy if possible, provided there is still something of value to be preserved. It may be said: "That is all very well, but to say that infidelity should be condoned is, in effect, to encourage adultery." The same argument could be applied against all forgiveness, and yet forgiveness, in general, is considered a Christian duty. And in fact forbearance often so increases affection as to prevent repetition of a first infidelity.

Not a few marriages are ruined by causeless jealousy. In the end, too often, the jealousy ceases to be causeless, although if it had not existed there would never have been any occasion for it. Jealousy is a feeling which most people cannot help having, but its intensity can be greatly increased or diminished by social conventions and received ethical codes. Where public opinion recognizes the "unwritten law," according to which the aggrieved party may murder the

adulterous couple or either of them, crimes of passion will be much
commoner than where a certain degree of self-restraint is expected. I
cannot help thinking that jealousy, though in some degree unavoidable, is regrettable and degrading, since it is based upon the indefensible feeling of property in another human being. Adultery and
jealousy, though they may be undesirable, are sure to occur not
infrequently; neither should be regarded as unforgivable, but both
should, as far as possible, be subjected to rational restraints.

There are some who hold that any man who does not approve of
legal penalties against adultery is, *ipso facto,* an advocate of adultery. This is as false as to suppose that opponents of prohibition
must be in favor of drunkenness. I hold that adultery should not be
subject to legal penalties, but I should still hold this opinion if I
thought as ill of it as do the most bigoted of my critics. A law which
cannot be enforced is a bad law. Every person who knows anything
of the lives of his acquaintances, and in particular every priest who
hears confessions, knows that adultery frequently occurs, and not
less frequently in New York State than where no law against it
exists. Where there is a law against it, it is almost a dead letter,
except in rare instances. Laws which are thus capricious in their
operation are indefensible. They do practically nothing to prevent
the acts that they forbid, although they provide an occasional outlet
for spite. Their most important effect is to weaken the general respect for the law. The effect of the prohibition of adultery as a
possible engine of tyranny is admirably set forth in Shakespeare's
Measure for Measure. This was pointed out to me when I was young
by my Victorian grandmother, one of the strictest moralists that
ever lived.

The real difference between me and my opponents goes much
deeper than the question of sexual morality. What is involved is the
whole concept of "sin." Are certain classes of acts, on the basis of
authority and tradition, to be called "sin," and forever removed
from rational discussion? Or should we recognize that in a changing
world ethical codes, like other things, must from time to time under-
go some modification?

For my part, I should contend that every ethical code must be
judged by its capacity to promote human welfare. This was the view
that Christ expressed when He said, "The sabbath is made for
man, and not man for the sabbath." His disciples, plucking ears of
corn on the Sabbath, appeared to their orthodox contemporaries

just as wicked as I appear to mine. All the greatest religious teachers have always taught that goodness is a matter of the heart, of the springs of action, not of external obedience to a code. In this I think they were in the right. I lay no claim to virtue in action, but I do believe that my conception of what constitutes virtue is nearer to that of the great teachers than is the conception of persecuting bigots.

To my mind, the sort of conduct that is to be commended is not that which fulfills certain rules, but that which springs from kindness and love of truth. Moral indignation is not the best attitude toward those whose actions we deplore. It is much better to seek to understand the causes of their behavior, and to search out its roots in individual psychology and social circumstances. Too often, in those who believe themselves to be lofty moralists, one detects a desire to inflict pain, and a use of the moral code to give an excuse. Christ protected the woman taken in adultery from punishment, but many of His professed disciples in the present day show no wish to imitate Him in this respect. In the penal code, and in the moral education of the young, it has gradually been found that great mitigations of traditional severity were desirable in the interests of moral improvement; but at each stage these mitigations have been opposed by those to whom punishment was the most attractive part of morality.

Love of truth, or (as it may be called) the scientific outlook, is, to my mind, only second to loving-kindness as an ethical principle. The man of science knows that it is difficult to ascertain truth, and probably impossible to ascertain it completely. He holds his opinions not as unalterable dogmas but only as what seems most likely to be true on the evidence hitherto available. Whatever opinions I have expressed, I hold in this spirit. There is not one of them that I am not prepared to abandon if new evidence of a convincing kind is brought to my notice; but equally there is not one of them that I am prepared to modify or suppress from fear of punishment or hope of worldly advancement.

It is difficult not to let one's opinion's harden into dogmas when one is attacked by furious dogmatists. But dogmatic or resistance and pusillanimous surrender are alike untrue to the scientific spirit. It is for the scientific spirit, not for any conclusions to which it may have provisionally led me, that I am prepared to fight with all my strength. For it is only by the scientific spirit wedded to loving-kindness that human life can be made less painful and less full of misery than it is now and has always been since the dawn of history.

24

A Liberal View of Divorce

In 1929 the Catholic Church held firm in its opposition to divorce, regardless of the grounds offered to support the dissolution of a marriage. In England and in many parts of the United States a couple could obtain a divorce only if proof of adultery was available, and even then, several states forbade divorce altogether.

Written in the same year as Marriage and Morals, *this essay argues for an easing of strict divorce laws. According to Russell, adultery, by itself, should not be grounds for divorce, since there can be other factors, such as insanity, habitual drunkenness, and criminal actions that should provide grounds for the dissolution of a marriage. Russell further argues that one should be able to obtain a divorce by mutual consent. By today's standards such a suggestion sounds reasonable enough; but in Russell's day, the law of England, like that of New York State, made it clear that there should be no divorce if both parties desire it. Russell considered such a view patently ridiculous.*

On few matters is there such diversity of law and custom as on divorce. The Catholic Church is opposed to divorce entirely on no matter what ground. The Soviet Republic allows divorce on the application of either party. The Scandanavian countries permit divorce by mutual consent. England admits only one ground, namely, adultery. Within the United States divorce laws differ widely. The law of New York State is the same as that of England. South Carolina has no divorce; Nevada is nearly as liberal as Scandinavia. Can we find any principle by which to judge as between these varying customs?

Originally published as *Little Blue Book* number 1582 (Girard, Kan.: Haldeman-Julius Publications, 1929).

Clearly the interests of children provide the main argument a-
gainst too easy divorce. When a marriage is childless the State has
no interest in its permanence, and it ought to be dissoluble on the
application of either party. Children are the one purpose of marriage, and no one should be tied to a union which fails in this
respect. But when there are children the matter is more complicated.
Divorce is apt to inflict psychological damage upon children, but at
least equal damage results from quarrels between parents and an
atmosphere of hostility in the home. There are therefore two opposite sets of considerations, between which a balance must be struck.

I do not think that adultery, by itself, should be a ground of
divorce. A large percentage of husbands and a not inconsiderable
percentage of wives, are occasionally and more or less casually unfaithful, particularly during enforced separations, without any desire to break up the home or any cessation of mutual affection. In
such cases it is the duty of the other partner to be tolerant, and not
to attach undue importance to a passing incident. The excessive
jealousy which at present makes such an attitude difficult would be
less difficult to control if it were not encouraged by public opinion,
which regards it as not merely justifiable but positively virtuous.

The most usual ground for divorce ought to be one which at
present is allowed in few countries, namely, mutual consent. The
law of England, like that of New York State, lays it down that there
shall be no divorce if both parties desire it. This is inherently absurd; there is nothing that makes a marriage of which both husband
and wife are weary better worth preserving than one which still
seems good to one of the parties. Moreover, as every one knows, the
law gives rise to evasions and perjuries; the great majority of divorces are in fact obtained by mutual consent, though lawyers and
judges have to pretend ignorance of this fact. It would be far better
to bring the law into conformity with what is really done, since
it is impossible to bring practice into conformity with the theory of
the law.

Another advantage of mutual consent is that it avoids the necessity for a public quarrel and for the villification of the "guilty"
party. The official adultery to which men have to submit in order
that their wives may divorce them is a sordid business, and not the
sort of thing that the law ought to demand and promote as it does
when adultery is the sole ground for divorce. Moreover, if mutual
consent is admitted, questions of alimony and custody of children
can be settled out of court by private treaty between husband and

wife, the Court being merely called upon to sanction whatever agreement has been reached. There is a fear that divorce would become commoner if mutual consent were permitted, but this fear appears to be groundless. Sweden, which permits this cause, has a much lower divorce rate than America. For these reasons I should advocate mutual consent as the ground wherever neither party has any special and unusual defect.

There remain, however, such matters as insanity, crime, and dipsomania. The failure to recognize these as grounds for divorce is an intolerable cruelty, not only to the husband or wife, but also to the children. Perhaps insanity is the clearest case. Our moralists are so much concerned that divorce shall only occur as punishment for sin that they have quite lost sight of the paramount consideration, namely, the welfare of children. They argue that since it is not wicked to be mad it ought not to be a ground for divorce. Thus men and women find themselves tied to partners who ought not to have access to the children, and commanded to have no more children unless they choose a lunatic for the other parent. This law can be understood on the hypothesis that it was made by lunatics, but on no other.

Very similar considerations apply to serious crime. If children have a jailbird for a father their welfare is not furthered by decreeing that their mother must be tied to him for life. Dipsomania, when it is sufficiently pronounced to need medical treatment in a home, and even when it only goes as far as habitual drunkenness, is a thing from which children should be shielded. In all such cases the refusal to allow the marriage to be dissolved is wanton cruelty and cannot be justified on any human or humane ground. Those who believe that religion enjoins such unnecessary suffering must have cruelty in their hearts, or else be incapable of freeing themselves from traditions that descend from a less merciful age.

While I hold that the legally permitted grounds for divorce ought to be extended as widely as they are in Scandinavia, I hold, nevertheless that as a matter of private morality parents ought to be slow to resort to divorce except for grave causes. The way to secure this, however, is not by harsh laws but by making parents more conscious of their obligations toward children and of the need of mutual forbearance resulting from these obligations. If a marriage brings lifelong happiness so much the better; but even if it does not, conscientious parents will hesitate to subject their children to the emotional strain and nervous damage too often entailed by separation or violent disagreement. This is a matter for the individual conscience and no good purpose is served when the law compels men and women to pretend to a degree of virtue that they do not possess.

To sum up: When there are no children divorce should be obtainable at the request of either party. Where there are children the usual ground should be mutual consent; other grounds should be insanity, grave crime, habitual drunkenness and venereal disease. Adultery *per se* should not be a ground.

Existing unduly severe laws can only be amended when there is a dominant political party not appealing for support to any of the churches. This means that in English-speaking countries the most that can be hoped is the maintenance of the *status quo*, at any rate for many years to come.

Part Five

Happiness

Introduction

Bertrand Russell was always aware that his rationalistic philosophy could be construed as gloomy. It was not uncommon for people to ask what his reasoned approach offered to replace restrictive dogmatism. What hope of happiness could he hold out to those who decided to abandon creed to walk the path of reason? Russell replied by saying: "In the first place, I do not say that I can offer as much happiness as is to be obtained by the abdication of reason. I do not say that I can offer as much happiness as is to be obtained from drink or drugs or amassing great wealth by swindling widows and orphans. It is not the happiness of the individual convert that concerns me; it is the happiness of mankind. If you genuinely desire the happiness of mankind, certain forms of ignoble personal happiness are not open to you. If your child is ill, and you are a conscientious parent, you accept medical diagnosis, however doubtful and discouraging; if you accept the cheerful opinion of a quack and your child consequently dies, you are not excused by the pleasantness of belief in the quack while it lasted."[1]

Russell taught that the beginning of wisdom and happiness rested in our acceptance of the fact that the universe was not concerned about our aspirations and that happiness and unhappiness were not distributed in accordance with what people deserve. "The secret of happiness," he observed during a television program celebrating his ninety-second birthday, "is to face the fact that the world is horrible." This point was elaborated earlier by Alan Wood in the penultimate chapter of his biography of Russell. Wood relates the story about how Russell's wife had expressed her opinion that it seemed horribly unjust that a young man who had been killed in war should not somehow or somewhere have a second chance to achieve happiness. "But the universe is unjust," Russell replied, "the secret of happiness is to face the fact that the world is horrible, horrible, horrible . . . you must feel it deeply and not brush it aside . . . you must feel it right here"—hitting his breast—"and then you can start being happy again."[2]

Russell believed that once a person has stopped believing that the universe has an overall sense of direction and purpose, he or she could then concentrate on what is attainable and not waste time in self-pity and cosmic complaints.

NOTES

1. Bertrand Russell. *The Impact of Science on Society* (New York: Simon and Schuster, 1953), p. 87.

2. Alan Wood. *Bertrand Russell: The Passionate Skeptic.* (New York: Simon and Schuster, 1957), p. 237.

25

What Makes People Unhappy?

Although this essay contains no profound philosophy or deep erudition, it contains Russell's extremely intelligent discussion of the causes of unhappiness. It was written in the hope that many unhappy people could become happy by well-directed effort.

Animals are happy so long as they have health and enough to eat. Human beings, one feels, ought to be, but in the modern world they are not, at least in a great majority of cases. If you are unhappy yourself, you will probably be prepared to admit that you are not exceptional in this. If you are happy, ask yourself how many of your friends are so. And when you have reviewed your friends, teach yourself the art of reading faces; make yourself receptive to the moods of those whom you meet in the course of an ordinary day.

> A mark in every face I meet,
> Marks of weakness, marks of woe

says Blake. Though the kinds are different, you will find that unhappiness meets you everywhere. Let us suppose that you are in New York, the most typically modern of great cities. Stand in a busy street during working hours, or on a main thoroughfare at a weekend, or at a dance of an evening; empty your mind of your own ego, and let the personalities of the strangers about you take possession of you one after another. You will find that each of these different crowds has its own trouble. In the work-hour crowd you

will see anxiety, excessive concentration, dyspepsia, lack of interest
in anything but the struggle, incapacity for play, unconsciousness
of their fellow creatures. On a main road at the weekend you will see
men and women, all comfortably off, and some very rich, engaged
in the pursuit of pleasure. This pursuit is conducted by all at a
uniform pace, that of the slowest car in the procession; it is impossible to see the road for the cars, or the scenery since looking aside
would cause an accident; all the occupants of all the cars are absorbed in the desire to pass other cars, which they cannot do on
account of the crowd; if their minds wander from this preoccupation,
as will happen occasionally to those who are not themselves driving,
unutterable boredom seizes upon them and stamps their features
with trivial discontent. Once in a way a carload of colored people
will show genuine enjoyment, but will cause indignation by erratic
behavior, and ultimately get into the hands of the police owing to
an accident: enjoyment in holiday time is illegal.

Or, again, watch people at a gay evening. All come determined
to be happy, with the kind of grim resolve with which one determines not to make a fuss at the dentist's. It is held that drink and
petting are the gateways to joy, so people get drunk quickly, and try
not to notice how much their partners disgust them. After a sufficient amount of drink, men begin to weep, and to lament how
unworthy they are morally, of the devotion of their mothers. All
that alcohol does for them is to liberate the sense of sin, which
reason suppresses in saner moments.

The causes of these various kinds of unhappiness lie partly in
the social system, partly in individual psychology—which, of course,
is itself to a considerable extent a product of the social system. I
have written before about the changes in the social system required
to promote happiness. Concerning the abolition of war, of economic
exploitation, of education in cruelty and fear, it is not my intention
to speak in this volume. To discover a system for the avoidance of
war is a vital need of our civilization; but no such system has a
chance while men are so unhappy that mutual extermination seems
to them less dreadful than continued endurance of the light of day.
To prevent the perpetuation of poverty is necessary if the benefits of
machine production are to accrue in any degree to those most in
need of them; but what is the use of making everybody rich if the
rich themselves are miserable? Education in cruelty and fear is bad,
but no other kind can be given by those who are themselves the
slaves of these passions. These considerations lead us to the problem

of the individual: what can a man or woman, here and now, in the midst of our ostalgic society, do to achieve happiness for himself or herself? In discussing this problem, I shall confine my attention to those who are not subject to any extreme cause of outward misery. I shall assume a sufficient income to secure food and shelter, sufficient health to make ordinary bodily activities possible. I shall not consider the great catastrophes, such as loss of all one's children, or public disgrace. There are things to be said about such matters, and they are important things, but they belong to a different order from the things that I wish to say. My purpose is to suggest a cure for the ordinary day-to-day unhappiness from which most people in civilized countries suffer, and which is all the more unbearable because, having no obvious external cause, it appears inescapable. I believe this unhappiness to be very largely due to mistaken views of the world, mistaken ethics, mistaken habits of life, leading to destruction of that natural zest and appetite for possible things upon which all happiness, whether of men or animals, ultimately depends. These are matters which lie within the power of the individual, and I propose to suggest the changes by which his happiness, given average good fortune, may be achieved.

Perhaps the best introduction to the philosophy which I wish to advocate will be a few words of autobiography. I was not born happy. As a child, my favorite hymn was: "Weary of earth and laden with my sin." At the age of five, I reflected that, if I should live to be seventy, I had only endured, so far, a fourteenth part of my whole life, and I felt the long-spread-out boredom ahead of me to be almost unendurable. In adolescence, I hated life and was continually on the verge of suicide, from which, however, I was restrained by the desire to know more mathematics. Now, on the contrary, I enjoy life; I might almost say that with every year that passes I enjoy it more. This is due partly to having discovered what were the things that I most desired, and having gradually acquired many of these things. Partly it is due to having successfully dismissed certain objects of desire—such as the acquisition of indubitable knowledge about something or other—as essentially unattainable. But very largely it is due to a diminishing preoccupation with myself. Like others who had a Puritan education, I had the habit of meditating on my sins, follies, and shortcomings. I seemed to myself—no doubt justly—a miserable specimen. Gradually I learned to be indifferent to myself and my deficiencies; I came to center my attention increasingly upon external objects: the state of the world, various branches of knowledge, individuals for whom I felt affection. External interests, it is true, bring each its own possibility of pain: the world may be plunged in war, knowledge in some direction may be hard to achieve, friends may die. But pains of these kinds do not destroy the essential quality of life, as do those that spring from disgust with self. And every external interest inspires some activity which, so long as the interest remains alive, is a complete preventive of *ennui*. Interest in oneself, on the contrary, leads to no activity of a progressive kind. It may lead to the keeping of a diary, to getting psychoanalyzed, or perhaps to becoming a monk. But the monk will not be happy until the routine of the monastery has made him forget his own soul. The happiness which he attributes to religion he could have obtained from becoming a crossing-sweeper, provided he were compelled to remain one. External discipline is the only road to happiness for those unfortunates whose self-absorption is too profound to be cured in any other way.

Self-absorption is of various kinds. We may take the sinner, the narcissist, and the megalomaniac as three very common types.

When I speak of "the sinner," I do not mean the man who commits sins: sins are committed by everyone or no one, according to our definition of the word. I mean the man who is absorbed in the consciousness of sin. This man is perpetually incurring his own disapproval, which, if he is religious, he interprets as the disapproval of God. He has an image of himself as he thinks he ought to be, which is in continual conflict with his knowledge of himself as he is. If, in his conscious thought, he has long since discarded the maxims that he was taught at his mother's knee, his sense of sin may be buried deep in his unconscious, and only emerge when he is drunk or asleep. Nevertheless, it may suffice to take the savour out of everything. At bottom he still accepts all the prohibitions he was taught in infancy. Swearing is wicked; drinking is wicked; ordinary business shrewdness is wicked; above all, sex is wicked. He does not, of course, abstain from any of these pleasures, but they are all poisoned for him by the feeling that they degrade him. The one pleasure that he desires with his whole soul is that of being approvingly caressed by his mother, which he can remember having experienced in childhood. This pleasure being no longer open to him, he feels that nothing matters; since he *must* sin, he decides to sin deeply. When he falls in love he looks for maternal tenderness, but cannot accept it, because, owing to the mother-image, he feels no respect for any woman with whom he has sexual relations. Then, in his disappointment, he becomes cruel, repents of his cruelty, and starts afresh on the dreary round of imagined sin and real remorse. This is the psychology of very many apparently hard-boiled reprobates. What drives them astray is devotion to an unattainable object (mother or mother-substitute) together with the inculcation, in early years, of a ridiculous ethical code. Liberation from the tyranny of early beliefs and affections is the first step towards happiness for these victims of maternal "virtue."

Narcissism is, in a sense, the converse of an habitual sense of sin; it consists in the habit of admiring oneself and wishing to be admired. Up to a point it is, of course, normal, and not to be deplored; it is only in its excesses that it becomes a grave evil. In many women, especially rich society women, the capacity for feeling love is completely dried up, and is replaced by a powerful desire that all men should love them. When a woman of this kind is sure that a man loves her, she has no further use for him. The same thing occurs, though less frequently, with men; the classic example is the hero of *Liaisons Dangereuses*. When vanity is carried to this height, there is no genuine interest in any other person, and therefore no real satisfaction to be obtained from love. Other interests fail even more disastrously. A narcissist, for example, inspired by the homage paid to great painters, may become an art student; but, as painting is for him a mere means to an end, the technique never becomes interesting, and no subject can be seen except in relation to self. The result is failure and disappointment, with ridicule instead of the expected adulation. The same thing applies to those novelists whose novels always have themselves idealized as heroines. All serious success in work depends upon some genuine interest in the material with which the work is concerned. The tragedy of one successful politician after another is the gradual substitution of narcissism for an interest in the community and the measures for which he stands. The man who is only interested in himself is not admirable, and is not felt to be so. Consequently the man whose sole concern with the world is that it shall admire him is not likely to achieve his object. But even if he does, he will not be completely happy, since human instinct is never completely self-centered, and the narcissist is limiting himself artificially just as truly as is the man dominated by a sense of sin. The primitive man might be proud of being a good hunter, but he also enjoyed the activity of the chase. Vanity, when it passes beyond a point, kills pleasure in every activity for its own sake, and thus leads inevitably to listlessness and boredom. Often its source is diffidence, and its cure lies in the growth of self-respect. But this is only to be gained by successful activity inspired by objective interests.

The megalomanic differs from the narcissist by the fact that he wishes to be powerful rather than charming, and seeks to be feared rather than loved. To this type belong many lunatics and most of the great men in history. Love of power, like vanity, is a strong element in normal human nature, and as such is to be accepted; it becomes deplorable only when it is excessive or associated with an insufficient sense of reality. Where this occurs it makes a man unhappy or foolish, if not both. The lunatic who thinks he is a crowned head may be, in a sense, happy, but his happiness is not of a kind that any sane person would envy. Alexander the Great was pyschologically of the same type as the lunatic, though he possessed the talent to achieve the lunatic's dream. He could not, however, achieve his own dream, which enlarged its scope as his achievement grew. When it became clear that he was the greatest conqueror known to fame, he decided that he was a God. Was he a happy man? His drunkenness, his furious rages, his indifference to women, and his claim to divinity, suggest that he was not. There is no ultimate satisfaction in the cultivation of one element of human nature at the expense of all the others, nor in viewing all the world as raw material for the magnificence of one's own ego. Usually the megalomaniac, whether insane or nominally sane, is the product of some excessive humiliation. Napoleon suffered at school from inferiority to his schoolfellows, who were rich aristocrats, while he was a penurious scholarship boy. When he allowed the return of the *émigrés,* he had the satisfaction of seeing his former schoolfellows bowing down before him. What bliss! Yet it led to the wish to obtain a similar satisfaction at the expense of the Czar, and this led to Saint Helena. Since no man can be omnipotent, a life dominated wholly by love of power can hardly fail, sooner or later, to meet with obstacles that cannot be overcome. The knowledge that this is so can only be prevented from obtruding on consciousness by some form of lunacy, though if a man is sufficiently great he can imprison or execute those who point this out to him. Repressions in the political mind and in the psychoanalytic senses thus go hand in hand. And wherever psychoanalytic repression in any marked form takes place, there is no genuine happiness. Power kept within its proper bounds may add greatly to happiness, but as the sole end of life it leads to disaster, inwardly if not outwardly.

The psychological causes of unhappiness, it is clear, are many and various. But all have something in common. The typical unhappy man is one who, having been deprived in youth of some normal satisfaction, has come to value this one kind of satisfaction more than any other, and has therefore given to his life a one-sided direction, together with a quite undue emphasis upon the achievement as opposed to the activities connected with it. There is, however, a further development which is very common in the present day. A man may feel so completely thwarted that he seeks no form of satisfaction, but only distraction and oblivion. He then becomes a devotee of "pleasure." That is to say, he seeks to make life bearable by becoming less alive. Drunkenness, for example, is temporary suicide; the happiness that it brings is merely negative, a momentary cessation of unhappiness. The narcissist and the megalomaniac believe that happiness is possible, though they may adopt mistaken means of achieving it; but the man who seeks intoxication, in whatever form, has given up hope except in oblivion. In his case, the first thing to be done is to persuade him that happiness is desirable. Men who are unhappy, like men who sleep badly, are always proud of the fact. Perhaps their pride is like that of the fox who had lost his tail; if so, the way to cure it is to point out to them how they can grow a new tail. Very few men, I believe, will deliberately choose unhappiness if they see a way of being happy. I do not deny that such men exist, but they are not sufficiently numerous to be important. I shall therefore assume that the reader would rather be happy than unhappy. Whether I can help him to realize his wish, I do not know; but at any rate the attempt can do no harm.

26

How to Be Free and Happy

Originally delivered as a lecture to the Rand School of Social Science in New York City under the auspices of the Young People's Socialist League on May 28, 1924, this essay was published by the Rand School later that year.

In this lecture Russell provoked a great deal of laughter by stating: "In America, I have spent most of my time by preaching idleness. I made up my mind when I was young that I would not be restrained from preaching a doctrine merely because I have not practiced it. I have not been able to practice the doctrine of idleness, because the preaching of it takes up so much time."

Here, Russell explains that idleness "is simply work or activity which is not part of your regular professional job." He deplored the excessive subservience of Americans to the ethic that "what we do is get on in our business, and get a fortune which we can leave to our descendants." According to Russell, the solution to an unhappy life could be found in obtaining wider interests; he maintains that under a good social system we should not have to work more than four hours a day. Responding to audience applause, Russell said: "Well, I am very glad to get that response from you, but when I made this remark to some other audiences in America a thrill of horror went through them and they said to me: 'What on earth should we do with the other twenty hours?' I felt, after that, that this gospel very much needed preaching."

The subject upon which I am supposed to be talking to you tonight is a very modest and easy subject—"How to Be Free and Happy." I do not know whether I can give you a recipe, like a cookbook recipe, which each one of you can apply. I do want, this last time that I am

---

Originally published by the Rand School of Social Science in 1924.

speaking in America, to say a few things which I believe firmly and consider, as far as my own experience goes, very important, and which I have not had much occasion, in previous talks, to say in this country.

Perhaps there may be some of you here, and certainly there are many elsewhere, who will say that the whole answer to my question "How to Be Free and Happy" is summed up in one simple sentence—"Get a good income!" That is an answer which I think is generally accepted. If I put that forward I should have won the assent of everyone that is not here. However, I think that it is a mistake to imagine that money, that income, is a very much more important thing in producing happiness than it actually is. I have known in the course of my life a great many rich people, and I can hardly think of one of them who appears to be either happy or free. I have known a great many people who were extremely poor—they also could hardly be happy and free. But in the intermediate realms you find most happiness and freedom. It is not great wealth or great poverty that brings most happiness.

My impression about it is this: that when you are talking of the external conditions of happiness—I am going to talk mostly of the conditions in your own mind, about the internal conditions—a person must have, of course, enough to eat and the necessaries of life and what is needed for the care of children. When you have those things you have as much as really contributes to happiness. Beyond that you only multiply cares and anxiety. So that I don't think enormous wealth is the solution. I should say, for the external conditions of happiness, that in this country, as far as the material problem of the production of goods is concerned, you have quite solved it. If the goods that are produced were distributed with any justice, that certainly would be a real contribution towards happiness. Your problem here is two-fold. It is first a political problem: to secure the advantages of your unrivalled production for a wider circle. On the other hand, it is the psychological problem of learning how to get the good out of these material conditions that have been created by our industrial age. That, I think, is where we modern people have failed most—on the psychological side, on the side of being able to enjoy the opportunities which we have created. I think that this is due to a number of causes.

I should attribute it partly to the effect of Puritanism in decay. Puritanism in its heyday was a conception of life which filled people's minds and made them in their way happy. Anything which fills people's minds makes them happy. But people nowadays don't believe in the Puritan way; they retain certain principles which are connected with Puritanism, though not perhaps quite obviously. They have, in the first place, a certain kind of moral outlook, that is, a tendency to be looking out for opportunities to find fault with others, a tendency to think that it is very important to keep up certain rules of conduct. There are a number of old, inherited taboos and rules which people don't think about but simply go on with because they always have been there. These do not touch the core of the matter. The thing that has survived most out of Puritanism is a contempt for happiness—not a contempt for pleasure, *a contempt for happiness!* You find among rebels a very great desire for pleasure but a very small realization of happiness as against pleasure, and that has gone through our whole conception of pleasure and of happiness.

For ages the Puritan outlook was devoted to making people think that pleasure was a base thing, and because of that belief the people who were not base did not devote themselves to producing the better forms of pleasure, such forms as art, etc., and pleasure, therefore, became just as base as the Puritans said it was. And that evil has tended to survive. It tends to be still the case that the nations, such as yours and mine, which have gone through this Puritan phase are unable to get happiness and even to get pleasure—pleasure that is not trivial. It is only the less worthy forms of pleasure which survive in spite of that Puritan domination. I think that perhaps that is the main reason why Puritanism, wherever it has existed, has proved itself so very destructive of art, because art, after all, is the pursuit of a certain kind, probably the most supreme and perfect kind, of pleasure; and if you think of pleasure as bad, art is bad. That is one thing that we owe to Puritanism.

Another thing that we owe to it is the belief in work. In America I have spent most of my time in preaching idleness. I made up my mind when I was young that I would not be restrained from preaching a doctrine merely because I have not practiced it. I have not been able to practice the doctrine of idleness, because the preaching of it takes up so much time. I don't mean idleness in the literal sense, for most people, the great majority of us white people, don't enjoy sitting in the sun and doing nothing; we like to be busy. What I mean by idleness is simply work or activity which is not part of your regular professional job. Under the influence of this dogma, Puritanism has forced us to retain in our operative beliefs the notion that the important part of our life is work. That, at any rate, applies to the major portion of mankind: that the important part of what we do is getting on in our business, and getting a fortune which we can leave to our descendants, and they, in turn, get a larger fortune to leave to theirs. This whole business has taken the place of living for Heaven, for in the old Puritan days we tried to forgo pleasures in life in order to get to Heaven.

Heaven has disappeared, but the idea of living in order to leave a large fortune has not disappeared, and the kind of a life which is required for the one purpose is much the same that is required for the other—the foregoing of enjoyment for the sake of future benefits. That we have retained from the old Puritan outlook, and that, I think, is not in its modern form a very fine or noble thing. In the old days there was something splendid about it, but in this modern form it is not anything that we should particularly admire, and for the sake of it we do forego everything that would make life civilized, free and happy.

By the way, let me tell you what I have often noticed when I have been traveling on the continent of Europe, where there are beautiful objects of art. I have seen the middle-aged American businessman being dragged about by his wife and daughter in a condition of almost intolerable boredom, because he was away from his office. It would be a better thing if, instead of getting concentrated upon work, people had larger interests. If we had a good social system we ought none of us have to work more than four hours a day. (Applause) Well, I am very glad to get that response from you, but when I made this remark to some other audiences in America a thrill of horror went through them and they said to me: "What on earth should we do with the other twenty hours?" I felt, after that, that this gospel very much needed preaching.

It is really a terrible thing to get the human being with all his capacities—to get him into blinkers with such a narrow outlook that he can only run along one little path. It is a disfigurement of the human being—it is something that every person who wants to see growth finds intolerable. A population of stunted human beings is growing up, shut out from the pleasures of human companionship, the pleasures of art, the pleasure from all the things that really make life worth living. Because, after all, to struggle all your days to amass a fortune is not really an end worthy of anyone.

I don't want to suggest to anyone that pleasure, mere pleasure, is an end in itself. I don't think it is, and, indeed, I think that the effect of the Puritan morality has been to emphasize pleasures at the expense of happiness, because, as base pleasures can be got more easily, they are less controlled by the censorship of official morals. We all know, of course, the sort of way in which the ordinary person who does not live up to the official morality of his time fails to do so: he seeks those ways which are most frivolous and have the least value in their own selves. That always will be the effect of a morality which is preached but not practiced.

I think the Chinese have shown their own wisdom by having an official morality which can be practiced. We in the West who have adopted the opposite plan, we have prided ourselves upon the extraordinary magnificence of the morality we profess, and thought that excused us from practicing it. I think that if we are going to have a true morality, if we are going to have an outlook upon life which is going to make life richer and freer and happier, it must not be a repressive outlook, it must not be an outlook based upon any kind of restrictions or prohibitions; it must be an outlook based upon the things that we love rather than those that we hate. There are a number of emotions which guide our lives, and roughly you can divide them into those that are repressive and those that are expansive. Repressive emotions are cruelty, fear, jealousy; expansive emotions are such as hope, love of art, impulse of constructiveness, love, affection, intellectual curiosity, and kindliness; and they make more of life instead of less. I think that the essence of true morality consists in living by the expansive impulses and not by the repressive ones.

What I am saying has, I am afraid, very revolutionary consequences to which I cannot hope to win the assent of everyone. There will be many who think that my deductions are not deductions to be accepted. For example, love and jealousy are—the one expansive and the other repressive. Now, in our traditional morality, when you subject it to psychological analysis and see whence it has sprung, you will all have to admit that jealousy has been the main-spring; it has been jealousy that has given rise to it. I don't myself feel that it is very probable that a code rising in that way and from that source can be the best possible. It seems to me far more likely that one arising out of the positive emotions would be better than one arising out of the negative, and that such restrictions as would have to be placed on freedom should arise out of affection or kindliness for other persons, and not out of the sheer repressive emotion of jealousy. If you apply *that* principle it leads to a better development of character and more wholesome type of person, a person freed from many of the cruelties which limit the conventional moralist.

There is a very strong element of cruelty in traditional morals—part of the satisfaction which every moralist derives from his morality is that it gives him the justification for inflicting pain. We all know that the infliction of punishment is to a great many people delightful. There was once a prime minister who traveled from Constantinople to Antioch, and spent there eight hours watching his enemy being tortured. I think that the impulse toward pleasure in the suffering of others is one which arises through people thwarting their natural emotions, through the fact that they have not been able to find a free outlet for their creative impulses.

I do not positively *know* whether that is really the basis of a great deal of cruelty, but I cannot help thinking that an enormous mass of the cruelty that we see in the world is from unconscious envy. That is a very deep-seated feeling in human nature, and when you have a nice, convenient code to embody it, of course it is very popular.

I don't know whether I can quite convey to you the kind of way in which it seems to me that one can live most happily. I find things in the Gospels which illustrate the sort of thing I mean—not texts which are very often quoted, but, for example, "Take no thought what ye shall eat, or what ye shall drink, or wherewithal ye shall be clothed." If you really lived upon that principle—which, by the way, forbids all discussion of the Volstead Act—you would find life very delightful. There is a certain kind of liberation, a certain kind of carefree attitude, which, if you can once acquire it, makes you able to go through the world untroubled, not distressed by all the minor annoyances that arise. The gist of the matter is to be rid of fear. Fear lies very deep in the heart of man; fear has been the source of most religions; fear has been the source of most moral codes; fear is our instincts; fear is encouraged in our youth, and fear is at the bottom of all that is bad in the world. When once you are rid of fear you have the freedom of the universe. Of course, you all know about the sort of dark superstitions of more barbarous ages, when men, women and children were sacrificed to the gods out of fear. This superstition we see to be dark and absurd, but our own superstitions do not strike us in the same light. Now, I am not prepared to say that no great disaster can ever overtake us, but I say this, that the fear of those things that might overtake us is a greater evil than the things themselves, and it would be far better to go through life not fearing, and come to some disaster, than go through life creeping, wise, and cautious, and burdened—never having enjoyed life at any moment and yet dying peacefully in your bed.

I think we want our lives to be expansive and creative, we want to live to a very great extent upon impulse; and when I say impulse I don't mean every transitory impulse of every passing moment—I mean those major impulses that really govern our lives. There are in some people great artistic impulses, in others scientific, and in others this or that form of affection or creativeness. And if you deny those impulses, provided that they do not infringe upon the liberty of another, you stunt your growth. I know, for instance, any number of men who are Socialists, and who spend their lives as journalists writing for the most conservative papers. These men may get pleasure out of life, but I don't believe that it is possible for them to get happiness. Happiness is at an end for any man who denies himself one of those fundamental impulses about which life ought to grow.

I should say precisely the same thing about the private affections. Where a really strong or powerful affection exists, the man or woman who goes against it suffers the same kind of damage—it is the same kind of inner destruction of something precious and valuable; all the poets have said so. We have accepted it when it was said in verse, because nobody takes verse seriously, but if it is said in prose and in public we think it is very dreadful.

I don't know why everybody is allowed to say a host of things in private that he is not allowed to say in public. I think it is about time we said the same things in public that we say in private. Walt Whitman, in praise of the animals, says: "They don't grunt and sweat over their condition—not one of them is respectable or unhappy throughout the whole world." I must say I have a very great affection for Walt Whitman. He illustrates what I mean—how the man who lives expansively lives in a kindly way; how he is free from cruelty, from the desire to stop other people from doing what they want.

I think it is very important to get that idea into one's head— that every artificial morality means the growth of cruelty. Of course, we cannot live like Walt Whitman's animals, because man has foresight and memory, and, having foresight, he has to organize his life into a unit. That is where we develop our superstitions. And you know quite well that it would not do if you followed each whim without a certain amount of discipline, and I don't want you to think that there is not a need of discipline. There is, but it should be that discipline that comes from within, from the realization of one's own needs, from the feeling of something which one wishes to achieve. Nothing of importance is ever achieved without discipline. I feel myself sometimes not wholly in sympathy with some modern educational theorists, because I think that they underestimate the part that discipline plays. But the discipline you have in your life should be one determined by your own desires and your own needs, not put upon you by society or authority.

Authority comes from the past and the old, and, speaking to a League of Free Youth, I suppose I need not speak, at my time of life, with that respect which I might be expected to show to it, because the old, although they are supposed to be wise, are not necessarily wise. We learn a great deal in youth and forget a great deal in age. We are at our maximum at thirty; at thirty we are at the moment when we learn at the same rate at which we forget. After that we begin to forget faster than we learn; so if we do have to have authority I should have a council composed of persons of thirty, but on the whole I think we can do much better without authority in those matters which do not directly affect the rest of the world.

Of course, it is your affair if you murder someone, but it is his affair also; so you cannot object to someone coming to interfere with your murdering him. But in those acts which affect ourselves it is absurd that the State or public opinion should have any voice at all. In the private relations of life society should take no part whatsoever—that is a matter for the individual. The welfare of children is, of course, a matter in which the community is concerned. It is not at present enough concerned. About children: you want that there should be enough, but not too many; you want them to be healthy and educated. Those are the things that the State should see to. At present it sees to some and not to others. All those things are affairs for the State. But where children are not involved, it seems to me that all interference is an impertinence—the State has no business in the matter whatsoever. Now, I don't want to talk only about that issue, because there are many other directions in which the same kind of thing applies. It applies, above all, in the aesthetic side of life. We in our industrial civilization have taken over from Puritanism, from Christianity, a certain utilitarian outlook, a certain belief that our acts should not be for their own sakes, for what they are now, but for a certain distant end. Things get to be judged by their uses and not by their real values. That is death to the aesthetic side of life, for the beauty of anything consists in what the thing is in itself and not in its uses.

I admit the sphere of the utilitarian, but not in judging of artistic matters. I find that we seem to have lost not only in the world of art—that is generally admitted—but we have lost something also in human companionship, in friendship, through not having so great a sense of intrinsic quality as we used to have. A man tends to be judged by what he does, and that is quite a different thing from the intrinsic quality of him; and so you will find that when a man has become a celebrity, everybody knows that what he says is very wonderful, whereas in his youth, when he was not recognized as a celebrity, he may have said far more wonderful things without being noticed. The excellence of a man's remarks, even if he is not famous, should be recognized, as well as vice versa.

In our private relations we all get so busy that we have not time to develop affections for others as they deserve to be developed; we have not time for sympathy, the understanding for all those things that make the beauty of human relations, because we all are so busy, and when we are not busy we are tired. You have in this country, on the average, if the goods produced in this country were divided equally, much more than anybody needs for happiness, and it would be possible to live on a very much smaller amount of work and yet have enough; you could then develop and cultivate those things that make for happiness. You would have freedom. A man does not have freedom if he has to indulge all day in an activity which is not one he likes; that is as bad as a treadmill. We cannot always be doing delightful things, but we can for the greater part of the day; and I think that in the advanced industrial nations a better ideal of private happiness is probably the thing that is most wanted. More important even than political and economic reconstructions is the realization of the things that really make for human happiness.

We should not be so ready to go to war if our lives were happier. It is to my mind quite an amazing thing to see the extraordinary feebleness in the modern world of what you might call the will to live. There is a will to work, but not a will to live; you don't find that the prospect of wholesale destruction is considered intolerable. You don't find that people are willing to sacrifice money and power in order that they may be rid of the menace of war; they don't really want to be rid of it. A happy nation would not be willing to sacrifice life, health and happiness for the idle business of fighting, and possibly winning. This comes because our lives are too collective and too little individual. We, living as we do, forced by the mechanical mold of our civilization more and more to resemble each other, we, I say, more and more live by mass emotions and less and less by the individual, personal ones. In that way the individual gets sacrificed. A life where the individual is sacrificed is not one where the individual is going to have a strong love for life.

We imagine we want all sorts of things, such as power and wealth, which are not the sources of happiness. You will find the sources far more truly portrayed in the Gospel. I am speaking of just the sort of thing that I quoted a moment ago, about taking no thought for tomorrow. If you have a human being that you love, or a child, if you have any one thing that you really care for, life derives its meaning from that thing, and you can build up a whole world of people whose lives matter. But if you start with the nation—"Here am I; I am a member of a nation; I want my nation to be powerful"—then you are destroying the individual. You become oppressive, because whether your nation is powerful depends upon the regimentation of people and you set to work to regulate your neighbor.

It is the individual that is important. You will think that, perhaps, is an odd thing for a Socialist to say. I believe the material side of life has got to be given over to Socialistic organization, but I believe that because I think the material side of life is the least important. So long as you have not enough to keep your life tolerable, material things are all-important—in most European countries there is such dire poverty that material things are of the utmost importance. But we can now, with our capacity of technical production, totally abolish the problem of poverty, that lingers because we are perfect asses. And when you think of the world you will have when poverty is eliminated, you see that in such a world material things will not be the important ones. You will have to settle, in a Socialistic community, whether the community is to work an extra hour a day and have an extra motor-car for each member. In such a community as that the spiritual goods will be more important, will be worth more than the things that are got through the collective community. The collective ocmmunity will give you your daily bread and your daily tasks. Your leisure you can devote, if you like, to other work, or football or movies, or whatnot.

I am sometimes asked: How can you ensure that people will use their leisure well? I don't want to ensure it. You are still in the realm of undue morality, of undue pressure of the community upon the individual, when you raise such a problem. As long as leisure is not used in any way to damage other people, it is a matter for the individual. Well, then, I say in the spiritual world we want individualism. It is in the material world that we want Socialism. We have Socialism now in the spiritual world and we have individualism now in the material world.

What you are to think, how you are to manage your emotions, are supposed to be matters for the State to settle; but whether you are to have enough to eat, that is not a matter of the State—there the sacred principle of liberty comes in. It has been put in exactly the wrong place. The thing that I am saying to you is really, after all, exactly what all great religious leaders have said, that the soul of man is the important thing. And that is the great thing to learn. The great thing is to feel in yourself that the soul, your own thoughts, your own understandings and sympathies, that is the thing that matters and that the external outward decor of life is unimportant so long as you have enough to keep you going and to keep you alive. It is because we are so immersed in competitiveness that we do not understand this simple truth.

I have been talking rather lightly to you, but the thing that I mean is something immensely living and a real kind of liberation— being free in this world, free of the universe, so that the things that happen to you no longer worry you, the things that occur no longer seem to matter. There is a kind of fire that can live in the soul of every man and woman, and when you have that you don't care any longer about the little things of which our lives are so full. You can live in that way—you can live freely and expansively. You will find that when you let those fears drop off you are closer to others, you can enjoy friendship in a different degree. The whole world is more interesting, more living—there is something there that is infinitely more valuable. Whoever has once tasted it knows that it is infinitely better than those things gotten by other methods. It is an old secret—it has been taught by all teachers and been forgotten by their priests; it is that secret of being in close contact with the world, of not having the walls of self so rigid that you cannot see what is beyond. The moralist is concerned to think "How virtuous I am," and he also is an egoist like the rest. It is not in that world of hard immorals that you will find the life that is happy and free. It is in the kind of life where you have lost fear because a little hurt is worth enduring—it comes from the knowledge of the fact that there is something better than the avoidance of hurt—there is the securing of a kind of intense union with the world, a kind of intense love, something glowing, warm, like a personal affection and yet universal. If you can achieve that you will know the secret of a happy life.

Bibliography

A COMPLETE LIST OF BERTRAND RUSSELL'S BOOKS*

1896 *German Social Democracy*

1897 *An Essay on the Foundations of Geometry*

1900 *A Critical Exposition of the Philosophy of Leibniz*

1903 *The Principles of Mathematics*

1910 *Philosophical Essays*

1912 *Problems of Philosophy*

1913 *Principia Mathematica* (with Alfred North Whitehead)
  Volume I (1910)
  Volume II (1911)
  Volume III (1913)

1914 *Our Knowledge of the External World*

1916 *Justice in Wartime*
  Principles of Social Reconstruction [*Why Men Fight*]

1917 *Political Ideals*

1918 *Mysticism and Logic*
  Roads to Freedom: Socialism, Anarchism and Syndicalism

1919 *Introduction to Mathematical Philosophy*

1920 *The Practice and Theory of Bolshevism*

American titles appear in brackets.—Ed.

1921   *The Analysis of Mind*

1922   *The Problem of China*

1923   *The ABC of Atoms*
       The Prospects of Industrial Civilization (with Dora Russell)

1924   *Icarus or the Future of Science*

1925   *The ABC of Relativity*
       What I Believe

1926   *On Education Especially in Early Childhood*
       [Education and the Good Life]

1927   *The Analysis of Matter*
       An Outline of Philosophy [Philosophy]
       Selected Papers of Bertrand Russell

1928   *Skeptical Essays*

1929   *Marriage and Morals*

1930   *The Conquest of Happiness*

1931   *The Scientific Outlook*

1932   *Education and the Social Order*
       [Education and the Modern World]

1934   *Freedom and Organization 1814-1914*
       [Freedom versus Organization 1812-1914]

1935   *In Praise of Idleness*
       Religion and Science

1936   *Which Way to Peace?*

1937   *The Amberley Papers* (with Patricia Russell)

1938   *Power*

1940   *An Inquiry into Meaning and Truth*

1945   *History of Western Philosophy*

1948   *Human Knowledge: Its Scope and Limits*

1949   *Authority and the Individual*

1950   *Unpopular Essays*

1951   *New Hopes for a Changing World*
       The Wit and Wisdom of Bertrand Russell
          (edited by L. Denonn)

1952   *Dictionary of Mind, Matter, and Morals*
          (edited by L. Denonn)
       The Impact of Science on Society

1953   *The Good Citizen's Alphabet*
       Satan in the Suburbs

1954   *Human Society in Ethics and Politics*
       Nightmares of Eminent Persons

1956   *Logic and Knowledge* (edited by R. C. Marsh)
       Portraits From Memory

1957   *Understanding History*
       Why I Am Not A Christian (edited by P. Edwards)

1958   *Bertrand Russell's Best* (edited by R. Egner)
       Vital Letters of Russell, Krushchev, and Dulles

1959   *Common Sense and Nuclear Warfare*
       My Philosophical Development
       Wisdom of the West (edited by P. Foulkes)

1960   *Bertrand Russell Speaks His Mind*

1961   *The Basic Writings of Bertrand Russell* (edited by
          R. Egner and L. Denonn)
       Fact and Fiction
       Has Man A Future?

1963   *Unarmed Victory*

1965   *On the Philosophy of Science* (edited by C. Fritz)

1967   *War Crimes in Vietnam*

1968   *The Art of Philosophizing*

1969   *Autobiography*
          Volume I (1967)
          Volume II (1968)

Volume III (1969)
Dear Bertrand Russell (edited by B. Feinberg and R. Kasrils)

1972   *The Collected Stories of Bertrand Russell* (edited by
B. Feinberg)

1986   *Bertrand Russell on God and Religion* (edited by Al Seckel)

The Collected Papers of Bertrand Russell Volumes 1-28

Currently available:

Volume 1 *Cambridge Essays, 1888-99*
Volume 7 *Theory of Knowledge: The 1913 Manuscript*
Volume 8 *The Philosophy of Logical Atomism and
Other Essays 1914-19*
Volume 12 *Contemplation and Action 1902-14*

SELECTED READING ON RUSSELL'S LIFE AND VIEWS

Aiken, Lillian. *Bertrand Russell's Philosophy of Morals*. New York: Humanities Press, 1963.

Ayer, A. J. *Bertrand Russell*. New York: Viking Press, 1972.

———. *Russell and Moore: The Analytical Heritage*. New York: Macmillan, 1971.

Buchler, Justus. "Russell and the Principles of Ethics," in *The Philosophy of Bertrand Russell* (Paul Schilpp ed.). La Salle, Illinois: Open Court, 1971). Fourth edition. pp. 513-535.

Clark, Ronald. *Bertrand Russell and His World*. New York: Thames and Hudson, 1981.

———. *The Life of Bertrand Russell*. New York: Alfred Knopf, 1976.

Copleston, S. J., Frederick. "Bertrand Russell's Moral Philosophy," in *A History of Philosophy*. Garden City, N.Y.: Image Books, 1967. Vol. 8, Part II. pp. 230-254.

Crawshay-Williams, Rupert. *Russell Remembered*. London: Oxford University Press, 1970.

Dewey, John (ed.). *The Bertrand Russell Case*. New York: Viking Press, 1941.

Edwards, Paul. "Russell: Life and Social Theories, Ethics and Critique of Religion," in *The Encyclopedia of Philosophy*. New York: Macmillan Publishing Co., 1967. Vol. 7, pp. 235-239, 251-258.

Feinberg, Barry and Ronald Kasrils (eds.). *Bertrand Russell's America: His Transatlantic Travels and Writings 1896-1945*. London: George Allen and Unwin, 1973.

———. *Bertrand Russell's America: 1945-1970*. Boston: South End Press, 1983.

Kohl, Marvin. "The Functions of Monogamous Marriage," in *Russell: The Journal of the Bertrand Russell Archives*. Vol. 5, no. 2 (Winter 1985-86): 162-68.

Kuntz, Paul. *Bertrand Russell*. Boston: Twayne Publishers, 1986.

Martin, Werner. *Bertrand Russell: A Bibliography of His Writings 1895-1976*. Connecticut: Linnet Books, 1981.

Matson, W. I. "Russell's Ethics," in *Bertrand Russell Memorial Volume* (George W. Roberts ed.). London: George Allen and Unwin, 1979.

Monro, D. H. "Russell's Moral Theories," in *Bertrand Russell: A Collection of Critical Essays* (David Pears, ed.). New York: Anchor Books, 1972.

Ruja, Harry. "Russell on the Meaning of Good," in *Russell: The Journal of the Bertrand Russell Archives*. Vol. 4, no. 1 (Summer 1984): 137-156.

Russell, Bertrand. "My Reply to Critics [on My Ethical Views]," in *The Philosophy of Bertrand Russell* (Paul Schilpp, ed.). La Salle, Ill.: Open Court, 1971. Fourth edition. pp. 719-729.

Schoenman, Ralph (ed.). *Bertrand Russell: Philosopher of the Century*. Boston: Atlantic Monthly, 1967.

Seckel, Al (ed.). *Bertrand Russell On God and Religion*. Buffalo, N. Y.: Prometheus Books, 1986.

Stapledon, Olaf. "Bertrand Russell's Ethical Beliefs," *International Journal of Ethics* 27 (1927):390-402.

Tait, Katherine. *My Father Bertrand Russell*. New York: Harcourt Brace Jovanovich, 1975.

Wood, Alan. *Bertrand Russell: The Passionate Skeptic*. New York: Simon and Schuster, 1958.

Index of Names

Aeschylus, 22
Agag (king), 77
Aiken, Lillian, 17, 338
Alexander the Great, 96, 320
Anthony, Saint, 214
Antony, Mark, 297
Aristotle, 66
Augustine, Saint, 91
Ayer, A. J., 338

Bagehot, Walter, 73
Bentham, Jeremy, 60, 89, 110, 132, 156
Blake, William, 315
Bright, John, 219
Brogan (Dr.), 149
Browne, Sir Thomas, 93
Buchler, Justus, 338
Buddha, 82, 84
Butler, Samuel, 118
Byron, Lord, 176, 177, 224

Caligula, 157
Calvin, John, 76
Charles V, 186
Christ (Jesus), 153, 174, 306, 307
Chuang-Tse, 79

Churchill, Sir Winston, 177
Clark, Ronald, 338
Cobden, 219
Confucius, 71, 174, 190ff.
Copleston, S. J., Frederick, 338
Corneille, 176
Crawshay-Williams, Rupert, 339
Cromwell, Oliver, 73

Dante, Alighieri, 214
David, 90, 93
Defoe, Daniel, 91
Dewey, John, 301, 339
Dickinson, Lowes, 109

Edwards, Paul, 339
Empedocles, 91, 185
Euripides, 77

Faraday, Michael, 145
Feinberg, Barry, 232, 250, 339
Fitzgerald, Edward, 40
Flanders, Moll, 91
Frederick II, 219
Freeman, R., 146
Freud, Sigmund, 207, 232

341

George I, 72
George III, 58
Gilais, Lionel, 191
Gladstone, William, 72
Gorki, Maxim, 152
Gregory the Great (pope), 91

Hamlet, 24, 31
Hammurabi, 174
Hannibal, 77
Haynes, E., 248
Hegel, Georg W. F., 120
Helena, Saint, 320
Herodotus, 117
Hertz, Heinrich, 145
Hitler, Adolf, 73

Iscariot, Judas, 59

James I, 93
Julius II, 217

Kant, Immanuel, 51, 110, 111
Kasrils, Ronald, 232, 250
Keats, John, 203
Kipling, Rudyard, 83
Kohl, Marvin, 339
Kropotkin, Peter, 89
Kuntz, Paul, 339

Lao-Tse, 79, 156, 191ff.
Lincoln, Abraham, 219
Lindsey, Judge Ben B., 250, 252ff.

Malthus, Thomas, 240, 252
Manning, Bishop William, 232, 301
Martin, Werner, 99, 339
Marx, Karl, 118, 207
Matson, W. I., 339

Maxwell, James Clerk, 145
McDougall, William, 249
Mendel, Gregor, 144
Michelangelo, 217
Mill, John Stuart, 132
Mohammed, 56
Moloch, 152
Monro, D. H., 339
Moore, George Edward, 15, 16, 17, 56
Moore, Tom, 176, 177
Müller-Lyer, 150, 151

Napoleon, 73, 118, 320
Nero, 88
Newsholme, A., 248
Newton, Sir Isaac, 93
Nietzsche, Friedrich, 60, 83, 110
Northcliffe, Lord, 142

Paul, Saint, 58, 71, 167, 255
Plato, 96, 175, 208, 210
Pythagoras, 90

Rabelais, Francois, 288
Rivers, 141
Rousseau, Jean Jacques, 135
Ruja, Harry, 339
Ruskin, John, 62

Samuel, 77, 85, 90, 174
Santayana, George, 15, 16
Sassoon, Siegfried, 147
Saul, 77, 174
Schilpp, Paul, 16, 113
Schoenman, Ralph, 340
Shaftesbury, Lord, 156
Shakespeare, William, 287, 304
Sidgwick, Henry, 89, 103, 105
Smith, Sidney, 51
Smollett, Tobias, 163

Socrates, 79, 88, 167, 264
Spartacus, 77
Spinoza, Baruch de, 26
Stalin, Joseph, 73, 82
Stapledon, Olaf, 340

Tait, Katherine, 340
Tawney, R. H., 85
Tolstoy, Leo, 30, 237

Uzzah, 90

Vesalius, Andreas, 186

Washington, George, 189
Watson (Dr.), 205
Webb, Sidney, 248
Wells, H. G., 160
Wesley, John, 156
Westermarck, Edward, 150
Whitman, Walt, 329
Wilson, Woodrow, 124
Wood, Alan, 109, 313, 314, 340
Wyatt, Woodrow, 179

Subject Index

Abortion, 252
Adultery, 72, 153, 154, 170, 172, 176, 203, 222-223, 225, 234, 235, 247, 256, 257, 261, 301ff., 307, 308, 310
Artificial insemination, 186
Asceticism, 225, 261
Authoritarianism, 119; in ethics, 72, 73, 85, 93, 94,

Bad, *see* Evil
Blameworthiness, moral, 36, 40, 42, 43, 55, 103, 131, 174
Birth control, 137, 223, 250, 252, 262, 263, 286
Bolshevik revolution, 115, 118, 124, 138
Boredom, 136, 159, 160, 284, 289
Buddhism, 27, 130

Capitalism, 58, 118, 121, 122, 123, 124, 138, 141, 208
Celibacy, 133
Censorship, 184ff.
Chinese morals, 115, 119, 142, 189ff.
Christian ethics, 58, 71, 72, 76, 77, 83, 151, 153, 158, 159, 167, 175, 192, 215, 262, 328
City College of New York, 232, 271, 301
Code of Hammurabi, 72, 174
Communism, 58, 96, 115, 208
Conduct, right and wrong, *see* Right and wrong actions
Conscience, (*see* also Intuitionism) 28ff., 47, 58, 59, 69, 94, 97, 169, 266
Consequences of actions, (*see* also Utilitarianism), 19, 20, 22, 28ff., 37, 39, 42, 43, 59, 65, 69, 81, 101, 104, 132
Cosmic Purpose, 57, 64, 89
Criminal code, 96, 157, 158, 181, 182
Cruelty, 26, 328

Darwinism (survival of the fittest), *see* Ethics (evolutionary)
Desirable, desire and desired, *see* Good, as satisfaction of desire
Determinism, 34, 37ff., 56

Deterrent justice, 52, 110
Disagreement, ethical, 35, 48, 50, 52, 55, 57, 60, 65, 83, 100, 101, 102, 110, 112
Disapproval, *see* Moral approval and disapproval
Divorce, 152, 153, 154, 158, 170, 210, 223, 224, 228, 231, 234, 236, 241, 247ff., 255, 257, 268, 275, 279, 286, 302, 303, 307ff.

Egoism, 44ff., 65, 130, 131, 139
Endogamy, 91
Ethical knowledge, 50, 61, 64, 66, 80, 82, 87, 88, 99, 100, 111
Ethical problems, nature of, 24, 25, 28, 32, 33, 34, 50, 51, 60, 61, 66, 88, 97
Ethics, definition of, 15, 19, 24, 28, 57, 61, 62, 64, 81, 87, 104; evolutionary, 26, 64, 65; objectivity in, 15, 16 30; and politics, 61, 83, 89, 94, 97, 111, 112, 181; as science, 15ff., 57, 60, 61, 87, 88, 99, 104, 154, 156, 157; skepticism in, 50, 52; subjectivity of, 15, 16, 24, 25, 50, 57, 64, 88, 99, 100, 105, 109, 110; universality in, 95, 96, 104, 105, 111
Eugenics, 163, 164, 211, 240, 241
Euthanasia, 175, 180
Evil or bad, concept and analysis, 17, 18, 20, 22, 25ff., 39, 42
Existence, as regards good and bad, 21, 22, 25, 26, 27, 38, 53, 55
Exogamy, 90

Fallacy of the aristocrat, 121ff.
Family strength, 151, 263

Fear, 328
Filial piety, 71
First World War, 18, 58, 124, 233
Free-will, 37ff., 43, 56

God, as evil, 158; as good, 25, 50, 52, 59, 60, 65, 120, 158
Good, concept and analysis of, 15, 16, 19ff., 38, 39, 42, 44ff., 59, 60ff., 87, 99, 100ff., 110, 111, 112; as happiness or pleasure, 19, 21, 23, 24, 45, 46, 54, 55, 60, 81, 82, 99, 102, 103, 105, 110, 111, 256; indefinability of, 24, 25, 100; as obedience to God, 24, 74, 93, 97; as satisfaction of desire, 21ff., 45, 47, 57, 61ff., 81, 82, 102, 111, 112
Good over evil, preponderance of, 28, 53
Good world, concept of, 25, 26, 28, 64, 65, 87, 120

Happiness, 125, 133ff., 141, 161, 313ff., 323ff.,
Heaven, 54, 326
Hedonism, 54, 55, 103, 161
Hell, 52, 64, 157, 182
Homosexuality, 104
Human Society in Ethics and Politics, 16, 69, 87, 99, 173
Human nature, 164
"Hypostatic Ethics," 15

Incest, 91
Industrialism, 117, 118, 120, 122, 123, 129, 132ff., 138, 143, 145, 146, 162, 192, 207, 222, 286, 291
Intrinsic value, 101, 102, 105

Intuitionism, 18, 28, 101

Jealousy, 139, 170, 203, 209, 222, 223, 225, 228, 257, 267, 280, 281, 293, 297, 303, 304, 327
Justice, 96, 97

Law, *see* Criminal code (*see also* Sex and the law)

Marriage and Morals, 109, 167, 207, 213, 231, 232, 249, 255, 261, 271, 302, 348
Marriage customs, changing of, 150ff., 164, 210, 223, 242, 246, 260
Marriage, good elements of, 231, 244, 245, 246, 256, 257, 258, 267, 269; indissolubility of, 152, 153, 158, 187, 234, 235, 247, 248, 253, 302, 307ff.
Meglomania, 320
Menstruation, 90
Monarchy, 73, 74
Monogamy, 151, 154, 222, 226
Moral approval and disapproval 28, 29, 30, 34, 35, 46, 56, 59, 103, 104, 105, 110, 182, 183, 222, 235, 236
Moral codes, 30, 31, 32, 57, 58, 59, 70, 75, 76, 79, 84, 90, 149, 173, 174; as effected by science, 155ff., 162, 165; as expressions of economic power, 75, 76, 77, 150, 151, 159; subjectivity of, 57, 58, 70, 104, 117, 150, 152, 153, 173, 176
Moral decay, 162, 163, 238, 239
Moralist's fallacy, 51, 52
Morality, definition of, 15
_ ~monism, 192

Narcissism, 319
New Testament, morality in, 94, 225

Objectively right acts, 30ff., 41, 42, 44, 55, 69
Old Testament, morality in, 76, 77, 78, 80, 89, 90, 93, 94, 96, 150, 174, 225, 259, 277
Oracle at Delphi, 75, 186
Ought, concept and analysis of, 21, 34, 37, 39, 44, 100, 101, 104

Pacifism, 202
Parental affection, 139, 140
Patriotism, 119
Personal morality, concept and analysis of, 69, 75, 78, 79
Persuasion in ethics, 60, 62, 63, 66, 102, 110, 111, 112, 169
Philosopher's fallacy, 51
Philosophical Essays, 15, 17, 44, 50
Pleasure, *see* Good, as happiness or pleasure
Polyandry, 164
Polygamy, 151, 211
Pornography, 185, 186, 224, 225
Positive morality, concept and analysis of, 69, 70, 74, 78, 131
Power morality, 70ff., 83, 94
Principia Ethica, 15, 17, 56
Probability, in deciding ethical actions, 32, 33, 34
Prohibition, 203
Propaganda agencies, 112, 163
Prostitution, 152, 154, 200, 223, 224, 251
Puritanism, 145, 146, 168, 200, 203, 206, 207, 214, 264, 265, 317, 324ff.

Rape, 184, 216
Reformative punishment, 52
Religious authority, 58, 71, 74ff., 80, 93, 94
Retributive punishment, 52
Right and wrong, actions, 18, 19, 28, 29, 30, 36, 37, 39, 59, 103, 104; concepts and analysis of, 17, 18, 28, 29, 30, 38, 175
Russell's dissatisfaction with ethical theories, 16, 99
Russian Revolution, 89, 90

Scientific outlook, 305
Self-control, 168, 170, 171, 216, 265, 267, 268, 280, 303
Self-sacrifice, 46ff.
Sex education, 171, 200, 201ff., 213, 226, 227, 231
Sex, religious attitude toward, 152, 184, 200, 201, 205, 213, 214, 215, 217, 221, 231, 232, 233, 250, 253, 255, 256, 262, 264, 301
Sexual morality, 154, 164, 169, 170, 183, 184, 199, 200, 201, 207, 208, 209, 216, 218, 225, 226, 228, 260, 261, 264, 266, 267
Sexual obsession, 184, 213ff., 218, 227, 228, 251, 252
Sexual relations, outside of marriage, 152, 209, 221, 222, 223, 231, 235, 236, 252; within marriage, 152
Sex and the law, 210, 234, 304, 307, 308, 309
Sin, 34, 58, 64, 65, 73, 80, 160, 161, 170, 175, 180, 182, 183, 195, 196, 203, 206, 211, 214, 222, 226, 234, 257, 262, 264, 268, 304, 316ff.
Social systems, good qualities in, 121, 123, 126, 129; methods of judging, 116ff., 129
Socialism, 118, 120, 122ff., 138, 142, 329, 332
Subjection of women, 71, 72, 78, 83, 151, 224, 225, 233, 236, 237, 243, 246
Suicide, 176
Sympathy, 82, 84

Taboo morality, 90, 91, 92, 95, 105, 170, 179ff., 184, 186, 187, 226
Tao, 79, 191, 192
Ten Commandments, 30, 31, 71, 93, 153, 175, 180
Trade unions, 138
Trial marriage, 251ff.

Unhappiness, 317ff.
Useless rules of conduct, 70, 75, 90, 91, 92, 149, 153, 167, 179, 180, 181
Utilitarianism, 28, 60, 69, 80, 81, 93, 132, 144, 145, 156, 330, 331

Venereal disease, 160, 211, 216, 226
Vindictive punishment, 101
Virtue, 34, 54, 59, 62, 80, 130, 132, 191, 195, 202, 227, 253, 319

Witches, burning of, 93, 104, 105